2.970,-

PHILOSOPHY OF MIND

An Overview for Cognitive Science

Tutorial Essays in Cognitive Science

Advisory Editors

Donald A. Norman
Andrew Ortony

PHILOSOPHY OF MIND

An Overview for Cognitive Science

WILLIAM BECHTEL
Georgia State University

LEA LAWRENCE ERLBAUM ASSOCIATES, PUBLISHERS
1988   Hillsdale, New Jersey   Hove and London

Lawrence Erlbaum Associates, Inc., Publishers
365 Broadway
Hillsdale, New Jersey 07642

Library of Congress Cataloging in Publication Data
Bechtel, William.
    Philosophy of mind: an overview for cognitive science /
William Bechtel.
        p.   cm.
    Bibliography: p.
    Includes index.
    ISBN 0-8058-0218-5.   ISBN 0-8058-0234-7 (pbk.)
    1. Mind-brain identity theory.   2. Mind and body.
3. Intentionality (Philosophy)   I. Title.
    [DNLM: 1. Mental Processes.   2. Philosophy.   3. Psychology.   BF
455 B392]
B105.M55B43 1988
128'.2'02415—dc19
87-30585
CIP
Printed in the United States of America
10 9 8 7 6 5 4 3 2

For my mother

Contents

Preface

As one of the several contributing disciplines to cognitive science, philosophy offers two sorts of contributions. On the one hand, *philosophy of science* provides a metatheoretical perspective on the endeavors of any scientific enterprise, analyzing such things as the goals of scientific investigation and the strategies employed in reaching those goals. Philosophy of science thus proposes a perspective from which we can examine and potentially evaluate the endeavors of cognitive science. On the other hand, *philosophy of mind* offers substantive theses about the nature of mind and of mental activity. Although these theses typically have not resulted from empirical investigation, they have often subsequently figured in actual empirical investigations in cognitive science, or its predecessors. Because the two roles philosophy plays in cognitive science are quite different, they are introduced in separate volumes. This one focuses on philosophy of mind, whereas issues in philosophy of science are explored in *Philosophy of Science: An Overview for Cognitive Science*.

The goal of this book is to provide a broad overview of the central issues in philosophy of mind and an introduction to the professional literature. Philosophers have adopted a variety of different positions on the issues I discuss and I have tried to describe as simply as possible some of the most prominent positions. I have also endeavored to cite a broad range of philosophical papers and books that the reader is encouraged to consult in order to develop a more thorough understanding of the various positions philosophers have taken.

I begin with a chapter that both discusses the methodology of philosophical inquiry and offers an overview of major figures from the history of philosophy whose ideas have been influential in philosophy of mind and cognitive science generally. Then in chapter 2, I discuss a variety of accounts of language that have been developed by analytic philosophers during the 20th century. Mind and language are obviously closely related phenomena and the perspectives developed in analyses of language have influenced philosophical accounts of mind. Hence, I make repeated references to this material in subsequent chapters. Philosophical analyses of language have also had considerable influence on work in other disciplines of cognitive science, including linguistics and cognitive psychology.

Many philosophers have viewed *intentionality* as the distinguishing feature of mental phenomena. Chapters 3 and 4 are devoted to explaining different accounts philosophers have offered of what intentionality is and how it has been taken to distinguish mind from other phenomena in nature. Some philosophers have viewed intentionality as so differentiating minds from other things in nature as to make it impossible to develop a science of mind. The claims of such philosophers are discussed in chapter 3. Chapter 4 is devoted to examining a number of attempts by other philosophers to show how intentionality can arise in the natural world and how the intentionality of mental events might be explained scientifically. Several of these attempts have been directly motivated by recent work in cognitive science, and the answers point to different types of research endeavors for cognitive science to pursue.

Perhaps the most widely discussed issue in philosophy of mind for the past 3 centuries has been the *mind–body problem*. This problem is a legacy of Descartes and numerous answers have been proposed to it. In chapters 5 and 6, I examine a number of these answers and their implications for cognitive science. Chapter 5 begins with an examination of different forms of dualism, focusing primarily on substance dualism. This position views minds as totally different kinds of things from bodies and hence seems to reject the possibility of ever developing accounts of mental activity using the strategies of natural science. In that chapter, I also discuss philosophical behaviorism, one of the first systematic attempts to reject dualism. Although philosophical behaviorism and behaviorism in psychology have different aims, both are opposed to using inner processing models to explain behavior, and hence are antithetical to the endeavors of cognitive science.

Chapter 6 examines a number of varieties of materialism, which holds that mental states are states of the brain. The Type Identity Theory was developed in response to work in the neurosciences that suggested a correlation between kinds of mental states and types of neural states. It proposed that having a certain kind of mental state was just to be in a particular neural state. Type Identity Theory is thus quite compatible with inner processing models of cognition, but links these models closely to neuroscience ones. Hence, it denies any autonomy to the investigations of cognitive science. Eliminative Materialism is even less sympathetic to an autonomous cognitive science, holding that mentalistic theories ought to be replaced by theories developed from neuroscience. A third form of materialism, the Token Identity Theory, is the attempted solution to the mind–body problem most congenial to cognitive science. It maintains that each individual mental state is also a brain state, but denies that the taxonomy of mental states corresponds to the taxonomy of neural states. Thus, it allows for cognitive accounts of behavior to be quite independent of neural accounts.

Cognitivism has raised a special issue that has been the focus of much recent work in philosophy of mind. In developing models of inner processing, cognitivists attempt to characterize mental events in terms of their causal efficacy. A philosophical theory called *Functionalism* tries to characterize this way of identifying and classifying mental events. This theory is the focus of the last chapter. I introduce several different versions of Functionalism that have been developed in philosophy of mind and also discuss a number of objections that have been raised against Functionalism. I conclude by describing an alternative form of Functionalism developed in philosophy of biology and show how it provides a potential more fruitful way to classify mental events.

For those not previously acquainted with philosophy, some comments about how to approach philosophical material are in order. Although it used to be widely proclaimed that philosophical claims do not require empirical evidence, this view is much less accepted today. A number of theses discussed in philosophy of mind were developed as analyses of empirical work done in psychology and other cognitive sciences. It remains the case, however, that philosophical claims tend to be fairly far removed from empirical evidence. Therefore, there tends to be much great room for argument as to the virtues of particular claims than is true in disciplines where empirical evidence is readily at hand.

In considering the views discussed in this book, the reader should remember the controversial and argumentative character of philosophical inquiry. Rather than simply accepting or rejecting a view, the reader should consider the possible kinds of arguments that mind be made on behalf of or against the view. The reader, thereby, enters into the argument itself, and does not remain a passive observer. Although the accumulated efforts of philosophers to address these issues provide a resource for anyone taking up these issues, the issues are not the exclusive prerogative of philosophers and scientists are encouraged to engage in discussing the issues themselves and to reach their own conclusions.

ACKNOWLEDGMENTS

I have received help and support from a number of institutions and persons in developing this text. First, thanks to Larry Erlbaum for inviting me to write this text. Although it was not as easy a project as it seemed it might be when he invited me, I have learned much from it. Special thanks are also due to Andrew Ortony for his valuable editorial advice and comments. Jim Frame was my research assistant through much of the writing of this text and provided invaluable assistance, particularly in organizing and coordinating bibliographical materials. Adele Abrahamsen, Robert McCauley, Donald Norman, Robert Richardson, and Douglas Winblad read various versions of this text and offered substantial comments for which I am most grateful. I used preliminary drafts of this text in my Philosophyy of Psychology course at Georgia State University in Fall 1985, and I am thankful to the students in that class for helpful feedback. Finally, a Georgia State University Research Grant provided essential support for developing the text, and is gratefully acknowledged.

1

Some Perspectives on Philosophy of Mind

INTRODUCTION: WHAT IS PHILOSOPHY OF MIND?

This book is devoted to introducing basic issues in philosophy of mind to the practitioners of other disciplines of cognitive science: cognitive psychology, artificial intelligence, cognitive neuroscience, theoretical linguistics, and cognitive anthropology. Philosophers were interested in the character of the mind long before these empirical disciplines arose. They asked such questions as: What are the distinctive features of minds? How should mental states be characterized? How are minds related to physical bodies? How are minds able to learn about the physical world? A variety of answers that philosophers have offered to these and other questions are examined in the subsequent chapters of this book. Before turning to the particular views philosophers have advanced, however, it is useful to put philosophical investigations of these issues into perspective.

Two questions cognitive scientists not trained in philosophy are likely to ask about philosophy of mind are (a) What methodology do philosophers employ to analyze mental phenomena? and (b) How do philosophical endeavors relate to the investigations carried out in other disciplines of cognitive science? I address these two issues in this first section of the chapter, and then offer an overview of some of the major historical traditions in philosophy that provide both the origins of many ideas now influential in cognitive science and the background to contemporary philosophical thinking.

In methodology, philosophy is distinct from the other disciplines of cognitive science in not having its own distinct empirical base.[1] Philosophers often distinguish between a priori knowledge, which can be discovered without empirical investigation, and a posteriori knowledge, which relies on empirical results. Many philosophers have thought that important truths about the mind could be established a priori. They hold that these truths can be established simply by reasoning about how the mind has to be or by analyzing the structure of our language through which we talk about minds. Other philosophers, although holding that their claims were ultimately a posteriori ones, have sought to establish truths about the mind by drawing out some of the logical consequences of results scientists have obtained through empirical inquiry.

Within philosophy, discussions about the nature of mind generally occur in two subfields: epistemology and metaphysics. *Epistemology*, which seeks to define what knowledge is and to determine how it is obtained, is concerned with those processes by which the mind is able to gather knowledge. *Metaphysics* has traditionally been characterized as the study of basic principles of the universe and of its origins. *Ontology,* a subfield of metaphysics, is concerned with identifying and characterizing the kinds of things that exist in the world.[2] It is particularly in this subfield that the character of mind is discussed. Some contemporary work in ontology is closely tied to the results of scientific investigations and analyzes what kinds of objects these sciences assume exist. Philosophers have been concerned with such matters as the criteria by which we determine whether theoretical entities posited in science (such as quarks or mental states) really exist or whether they are simply useful fictions for doing science. Quine (1969a) advanced the maxim (which not all agree with) that what we take to exist are the entities posited in our scientific theories. Quine's approach ties investigation of metaphysical issues closely to work of empirical science, but there remains the question of when we should accept a scientific theory as giving an accurate account of nature. Quine thought that theories purporting to talk about mental states are not acceptable scientific theories (see chapter 3).

Most philosophers today would maintain that empirical science is relevant to both epistemological and ontological discussions of the mind, but still maintain that the philosophical issues are distinct from the empirical issues addressed in other disciplines of cognitive science. Generally, the distinction is thought to result from the fact that philosophy is concerned with fundamen-

---

[1]Within cognitive science there are now philosophers who do engage in empirical investigations, most frequently by developing artificial intelligence (AI) simulations. These philosophers are returning to an older tradition in philosophy, exemplified by Aristotle, Descartes, and Kant, who carried out both empirical inquiries and developed more purely conceptual analyses. Such hybrid endeavors had not been popular in this century until the past decade.

[2]See Bechtel (in press b) for more on the nature of epistemology and metaphysics as well as a discussion of the other main fields of philosophy—logic, and moral theory.

tal conceptual issues. Such issues concern the adequacy of a particular theoretical framework to accommodate features of mental states such as their intentionality (chapters 3 and 4) or their affective or qualitative character (chapter 7). These are issues for which we cannot simply devise empirical experiments. Hence, attempts to answer them often involves complex arguments that take us quite far from empirical results.

The fact that philosophical claims lie so far removed from empirical inquiry poses a challenge to anyone turning to philosophical investigations from training in experimental research. In order to evaluate a philosophical claim you must follow the often complicated chain of reasoning offered in support of the claim. This, however, is not meant to deter outsiders from entering the philosophical arena. Indeed, such participation is most welcome; one of the benefits philosophers can gain from participating in the interdisciplinary research cluster of cognitive science is learning of new perspectives on the mind from other cognitive scientists.

All that is required for the nonphilosopher to get involved with philosophy of mind is to begin to confront the issues. This means becoming an active participant in the debates by offering arguments for or against different positions. It is not enough simply to turn to philosophers as authorities and cite what a particular philosopher has said as an answer to one of these foundational questions. Given that philosophical views depend on a long chain of argument, they are frequently controversial. Different philosophers maintain a variety of different views about these issues. This becomes evident as we take up various issues in the following chapters. Rather than simply accepting an authority, it is necessary to explore the issues and to evaluate the arguments advanced for competing claims. On this basis, you can hope to make a rational decision about what position to accept.[3]

Nonphilosophers, upon recognizing the controversial nature of philosophical claims, sometimes decide that such fundamental questions cannot be resolved. They form the view that there are simply a variety of different views and it does not matter much which one you accept. The fact that philosophers have been addressing some of these questions for 2,500 years and still disagree on how to answer them would seem to be provide good support for such a claim. But what that claim fails to recognize is that there often is a close interaction between philosophical claims and empirical research efforts such that those engaged in an empirical investigation frequently assume, consciously or unconsciously, a particular philosophical stance. Historically, these connections can be demonstrated in the history of physics and biology, but here it suffices to consider some ways philosophical views have had or are having broad impact on cognitive science.

The cognitive approach to mental phenomena, which unites current work

---

[3]For a useful introduction to philosophical methodology, see Woodhouse, 1984.

in cognitive science, is not the only possible approach. Two other approaches are to characterize mental activities in terms of propensities to behave or in terms of neural processes. The focus on behavior was characteristic of behaviorism, which dominated much of experimental psychology (and had consequences for linguistics and anthropology) for much of this century. The behaviorist approach was supported by a number of philosophical arguments that I consider in chapters 3 and 5. Although the behaviorist approach is now largely out of fashion, both in philosophy and psychology, the neural approach is not. Serious endeavors are now developing to explain mental life in terms of neural processing. This approach too is supported by philosophical perspectives, including the mind–brain Identity Theory and Eliminative Materialism, which are discussed in chapter 6.

The cognitive approach is characterized by the attempt to identify mental states functionally, that is, in terms of their causal interactions with other mental states. Recognizing the possibility of identifying these states through their causal interactions is part of what enabled cognitivists to overcome the strictures of behaviorism. Moreover, it is the prospect of characterizing these states independently of their material realization in the brain which, for cognitivists, licenses the autonomy of psychology from neuroscience. Over the past 2 decades philosophers have tried to develop a functionalist account of mental states to ground the cognitivist program. As I discuss in chapters 4 and 7, however, there have been a number of criticisms of the coherence of this approach that in turn may have implications for the cognitivist program.

Language has figured centrally in the study of cognitive processes. A great deal of philosophical theorizing has focused on language and on the ability of language to carry meaning. Some of these views have been adopted directly in various programs in psychology and linguistics, including the distinction between the *sense* of an expression and its *referent* (see chapter 2). Formal logical analyses of language, such as predicate calculus,[4] have been employed in endeavors in artificial intelligence to model human reasoning. Other aspects of the philosophical analysis of language, such as challenges to the claim that words have objective meanings, have figured in some of the criticisms of artificial intelligence and in the development of recent views of concepts and categorization in psychology and linguistics.

As I discuss different philosophical views in this text I point out ways in which they are relevant to work in other disciplines of cognitive science. As the brief sketch just given indicates, however, many of the views advanced within philosophy have had and are having ramifications for cognitive science.

---

[4]See Bechtel (in press b) for a basic introduction to modern logic and its relevance to cognitive science.

One consequence of linking philosophical ideas with the empirical inquiries in other parts of cognitive science is that empirical evidence becomes relevant to addressing the adequacy of particular philosophical views. This may suggest, mistakenly, that the only way now to evaluate these philosophical views is to await the judgments of the empirical investigations based upon them. Although those judgments will certainly be relevant, philosophers bring some additional resources that can help in our contemporary evaluations of these endeavors. One is training in developing and evaluating complex and often abstract arguments. A second is knowledge of the long history of attempts to grapple with these issues. It is within this history that we can often locate the sources of modern ideas. But more importantly, we can discover a rich source of arguments that suggest why particular positions are plausible and why others are not viable.

Many of the ideas that underlie research endeavors in contemporary cognitive science are direct descendants of ideas that were first developed by philosophers of earlier eras such as Plato, Descartes, Hume, and Kant. Moreover, contemporary philosophical theorizing about minds is also the heir to this tradition. Therefore, the remainder of this chapter offers a brief overview of relevant figures in the history of philosophy, focusing on how they understood mind and the ideas they contributed to current discussions.

RELEVANT ASPECTS OF MAJOR HISTORICAL APPROACHES TO PHILOSOPHY

In a short discussion it is not possible to do full justice to any of the major historical figures in philosophy that have influenced contemporary thinking about mind. To present a manageable account of this material I focus on a number of traditions within the history of philosophy, each of which offered a general perspective on important issues relevant to our understanding of mind. I briefly indicate some of the major members of these traditions and the central tenets advanced by the members of the school. The reader should be advised, however, that there is intense debate surrounding the interpretation of most ot these philosophers and one would need to enter into a careful examination of these debates to reach a definitive interpretation of any of them.

The Classical Philosophers: Socrates, Plato, and Aristotle

Three Greek philosophers working in the fifth and fourth centuries B.C. set the agenda for much of subsequent thinking about science as well as philosophy in the Western world, including our attempts to understand mind.

Socrates set the questions. Plato was his student, and in turn was the teacher of Aristotle, but Plato and Aristotle offered quite different sorts of answers to Socrates' questions.

Socrates (c. 470–399 B.C.) is often taken to be the first major philosophical thinker. He is rather unusual in that he did not defend any philosophical theses. He also left no writings, so what we know of Socrates largely stems from Plato's presentation of him as the central figure in a number of dialogues. Rather than defending theses, Socrates developed a mode of inquiry, commonly referred to as the *Socratic Method*. This method involves dialogue that begins with a request for a definition, such as: what is knowledge? or what is beauty? Once a definition is proposed (e.g., knowledge is true belief), the questioner pursues additional questions to evaluate the adequacy of the answer. Often such questioning generates counterexamples that show that the initial definition is inadequate. (For example, a true belief acquired quite by chance would not seem to be a case of knowledge.) Once the definition is found to be deficient, the questioner asks for a new definition that overcomes the objections to the previous attempt, and the process is repeated. For Socrates, the goal of this activity was to discover universally true definitions for our concepts. In seeking such definitions, Socrates opposed the Sophists, many of whom maintained that precise definitions were impossible because words meant different things in different contexts.

Socrates focused on trying to define ethical terms like *virtue* and *justice*, but the method can clearly be applied to any concept. Socrates would maintain that we cannot acquire knowledge in any field until we develop adequate definitions of the concepts used in that field. The issue of whether there are definitions for our concepts that meet Socrates' requirements of adequacy is clearly a critical one for cognitive science. Early cognitive scientists, especially in artificial intelligence, tended to assume that there were such definitions and that these could be encoded in programs. Moreover, many studies of meaning or semantics by philosophers and linguists have assumed that our concepts can be defined. But recent developments in psychology (Rosch, 1975) and linguistics (Lakoff, 1987), as well as in philosophy (Wittgenstein, 1953), have challenged the view that most of our concepts are grounded in the kind of definitions Socrates sought.

Socrates never seemed to find adequate definitions,[5] but the quest was taken up by Plato (c. 428–347 B.C.), who thought he could provide a framework for answering Socrates' questions. One of Socrates' frequent objections was that, in trying to provide definitions, interlocutors would cite examples. He found examples inadequate as definitions because they did not

---

[5]For Socrates this was not necessarily a failure. Although no positive results were achieved, he seemed to view the discovery that we lacked knowledge and were really ignorant as the first fundamental step toward wisdom.

tell us the range of things to which the concept would apply. For instance, an example of a just action would not tell us what other actions were just. Plato saw Socrates' demand for general definitions as unanswerable as long as we confined ourselves to the physical world. He therefore proposed the existence of an abstract world of *Ideas* or *Forms*. These entities would provide the perfect exemplars for our concepts, and we could judge instances in this world as being more or less good imitations of these Ideas. Thus, for Plato, to answer Socrates' request for a definition, it was necessary to identify the Idea, not a worldly instance. The human predicament, however, is that all we experience are the imperfect examples of the concepts found in the physical world around us. We never see a truly straight line, but only an imperfect approximation to a straight line drawn on paper. In order to clarify our thinking, Plato maintained, we need to redirect our thinking to the Ideas themselves and not remain focused on the objects of the physical world.

To explain how our knowledge is based on the Ideas, Plato develops an elaborate account of how we once perceived the Ideas directly, but through birth had forgotten this experience. It is necessary to rekindle these memories so that we can ground our thinking on the Ideas themselves. The physical objects of experience, because they are imitations of the Ideas, can facilitate this rekindling if we conduct the right kind of Socratic inquiry about these objects and do not become preoccupied with the distortions induced by these imitations. In the dialogue *Meno*, Plato tries to show how knowledge of mathematical principles is innate in an untutored slave boy, but must be elicited through an inquiry in which the boy tests the adequacy of various hypotheses he himself puts forward until he is able to once again recognize the true principles embodied in the Ideas. (For Plato's dialogues, see Hamilton & Cairns, 1961.)

Plato's theory of Ideas and his proposal that knowledge of these Ideas is innate has had a continuing legacy in both philosophy and other disciplines in cognitive science in the context of theorizing about innate knowledge. The proposal that certain knowledge is innate is generally put forward when it seems impossible to explain how we could acquire that knowledge through experience. Chomsky (1959) argued that knowledge of syntactic rules must be innate since an infant does not have enough experience to learn them by induction. Similarly, Fodor (1975) has argued that concepts must be innate because there is no conceivable way we could learn them. (See further Fodor, 1981; Stich, 1979; and papers in Piattelli-Palmarini, 1980.)

One of Plato's most controversial claims is that our knowledge is really about abstract Ideas, not things in this world. This claim has had its most enduring impact in highly theoretical sciences, particularly in mathematics. In geometry it is not uncommon to think of pure figures like triangles existing separate from any drawings of them. Similarly, the distinction between numbers and numerals seems to capture this distinction between the pure objects and our representations of them. But many have found Plato's conclusion that our knowledge is not of things in this world untenable. Plato himself presented some of these difficulties in his later dialogues, but it was his student, Aristotle (384–322 B.C.), who emphasized them and offered an alternative philosophical scheme that redirected attention to objects of this world. Aristotle preserved something of Plato's notion of Ideas with his concept of Forms, but he argued that Forms are in the objects we experience, not in some abstract space. Aristotle construed objects of the world as consisting of a Form imposed on matter (e.g., a cup consists of the imposition of the form CUP on the clay out of which it is made). He maintained that the Form determined the kind of object something was and fixed many of its basic properties.

To acquire knowledge of an object for Aristotle required recognition of the Form in it. Like modern cognitive scientists, Aristotle was concerned with how we can represent in our minds the objects in the world. He developed a theory of perception whereby the Form that defined the object would be transferred to the mind of the perceiver. Thus, to perceive a table required actually taking the form of the object (but not its matter) into the mind of the perceiver. Thus, Aristotle held an early version of the representational theory (see chapter 4).

Aristotle's account of Forms was critical to the scientific theories that he developed and that endured until the 17th century. He allowed that the Form that defined an object could be changed as, for example, when a carpenter would take a tree and make it into a table. On the other hand, Forms provided organization and direction to natural objects so that these objects behave in accord with their form. At least in the case of living organisms, the Form of the object specified the goal state towards which it was developing (see chapter 5). In this respect, Aristotle's view of nature is quite different from the modern. For Aristotle (as well as for Plato[6]), nature is *teleological* or goal directed. Whereas we generally view objects as passive, he viewed objects as seeking certain objectives determined by their Form. When Aristotle attempted to analyze change in nature, he focused not just on what we would call the "cause" of that change, but on four factors: the matter that underwent change, the event that induced the change, the form that was realized as a result of the change, and the goal toward which the change was directed.[7] The applications of this view are found in Aristotle's account of how different kinds of objects seek their own place in nature (e.g., fire strives

---

[6]The difference for Plato was only that the objectives were defined by the abstract Ideas. not embodied Forms.

[7]These factors are commonly referred to as Aristotle's *four causes*. The term *cause* in this context is rather misleading, and hence I have spoken of factors that need to be considered in explaining the change.

to rise, whereas earth tries to go to the center of the universe) and in his view of living things as seeking to fulfill their form. (For writings of Aristotle, see McKeon, 1941.)

Modern science, which has been developed since the 17th century, has repudiated the idea of a teleologically oriented universe in favor of a mechanistic model. Although it has proven quite easy to eliminate the notion of teleology from our accounts of purely physical phenomena, it has been much harder to do without it in accounting for biological and cognitive phenomena, for these do seem to be goal-directed phenomena. Thus, one of the philosophical problems we face in giving an adequate conceptual analysis of modern biology and cognitive science is to provide a framework that can accommodate the teleological character of living things and cognitive systems without going beyond the type of mechanistic framework originally developed within the physical sciences (see chapter 7).

The views of Socrates, Plato, and Aristotle, although no longer accepted in their original form, continue to influence thinking in cognitive science in a variety of ways. Moreover, they have had a lasting impact on science and an even longer impact on our folk science (McCloskey, 1983). Aristotle's account of objects in particular provided a comprehensive structure in which to describe and categorize natural phenomena that served as a basis for science until the 17th century. What it did not provide, though, was an adequate structure for understanding dynamic processes of nature. The scientific revolution largely involved the development of a dynamic view of nature in which the focus was not on identifying the essence of objects but on modeling change in terms of the movements induced in physical matter. This involved the development of a mechanical conception of the universe. Two new philosophical perspectives—*Rationalism* and *Empiricism*—developed as attempts to provide a conceptual framework for understanding the new mechanistic science of Copernicus, Galileo, and Newton. Although the mind was not taken as a central object of scientific study in this new science, the Rationalist and Empiricist accounts of how we could know the claims of this science have had lasting impact on theorizing about mind.

Rationalism

Rationalism emerged as the dominant philosophical tradition on the European continent during the 17th and 18th centuries. Its three foremost representatives were Descartes (1596–1650), Leibniz (1646–1716), and Spinoza (1632–1677). To understand the Rationalists we must bear in mind that they were deeply involved both in the actual development of modern science and in providing a coherent philosophical account of it. Today their philosophical views often are taken up independently of their contributions to the development of science, but this misrepresents their approach to philosophy.

What is distinctive of Rationalism is a strong reliance on *reason* as the tool for discovering the processes operating in nature. The senses had a role to play for the Rationalists, but it was secondary to that of reason. Part of the attraction of reason for the Rationalists was a conviction that nature had to be designed in a logically sensible manner. If this was true, then careful logical inquiry could lead us to fundamental truths. The character of such logical inquiry is exemplified in Descartes' *Meditations on First Philosophy* (1641/1970). He begins the *Meditations* with a program of radical doubt through which he questioned every belief of which he was not certain. To extend his doubt maximally, Descartes contemplated the possibility that he was under the control of an evil genius whose endeavor was to deceive him maximally. Descartes claims that the motivation for raising these doubts was to clear his mind of all dubious propositions that had not been fully demonstrated. He attributed much of our mistaken thinking about nature to careless acceptance of ideas that had not been carefully examined.

Once the ground had been cleared of mistaken ideas, Descartes' goal was to build a new edifice of scientific truths that would be carefully reasoned from indubitable foundations. The first indubitable truth he thought he discovered was his own existence, which he took to be a necessary consequence of the fact that he was thinking when he raised these doubts. Even the evil genius could not arrange a situation where Descartes both thought something and did not exist. (This is the context of Descartes' famous expression "Cogito ergo sum" or "I think, therefore I am.")

In establishing that his existence could not be doubted, Descartes thought he had discovered a method for establishing claims about which he could be certain. He claimed that the idea of his own existence was "clear and distinct." For him, an idea was clear when we grasped its essence; it was distinct when we perceived it differentiated from other ideas. Descartes formed the hypothesis that all clear and distinct ideas are true and set out to justify it. To do so, he tried to show that the idea of an evil genius was incoherent and that instead there was a nonmalevolent God who provided him with his ideas. Once he had accomplished this, he reasoned that because God was nonmalevolent, he could trust his ideas as long as he adhered to principles of proper reasoning in synthesizing knowledge from his clear and distinct ideas. Thus, the method of reasoning through clear and distinct ideas was vindicated.

Descartes' argument for the existence of God has been much criticized in the philosophical literature, but that need not distract us from considering his overall program, which was to develop the conceptual foundations for the new physics. What Descartes thought his clear and distinct ideas showed was that nature was a corpuscularean system (see Descartes, 1644/1970). All physical objects were composed of tiny corpuscles, and the basic properties of these corpuscles—their size, shape, and motion—determined the behavior of physical objects. The motion of a corpuscle resulted from the forces impinging on it from collisions with other corpuscles. Further, Descartes reasoned that there could not be space that was unoccupied by corpuscles and that all interactions between corpuscles resulted from direct physical contact. In terms of these basic principles, Descartes tried to develop theories that could explain the observed behavior of physical objects. He thought that nearly all natural phenomena, animate and inanimate, could be so explained in terms of physical interactions of corpuscles. Descartes made an exception only in the case of the human mind (see chapter 5). This was the source of Cartesian "dualism" (the view that the mind is separate from the body), but from his vantage point of trying to provide a foundation to a physics that could explain nature, this was a relatively minor exception.

I have focused on Descartes because his program is prototypical of the Rationalists' endeavors. From the vantage point of cognitive science, what is most important about the Rationalist program is not the attempt to provide certainty to our knowledge, but the emphasis on the importance of reasoning in arriving at our knowledge. The Rationalists, like Plato before them, took their model of knowledge from mathematicians, who tried to derive theorems from principles they took to be indubitable. Although the assumption that mathematical postulates are indubitable has been challenged in the past two centuries, the conception of mathematics as relying on logical reasoning from postulates has remained. Many cognitive scientists have shared the view that cognition is primarily a process of reasoning. This is particularly true of those in artificial intelligence (AI) who have devised programs in which basic principles of knowledge are encoded and conclusions are drawn through various devices of logical reasoning. Although the materialistic aspect of the claim that a computer can simulate reasoning was foreign to Descartes, the ability of the computer to carry out logical inferences would recommend the computer to a Rationalist as a tool for modelling thought. Similarly, it is not surprising that a linguist like Chomsky (1966), who thinks of language structures as being produced through the application of rules, would characterize his program as "Cartesian linguistics."

Empiricism

While Rationalism was developing on the European continent, a radically different view, known as Empiricism, was developing in Britain during the 17th and 18th centuries. Although still important, reason plays a far less central role for the Empiricists. Sensory perception, instead, provides the foundation. A precursor to the Empiricist movement, Francis Bacon (1561–1626), attributed the errors of Aristotelian science to an overreliance on reason, and argued that only a thoroughgoing allegiance to sensory evidence could ground the building of a new science. Bacon's proposal was to build knowledge of general truths by following principles of induction on the evidence provided by the senses (Bacon, 1620).

In many respects, Locke (1632–1704) set the pattern of analysis for the Empiricists. He traced all knowledge back to sensory experience and tried to show how experience gives rise to simple or elementary ideas. He also set out to analyze how the mind would associate ideas of particular objects to form complex ideas as well as general and abstract ideas needed for science. The principle that the mind operates chiefly by associating simple ideas from experience provided the basis for a long-enduring tradition that cognitive scientists recognize as *Associationism* (Locke, 1690/1959).

Of the major Empiricists, Locke was the greatest devotee of Newtonian science. His objective was to show how Newtonian science could be grounded on an empiricist epistemology that began with experience and developed all other knowledge through principles of association. In particular, he thought he could justify the basic Newtonian view of a mechanistic universe that operated in a manner much like a clock.[8] In contrast, both Berkeley and Hume in various ways challenged some of the features of Newtonian science and tried to place it in what they took to be a better light.

Berkeley (1685–1753) was appalled by the possibility that the Newtonian mechanistic world view would leave no place for God.[9] His remedy to the mechanization of the world was radical—he denied the existence of the physical world as an object existing outside of thought. He argued that the claim that our ideas are about physical objects external to our ideas was incoherent, maintaining that our thoughts could never inform us about anything but our ideas. Thus, we could never know about a separately existing physical world, if such existed. Moreover, the truth of science, Berkeley argued, did not depend on the existence of an external physical world. Ideas and minds that thought them were the only kinds of objects needed. He appealed to God to explain the regularities and coherence among the ideas we acquire from sensory experience. Even when we did not have ideas of things, God could have them and the objects would therefore exist in the mind of God. Thus, although denying the existence of an external, physical world, he did not deny the existence of objects and the legitimacy of scientific investigations. He simply contended that these objects were presented in ideas

[8]This Newtonian conception differed from the Cartesian conception in some important respects. For example, Newton and Locke accepted the idea of empty space and of action at a distance. The latter concept was needed to account for Newton's gravitational laws. Descartes, on the other hand, tried to explain gravitation through the direct contact and interaction of a series of corpuscles so that action at a distance could be avoided.

[9]The Newtonians themselves were inclined toward deism, a theology according to which God was a creator of the world but subsequently left the world alone to operate according to its own principles. Many Christians, including Berkeley, thought this view removed God too far from the ordinary world.

and that what science was about was the order of ideas as they were presented to us by God (Berkeley, 1710/1965).

Hume (1711–1776) departed from the Newtonian scheme in a different direction. Like Descartes, Hume began his inquiry in a skeptical vein. He challenged our claims to know a variety of things that many people claimed to know. One of his chief targets was *causality*. Hume argued that experience could never reveal to us the relationship that holds together cause and effect. Experience can show us that one type of event is regularly followed by another, but not any intrinsic connection between them. In making this claim, Hume was undercutting a fundamental principle of the new Newtonian science, but he argued that the consequences were not as drastic as they might seem. Unable to find any experiential grounds for our belief in causality, Hume traced it to a natural disposition of human beings to form associations between events that are regularly conjoined in experience. Our beliefs about causal relations are not something about the world that can be inferred by reasoning about our sensory experience, but are simply reflections of our basic character and the way we experience nature (Hume, 1748/1962, 1759/1888; for a discussion of Hume's contributions to cognitive science, see Biro, 1985a).

Although they reached this conclusion in different ways, both Hume and Berkeley held that pursuing the basic empiricist principle of tracing knowledge claims back to sensory experiences and inferences we draw from them resulted in greater restrictions on what could be known than Locke thought. In this they saw themselves as more thoroughgoing Empiricists than Locke. Imposing limits on what humans can know has been part of the enduring legacy of empiricism. We see this in both Associationism and Behaviorism, which, as heirs of the Empiricists, have argued for limits on what we can know based on theories about how we acquire knowledge from experience.

The Kantian View

Of all the historical figures in philosophy, Kant (1724–1804) offered views that are most closely aligned with those advanced in contemporary cognitive science, although Kant would certainly not have endorsed cognitive science. Kant can be seen in part as synthesizing the Empiricist and Rationalist traditions. He began by trying to answer Hume. He saw Hume's skepticism as leading to disastrous results, particularly as it undercut the potential for knowledge of the causal relationships in nature, posited in Newtonian science. He took our ability to know Newtonian science as a given, and set out to show how such knowledge was possible. He agreed with Hume and other Empiricists that our knowledge of physical processes depends on experience and is not discovered simply by reasoning about our innate ideas. However, he also saw Hume's skepticism as the inevitable consequence of allegiance to the empiricist principle that tried to extract all knowledge from experience. The only option, he saw, was to launch his "Copernican Revolution" in philosophy through which he reversed the relation of humans to the natural world. Whereas all previous philosophy assumed that the objects of knowledge exist independently of us and then asked how we could know them, Kant contended that our cognitive activities were partly constitutive of the objects that we experience. He further maintains that it is our own participation in the construction of the objects of perception that makes it possible for us to know them.

In explaining how our cognitive activity is constitutive of the phenomena that we experienced, Kant partly endorsed the Rationalist approach. He claimed that our ability to perceive and think about nature depended on concepts or categories of the understanding that we bring to experience, categories that we possess innately. But the categories Kant had in mind were not the categories through which we classify objects. Rather, his categories specify the general character of objects and the relations in which they stand. Thus, he includes *cause and effect* as a category. Moreover, these categories are not represented in the mind as concepts that can be analyzed in order to derive knowledge of nature, as Rationalism maintained. Rather, these categories had to be applied to the sensory input that we received in order to constitute a world of experience. To make this possible, Kant claimed that the categories had to be schematized—that is, they had to be given interpretations in terms of the spatial–temporal character necessarily exhibited by all sensory stimuli. The schema for cause is, for example, the constant succession of one state by another. For us to experience an object, the intellect must apply the schematized categories to our sensory input. Thus, the objects that we experience are the product of applying the schematized categories to raw sensory input. Our knowledge is limited to these constructed objects.

Kant held that raw sensory experience that is not brought under the categories and the objects that give rise to these sensory experiences (which Kant termed *things in themselves*) are unknowable by us. Hence it makes no sense to inquire as to what things in themselves are really like. On the other hand, the objects of phenomenal experience, those constructed by applying the categories to sensory stimuli, are within our domain of knowledge. Because these objects have been constructed in accord with our categories, we can be sure that they adhere to the principles set out in those categories. For example, because we construct the world so that every event has a cause, we know with certainty that every event has a cause. Because principles like causation are used in constructing the world, Kant claimed that we could know with certainty that the principles of Newtonian physics are true.

Kant called the principles that are the necessary result of applying the categories to experience *synthetic a priori*. Explaining what he meant by this will help place Kant's position in perspective and show how it is linked to modern cognitive science. Previously, I distinguished a priori knowledge, which is knowable without experience, from a posteriori knowledge, which depends on experience. We now need to introduce a second distinction between analytic and synthetic statements. *Analytic* statements are statements that are true in virtue of the meaning of the words. For example, the statement "a bachelor is unmarried" is true in virtue of the meaning of the word "bachelor." *Synthetic* statements are ones that put concepts together in ways that may be false. For example, the statement "the car is red" is not true in virtue of meaning and may be false. Only synthetic statements make substantive claims about the world.

It is traditional to think of analytic statements as known a priori because they depend on the meanings of words, and of synthetic statements as known a posteriori because they make substantive claims about the world and so require experience to be known. Kant rejected this view and treated some synthetic statements as knowable a priori. He is thus maintaining that prior to actual experience we can know how things must be in nature. This is because of the role the categories play in the way we experience objects. In the vocabulary of modern cognitive science, Kant is introducing top-down processing into our cognitive processes, including perception, and claiming that this processing constrains the knowledge process. However, Kant would likely disown this interpretation of his view because the processing views of modern cognitive science are taken to be parts of empirical science, whereas he thought that the role of the categories in cognition could not be studied empirically, but only ascertained by inquiring into the necessary conditions for experience. (But see Biro, 1985b.) Kant spoke of such inquiry as transcendental (Kant, 1787/1961).

Kant's proposal constituted a kind of watershed in philosophical thinking because it opened the possibility that the world we know is the world we construct and not some independent world with which we must struggle to have contact. One of Kant's views that was most controversial was his claim that the concepts and categories he identified were those that had to be used to have any experience at all. Thus, he thought that not only Newtonian science but also Euclidian geometry were necessarily true, not just empirically true. The introduction of non-Euclidean geometries and subsequently of non-Newtonian physics undercut the supposition that Kant's categories were necessary.

Amongst the various modifications of Kant's approach that have been considered, one of the more influential was the development of *Pragmatism*, particularly through the work of the American philosopher Charles Sanders Peirce (1839–1914). Peirce surrendered the claim that there is a set of categories that we must employ to conceptualize nature, but with Kant he maintained that we in fact supply the organizing concepts that we use to conceptualize nature. Instead of arguing that these concepts have legitimacy because they are ones that we must use, Peirce proposed that they gain legitimacy as they prove fruitful in our attempt to develop adequate theories of nature. Peirce focuses on inquiry as an ongoing, corrective processes. Inquirers, for Peirce, adopt concepts and theories and try to organize their experience in terms of them. These concepts and theories give rise to expectations, expectations that may fail. When they fail, inquirers must modify their concepts and theories in order to generate expectations that better accord with what happens. This is an ongoing enterprise, but one that Peirce claims will ultimately yield a set of concepts and theories that will not require subsequent modification. Although we will not know when we have reached the point where no future experience will contravene our expectations, when we do so we will have knowledge of the way the world is.[10] (See Peirce, 1877/1934, 1878/1934.)

Two Contemporary Traditions: Continental and Analytic

Just as for many other periods of history, the philosophical community in the Western world is currently split between two different approaches. The *Analytic* tradition has been the major tradition in the English speaking world during this century, and has periodically also attracted adherents in Germany, Holland, and Scandinavia. In contrast, the *Continental* tradition has been most influential in Europe, although it has increasingly attracted interest in the English speaking world.

Most of the work in philosophy of mind that has been discussed by cognitive scientists has originated within the analytic tradition. The philosophical views described in subsequent chapters, therefore, provide an introduction to the character of analytic philosophy. Here I simply note two of the factors that shaped the development of this tradition. One is a reliance on the use of symbolic logic as a tool for analysis. (See Bechtel, in press b, for a brief introduction to symbolic logic and how it figures in modern philosophy of science). A second is a concern with language. This concern has taken two forms. On the one hand, analytic philosophers often have thought that philosophical problems could be solved by clarifying our use of language. As a result, analytic philosophers often have engaged in the practice of conceptual analysis, trying to clarify the meaning of particular concepts, such as *belief*, *freedom*, or *truth*. On the other hand, analytic philosophers have been interested in language itself and accounting for how it functions. In particular, analytic philosophers have been interested in how words

---

[10]Thus Peirce also rejected Kant's claim of a domain of things-in-themselves beyond our realm of knowledge. We will know all that there is to know when inquiry reaches this point of no further revision.

have meaning so that sentences can say things. Various accounts of language advanced by analytic philosophers are described in the next chapter.

The Continental tradition has been less committed to the logical analysis of language and much more concerned with accurately describing basic features of human existence. Within the Continental tradition there have been two central schools which have focused on different aspects of human experience. The *Phenomenogical* school emerged in the late 19th century in the work of philosophers like Husserl and has continued through philosophers like Merleau-Ponty. It has sought to analyze the content of human experience and the processes by which our phenomenal experiences are shaped. The *Existential* school, represented by philosophers like Heidegger and Sartre, has focused more on the context of experience and the demands to act in such contexts. Thus, Sartre spoke of humans finding themselves thrown into existence and needing to create for themselves principles by which to make decisions.

More recently, a new movement has arisen in the Continental tradition. The *hermeneutical* school, associated with Derrida, emphasizes the process of interpretation, both of texts and of culture generally. The basic idea is that one must "deconstruct" the text or the culture so as to discover the fundamental assumptions that are being made in it. These assumptions are not to be justified or refuted, but simply exposed.

CONCLUSION: READY TO CONFRONT
THE ISSUES

This chapter has been preparatory to the main endeavor of this book, that is, providing an introduction to contemporary philosophy of mind. I have briefly characterized the endeavors of philosophy of mind with regard both to the philosophical method of addressing issues about the mind and to the relevance of philosophical views to cognitive science itself. I also provided brief accounts of major figures in the history of philosophy who are relevant to current philosophical theorizing and research in cognitive science. In the following chapter, I discuss research in philosophy of language that has contributed to philosophy of mind and has been influential in various of the cognitive sciences, including linguistics and artificial intelligence.

2

Philosophical Analyses of Language

INTRODUCTION

Analysis of language has been a major endeavor of analytic philosophers. Philosophers, however, have not been the only investigators who have tried to analyze language and so, to set the framework for discussing philosophy of language, it is useful to indicate how philosophical analyses of language differ from those advanced in other cognitive science disciplines. Psychologists have been principally interested in the processes internal to the mind that make language use possible. In contrast, philosophers have viewed language as an object to be analyzed in its own right, without raising questions about internal psychological processes. In this respect, philosophy of language is closer to linguistics. But philosophical analyses also differ from those of linguists. Linguists have been principally interested in developing abstract characterizations of either the syntax or semantics of a language, and often have produced generative accounts that try to predict the infinite set of sentences that can arise in a language from a finite number of principles. Philosophers, on the other hand, have attempted to provide general accounts of what constitutes the meaning of linguistic expressions without trying to develop detailed theories to account for the types of utterances that appear in actual languages. Although the aims of philosophers, psychologists, and linguists are distinct, the endeavors are clearly related so that contributions in one discipline have been employed in the others.

Philosophers have actually developed quite a variety of different and competing analyses of linguistic meaning over the past century. My discussion follows the historical order in which these ideas were advanced. In many cases subsequent analyses were proposed to overcome problems or perceived problems with earlier analyses. This does not mean that the later analyses are superior and that the earlier positions are of merely historical interest. Many philosophers still endorse the earlier positions and have tried to overcome objections to them. Hence, each account of linguistic meaning should be evaluated for its adequacy and not discounted because other views have subsequently become fashionable.

REFERENTIAL ANALYSIS OF MEANING: MEINONG, FREGE, RUSSELL, AND EARLY WITTGENSTEIN

The concern with the meaning of words and sentences in language emerged at the very beginning of analytic philosophy in the work of Meinong, Frege, Russell, and Wittgenstein. These philosophers made *reference*—the phenomenon of words referring to or denoting things in the world—central to their analyses of meaning. The meaning of a word like "hammer," they maintained, consisted in the object, a hammer, to which that worked referred.

The philosophers who advocated the referential approach were the very ones who were responsible for the development of modern symbolic logic. Their referential analysis is a natural consequence of that logic which takes as paradigmatic what is called *extensional discourse.* In extensional discourse the symbols of the language stand for objects or properties of objects and the claims made in sentences of the language are taken to characterize (truly or falsely) these objects and their properties. Extensional languages adhere to what is known as *Leibniz's Law*, according to which we can substitute one term for another that refers to the same object without changing the truth value of the sentence. For example, in the sentence "The green Buick hit the red Ford" we can substitute "Lesley's old car" for "the green Buick" if they both refer to the same car, and if the first sentence is true, then the second sentence will also be true. In such extensional discourse the reference relation between the linguistic names of objects and the objects themselves is absolutely fundamental. But this relationship turns out to be problematic in at least some cases. The problems were expressed in a number of logical puzzles and the theories of language that the early analytic philosophers advanced were designed to resolve these puzzles.[1]

One puzzle was generated by Alexius Meinong (a philosopher only

---

[1]The role of such puzzles in the development of modern philosophy of language is clearly brought out by Russell (1905): "A logical theory may be tested by its capacity for dealing with puzzles, and it is a wholesome plan, in thinking about logic, to stock the mind with as many puzzles as possible, since these serve much the same purpose as is served by experiments in physical science" (p. 47).

tangently related to the analytic movement). His puzzle concerns judgments about non-existent objects such as the judgment "the round square does not exist" or the statement "the golden mountain does not exist" (Meinong, 1904/1960). The expressions "round square" and "golden mountain" are the subjects of these sentences and so we seem to be referring to a round square and a golden mountain. This seems paradoxical because we are referring to the object and so affirming its existence in the very act of denying its existence. To resolve such puzzles Meinong argued that we must invoke a broader conception of objects wherein we countenance objects without them existing. Meinong proposed that there are pure objects, beyond being and nonbeing, which could be the referents of our linguistic terms even when there are no corresponding actual objects. In effect, what Meinong is doing is distinguishing the reference relation that holds between a linguistic term and its referent from ordinary relations between objects. For someone to instantiate the ordinary relation of buying bread there must actually be bread that the person buys. But this is not true of referring—for someone to refer to bread does not require that there actually be bread which is referred to. Meinong's solution, which allowed that there were objects different from actually existing objects to which we can refer, struck subsequent philosophers, such as Russell and Ryle, as worse than the problem itself. They see Meinong as unnecessarily positing new kinds of objects and so have preferred other solutions to this puzzle.

In 1892 Gottlob Frege, one of the main contributors to the development of modern logic, raised a different kind of puzzle for the analysis of language. This one focused on the identity predicate, represented in English by the verb "is" in statements of the form "X is Y." Sentences of this form seem to portray a relation between two objects, but Frege shows that the two most natural accounts of the identity relation fail to capture the significance of such statements as "Venus is the Morning Star." One account views identity as a relation holding between an object and itself. If that were the case, then we could equally substitute one name for the other, thereby rendering the statement as "Venus is Venus." This, however, lacks the informativeness of the original sentence. The other account views identity as a relation between names—they stand in the relation of naming the same thing. But on this account "Venus is the Morning Star" states nothing more than our acceptance of a linguistic convention to use the two names co-referentially. As such, it does not make an empirical claim.

To explicate such statements, Frege introduces the distinction between the *sense* and *referent* of a term. The referent is the object named or otherwise referred to by the term, whereas the sense involves the "mode of presentation" whereby the referent is presented to us. Using this distinction, Frege resolves the puzzle about the statement "Venus is the Morning Star." The statement tells us that two terms with different senses actually have the same referents. Thus, it is informative in the way "Venus is Venus" is not. But it does not simply state a linguistic convention. Rather, it describes an actual astronomical discovery. It reports that two terms, whose senses were already fixed so that they might refer to different objects, have been found to refer to the same object.

Frege's distinction between sense and reference has been very influential in subsequent analyses of language, so it is useful to develop some other aspects of his discussion. Frege proposed that in certain contexts a term may change from having its *customary* sense and reference to having an *indirect* sense and reference. The indirect reference of a term is its customary sense. This allows Frege to solve another logical puzzle that arises with sentences that contain verbs such as "knows," "believes," and "thinks" followed by a proposition. These sentences violate Leibniz's Law (previously noted). For example, in the sentence "Oedipus knew that he killed the man in the chariot" we cannot substitute "his father" for "the man in the chariot" without changing the truth value of the sentence. Frege's solution is that in contexts governed by verbs like "know," referring terms no longer have their customary reference, but rather their indirect reference. Because the indirect reference (i.e., customary sense) of "his father" and "man in the chariot" are different, the two terms cannot be substituted and no violation of Leibniz's Law results.

Frege extended his doctrine of sense and reference beyond single terms to whole sentences. To identify the referent of a sentence, Frege relied on a central idea of modern logic according to which a function is associated with a sentence that takes a set of words into a truth value. Invoking this idea, Frege treated the referent of a sentence as its truth value. Thus, all true sentences refer to "the True" and all false sentences refer to "the False." This approach of Frege has had lasting impact in formal semantics and figures in arguments such as Putnam's demonstration that model theoretic semantics is impossible (see Lakoff, 1987; Putnam, 1981).[2] Frege identified the sense of a sentence as the thought that it expresses. Frege, however, rejected any psychological interpretation of thoughts. He held that logic, including the logical analysis of ordinary language, is directed at objective phenomena, not subjective psychological states. So thoughts, for him, were not states of an individual's mind, but objective entities. What Frege had in mind by thoughts might best be understood as what other philosophers have referred to as *propositions*, entities posited as presenting the meaning of a sentence and shared by different sentences with the same meaning (e.g., "Snow is white" and "Schnee ist weiss").

Bertrand Russell was dissatisfied with both Meinong's and Frege's treatments of these logical puzzles and offered his theory of descriptions as

---

[2]It is worth noting, however, that there is another way we might identify the referent of a sentence—we could take it to be the fact or state of affairs described by the sentence.

an alternative way to deal with them. Russell's (1905) theory was designed to answer not just the puzzles described by Meinong and Frege, but two additional ones. One of these was already suggested in the discussion of Frege's theory. Consider the sentence "George IV wished to know whether Scott was the author of Waverly." Russell notes that applying Leibniz's Law in this context not only loses the cognitive importance of the identity claim (as it did in the sentence about Venus) but also leads to a false statement. For example, substituting "Scott" for "the author of *Waverly* produces "George IV wished to know whether Scott was Scott," which presumably is false even if the statement "George IV wished to know whether Scott was the author of Waverly" was true. A valid logical principle should not allow us to infer a false statement from a true one. Russell's second additional puzzle stemmed from the classical logical principle of the *excluded middle*, which holds that a statement or its contradictory must be true. But consider the statement "The present King of France is bald." To evaluate the truth of that statement, we look at the list of bald things and, not finding the present King of France there, conclude that it is false. But now consider its contradictory, "The present King of France is not bald." Because the present King of France is also not on the list of non-bald entities, this sentence is also false, in apparent violation of the law of excluded middle.

As an alternative to Meinong's and Frege's accounts of these puzzles, Russell advanced his theory of descriptions. According to this theory, the class of names is restricted to expressions that directly designate actually existing individuals and do so in their own right, without depending on the meaning of other terms. (This requirement is intended to exclude from the class of names terms like *Socrates*, which, for us, are only connected to their referent through some defining expression. We only have names for objects which we directly confront in experience.) Other referring terms, including many apparent names like *Socrates* and descriptive terms like *the morning star*, are construed as descriptions. Thus, the expression "the morning star" is analyzed as having the logical form "the unique object which has the property of being the last star still visible in the morning."

Using this mode of logical analysis, Russell proposed to dispel all of the aforementioned puzzles. First, the statement "The round square does not exist" is analyzed as "There is no object which is both round and square." In this analysis there is no subject term that attempts to refer to the object whose existence is denied, so the puzzle is resolved. Second, "Venus is the Morning Star" is analyzed as "There exists a unique object which is the morning star and it is Venus." The term *Morning Star* ceases to be a name and the sentence is viewed as attributing the property of being the morning star to the named object, Venus. Analyzed this way, the sentence does not present an identity claim and hence cannot be rendered trivial in the way Frege feared. Third, "George IV wanted to know whether Scott was the author of *Waver-*

ly" is analyzed as "George IV wanted to know if one and only one person wrote Waverly and if Scott was that person." In this paraphrase "the author of *Waverly*," does not appear as a name and so "Scott" cannot be substituted for it. Rather, George IV is construed as asking whether Scott was the person to whom the predicate "wrote Waverly" applies. Finally, "The present King of France is bald" is analyzed as "There is one and only one person who is the present King of France and he is bald." Its contradictory is now seen to be "It is not the case that [there is one and only one present King of France and he is bald]". (The square brackets indicate that the negation covers the whole statement, not just the first conjunct.) Although the first sentence is false, its contradictory is true, and the law of excluded middle is not violated.

What Meinong, Frege, and Russell each tried to do in response to these puzzles was to articulate a theory of meaning. The core of all of their theories was the notion of reference: the meaning of a term consisted primarily in the object to which it applied. Frege's notion of sense and Russell's account of descriptions were added to the referential account in order to avoid certain of the logical puzzles that seemed to confront the theory. They, however, constituted an addition and did not remove the core of the theory, the concept of reference. (For further discussion of Meinong, Frege, and Russell, see Linsky, 1967.)

The core conception of language as functioning by referring to things in the world was further developed by Ludwig Wittgenstein, particularly in his *Tractatus Logico-Philosophicus* (1921/1961). Wittgenstein's endeavor was to explain how language can be used to present information about the world. The tools of sentential logic allowed the analysis of statements about the world into simple statements or propositions. These propositions presented simple facts about the world. Wittgenstein's principal interest was in how these propositions represented facts. Here Wittgenstein developed what is known as the *picture theory of meaning*. His proposal is that propositions represent features of the world in the same way as drawings or maps do. The lines and shapes in a drawing stand for the things drawn and the relation of the lines and shapes is supposed to show the relation between these things. Similarly, Wittgenstein proposed that the words of a proposition stand for things in the world and the relationship of the words represent the relationship of these things. When the world is as the proposition pictured it, then the proposition is true. In this conception of how language describes the world, all terms are taken as serving as names and so the naming relation is central.

The referential analyses of language were further developed by a group of philosophers commonly referred to as the Logical Positivists. The Logical Positivists, which included such figures as Carnap, Reichenbach, and Hempel, are discussed more fully in Bechtel (in press b); I only mention one aspect of their endeavor here. Russell, in proposing his theory of descriptions, seemed to hold that ordinary language might not manifest its logic in the clearest possible way and might need reformulation. One of the things the Positivists sought to develop was a logically proper language that would clearly exhibit the logic. With such a language, people would no longer be misled by such features of natural languages as nonreferring expressions. The principal focus of the Logical Positivists was the language of science. They saw science as our greatest tool for discovering truths and sought to understand the logic of scientific inquiry and the manner in which scientific discourse acquired its meaning. They proposed that the meaning of scientific terms was grounded in the experiences by which scientists could determine whether the terms were satisfied. Such determination might be achieved through simple observations or experimental endeavors. The requirement that terms be so grounded in experience became known as the "verifiability theory of meaning." Having maintained that such reliance on verification was crucial to science, the Logical Positivists proposed to extend the verifiabilty requirement to other areas of human inquiry and advocated a general requirement on meaningful discourse. They thus proposed a modification of ordinary language through which we would expunge terms that lacked such verifiability. In developing this verifiability theory of meaning the Positivists adopted the referential approach to language and embedded it within an analysis of how we could acquire knowledge.

WITTGENSTEIN'S LATER CRITIQUE
OF THE REFERENTIAL THEORY

In the previous section we saw that at one time Wittgenstein endorsed the referential analysis of meaning. After defending it in the *Tractatus*, he left philosophy for better than a decade. When he returned in 1929 he began to question his earlier views. This questioning culminated in his *Philosophical Investigations*, published posthumously in 1953. In this statement of his new philosophical views, Wittgenstein focused on the variety of ways language is used and particularly on the fact that it can be used to do more than state facts. Rather than looking for the meaning of linguistic expressions in the way words refer to objects, Wittgenstein claimed that we first should focus on how we use language. To capture the idea that there are a variety of uses of language, Wittgenstein introduced the idea that particular uses of language can be construed as particular linguistics activities or *language games*. Wittgenstein claimed that there are a variety of language games, each with its own mode of play and its own rules. At one point Wittgenstein (1953) offers the following list of language games (not meant to be exhaustive):

Giving orders, and obeying them—

Describing the appearance of an object, or giving its measurements—
Constructing an object from a description (a drawing)—
Reporting an event—
Speculating about an event—
Forming and testing a hypothesis—
Presenting the results of an experiment in tables and diagrams—
Making up a story; and reading it—
Play acting—
Singing catches—
Guessing riddles—
Making a joke; and telling it—
Solving a problem in practical arithmetic—
Translating from one language into another—
Asking, thanking, cursing, greeting, and praying—. (Wittgenstein, 1953, I, 23)

In these various language games words are actually used in different ways. They are not always used to refer to objects. Accordingly, Wittgenstein thought we radically misunderstand ordinary language if we analyze it purely referentially.

Pain is one term Wittgenstein thought we misunderstand if we treat it referentially. In chapter 5 I discuss Wittgenstein's proposals as to how we should understand mental phenomena, but alluding to this example draws out one of the central aspects of his philosophy. He contends that many philosophical mistakes result from not attending carefully to the nature of particular language games and the rules that govern them. Such failures lead philosophers to create pseudoproblems. The very statement of these problems represent confused use of language. The proper task of philosophy, he contends, is not to solve these problems, but to dissolve them by showing how they originated from a failure to attend to the way language is really used. Consider the use of a term like *pain*. If we do not attend to how this term is used, we might think that a sentence like "I have a pain" is comparable to the sentence "I have a cat." This could mislead us into asking for evidence that a person has a pain and into trying to characterize pains as private things. But Wittgenstein asks us to attend to the circumstances in which we would use the expression "I have a pain." In using this expression we are not reporting something private, he maintains, but giving expression to our pain.

One of the philosophical doctrines about language that Wittgenstein criticized holds that in order for a general term (e.g., *dog* or *book*) to apply to an object, the object must possess the proper essence or defining properties. The idea that there must be defining properties for a general term goes back to Socrates (see previous chapter) and has been held by many philosophers since. Wittgenstein denies this assumption, maintaining that for many important terms in language we cannot specify defining or essential properties.[3] This is not because of our inadequacy, but because language does not require that things have essences. To try to convince readers of this claim, Wittgenstein uses the example of the simple term *game* and contends that there is no property shared by all and only games. Hence, there is no defining property of games shared by all and only games but only an overlapping variety of similarities between different games:

> Consider for example the proceedings that we call "games". I mean board-games, card-games, ball-games, Olympic games, and so on. What is common to them all?—Don't say: "There *must* be something common, or they would not be call 'games' "—but *look and see* whether there is anything common to all—For if you look at them you will not see something that is common to *all*, but similarities, relationships, and a whole series of them at that. To repeat: don't think, but look! . . . Are they all 'amusing'? Compare chess with noughts and crosses. Or is there always winning and losing, or competition between players? Think of patience. In ball games there is winning and losing; but when a child throws his ball at the wall and catches it again, this feature has disappeared. Look at the parts played by skill and luck; and at the difference between skill in chess and skill in tennis. Think now of games like ring-a-ring-a-roses; here is the element of amusement, but how many other characteristic features have disappeared! . . .
>
> And the result of this examination is: we see a complicated network of similarities overlapping and criss-crossing: sometimes overall similarities, sometimes similarities of detail. (Wittgenstein, 1953, I, 66)

Wittgenstein introduced the notion of "family resemblance" to describe his alternative view of what groups things into kinds. Just as members of a human family may resemble each other without there being one or more characteristics shared by all, Wittgenstein argued that instances of games will resemble each other and thereby form a linked network, without there being a single property shared by all games. This view of Wittgenstein's has become influential in recent cognitive science through the work on concepts and categorization by Eleanor Rosch (1975) and others (see Smith & Medin, 1981, for a review). Rosch, too, rejects the view that there are necessary and sufficient conditions that determine membership in a category and instead

---

[3]Socrates, for example, maintained that one could gain understanding of knowledge or justice only by discovering the essential property that would make something an instance of knowledge or justice. Wittgenstein, (1958) responds:

> The idea that in order to get clear about the meaning of a general term one had to find the common element in all its applications, has shackled philosophical investigation; for it has not only led to no result, but also made the philosopher dismiss as irrelevant the concrete cases, which alone could have helped him to understand the usage of the general term. When Socrates asks the question, 'what is knowledge?' he does not even regard it as a preliminary answer to enumerate cases of knowledge. (pp. 19-20)

explores how members of a category manifest similarity to an exemplar. (Wierzbicka, 1987, challenges the claim that terms like *game* lack a set of defining properties. For further discussion of this issues, see Barsalou, in preparation.)

Wittgenstein's later approach to language is radically different from that of philosophers who have claimed that ordinary language must be reformed because of its deficiencies. Wittgenstein's approach represents one version of what is often referred to as *ordinary language philosophy*. This term represents a commitment to the adequacy of already existing language and a need for attending more carefully to how this language is actually used. In fact, Wittgenstein represents a radical version of ordinary language philosophy insofar as he holds that philosophical problems arise "when language *goes on holiday*," that is, when we misuse ordinary language, and that the solution comes not in answering the problems philosophers pose but by dissolving the philosophical problems by appealing to how we ordinarily use the language.

SPEECH ACT THEORY:
AUSTIN, SEARLE, AND GRICE

Wittgenstein was not the only philosopher to turn to ordinary language for insight. Austin, Searle, and Grice have all concurred with Wittgenstein's judgment that rather than trying to reform ordinary language, philosophers should attend more carefully to how it functions. They developed a somewhat different perspective from Wittgenstein, however, insofar as they emphasized the use of language as a kind of action and analyze it accordingly.

The idea of treating language use as a kind of action was developed by J. L. Austin. In some of his early work, Austin advocated a distinction between *performative* utterances, such as issuing a command, and *constantive* utterances. The latter category encompassed the basic assertions that had been analyzed by Frege, Russell, and the early Wittgenstein. Austin's focus was on the former kind of utterance, which involved using language to carry out actions such as commanding and questioning. He took these uses to constitute actions. However, by the time he gave his William James' Lectures in 1955 (published posthumously as *How To Do Things with Words*, 1962a), he came to treat all speech acts, including ordinary assertions, as actions, and so themselves performatives. In analyzing these acts, Austin introduced a distinction between three sorts of acts that might be performed in making an utterance, which he termed *locutionary*, *illocutionary*, and *perlocutionary* acts. The locutionary act consists in making statements with words, where words are used with particular senses to refer to particular objects. The illocutionary act consists in the action the speaker performs in making the utterance. This might be informing warming, or promising. To distinguish the illocutionary act from the meaning of the words (which is part of the locutionary act) Austin speaks of these different uses of language as involving different *illocutionary forces*. Finally, the perlocutionary act consists in the effect the utterance has on the hearer. This might, for example, be to bore the hearer or convince him or her to take a certain action.[4]

Once we distinguish the illocutionary act performed in saying something from the locutionary act of uttering the words, we are in a position to note a variety of ways in which the act can fail or go wrong. For example, I can utter the words "I promise to give you a hammer" when I do not have a hammer, thereby being irresponsible, misleading, or imprudent. This has led to an inquiry into the conditions that must be fulfilled in order for a speech act to have a particular illocutionary force or for it to have its intended perlocutionary uptake. Austin began such inquiry, and it has been pursued more extensively by John Searle (1969, 1979). For example, Searle proposed that in order for one person to request another person to do something, the following conditions must be satisfied: The second person must have the ability to do the action and the first person must want the action done, must believe that his or her utterance will accomplish that end, and must have reasons for wanting it done. If any of these conditions are not satisfied, an action of requesting has not occurred.

Speech act theorists have also focused on another feature of the actions performed in using language—the cooperation required between speakers. Grice (1975) articulated four classes of maxims that specify ways in which speakers generally or conventionally cooperate in conversations:

1. Maxim of Quantity: Provide as much information as is needed in a context, but not more information.

---

[4]Austin not only developed this analysis of speech acts, but invoked the analysis of the use of language as a tool for solving philosophical problems. This tool required first collecting the vocabulary and idioms used to talk about a particular domain, like responsibility, and then examining in detail the nuances involved in the use of the terms and idioms. To collect the terms and idioms Austin recommended such techniques as free association, reading of relevant documents (e.g., legal findings about responsibility), and examination of dictionaries. The second steps involved constructing statements that might actually be used in the language, paying close attention to what terms would be used in normal speech and which ways of saying things would be preferred to others. For Austin, this activity had to be carried out prior to any philosophical theorizing, since such theorizing could contaminate the evidence and destroy sensitivity to how people actually use the language. The point of this exercise is to uncover the subtle distinctions made in the language that may then be of use when one begins to construct philosophical theories. The third step is to construct philosophical theories that both account for how the terms and idioms of the langauge are normally used and draw upon the insights about ordinary usage discovered in the earlier steps. It is in this last step that Austin's approach departs from Wittgenstein. For him, analysis of ordinary use of language is a tool to be used in solving philosophical problems, it does not lead us to dissolve the problems. Austin illustrated this method in numerous studies on topics of philosophical importance, such as the nature of human responsibility (Austin, 1956-1957) and the process of perception (Austin, 1962b).

2. Maxim of Quality: Speak true information.
3. Maxim of Relation: Make your contribution relevant to the context in which you are speaking.
4. Maxim of Manner: Speak as clearly as possible, avoid ambiguity, say things as simply as possible.

When you violate these maxims, Grice contended, you may mislead the person to whom you are speaking. For example, if you know the Reds won the game but say "Either the Reds or the Pirates won" in response to the query "Who won the game?" you mislead your audience into thinking that you do not know who won. You have violated the principle of providing as much information as is needed in the context. These principles affect not only the perlocutionary uptake of an utterance, but also the illocutionary force. This is due to the fact that by relying on these maxims you can often intend to mean things without actually saying the appropriate words. For example, if, in response to someone saying "I ran out of gas" you say "There is a gas station around the corner" you may be performing the illocutionary act of telling someone where they can get the needed gas. But this depends on the fact that your response is relevant to the context and you are giving maximal information. If you know the station is closed or out of gas, you would violate the quantity maxim and fail to perform the illocutionary act of informing the person where to get gas.

Relying on these maxims to perform an illocutionary act generates what Grice refers to as *conversational implicatures*. As Grice notes, you can also violate these principles to produce other conversational implicatures. For example, if, in writing a recommendation for a student, a professor fails to comment on pertinent items such as the student's scholarly abilities, and focuses on irrelevant details, like the student's reliability in attending classes, the faculty member makes a statement about the student's performance as a student and future professional. Without explicitly denigrating the student's ability in words, the faculty member nonetheless does so.

The speech act theorists Austin, Searle, and Grice, together with Wittgenstein, attempted to transform radically the task of philosophy of language. Rather than focusing on the meaning of words in a language, these philosophers tried to shift philosophers' focus to the activity of using language. For a number of years this approach attracted considerable philosophical interest, but this has largely expired as most philosophers of language have returned to analyzing the formal structure of language and attempting to articulate the logic of language. Questions about how language is used, though, have been taken up in linguistics as part of pragmatics (see Green, in preparation, for more details). Moreover, many of the issues discussed by these philosophers, especially Austin's distinction between locutionary, illocutionary, and perlocutionary forces in speech acts, have gained currency in psychological investigations of language comprehension and in artificial intelligence work on natural language processing.

HOLISTIC ANALYSES OF MEANING:
QUINE AND DAVIDSON

During the same period in which ordinary language philosophers were challenging the referential approach to language, Quine raised a different kind of objection to that program. Quine claimed that he was carrying the program of the Logical Positivists, especially Carnap, to its logical conclusion. In an early influential paper, Quine (1953/1961a) attacked two tenets held by many empiricists, which he took to be misguided dogmas that ought to be removed from Empiricism. These were the assumption that some statements were analytically true, that is, true in virtue of the meanings of the words (see chapter 1, this volume), and that meaningful discourse could be reduced in a systematic way to sensory experience.

The notion of analytic truth has been particularly important to philosophers in the analytic tradition, whose objective has been to discover truths by analyzing the meanings of philosophically important terms. But Quine argued that there is no noncircular definition of analyticity. If we define analytic truths as statements true by virtue of the meaning of their terms, then we must define meaning, and Quine argued that this leads us back to the notion of analyticity. Quine argued that this inability to define *analytic* is symptomatic of a larger problem, which is that words do not have specific meanings, but only meanings in the context of a whole network of other words to which they are connected in the sentences we take as true.

Similarly, Quine argued that successive failures to reduce scientific language to sensory experience is also symptomatic of the same problem. The remedy he recommended was abandoning the idea that words or even sentences have discrete meanings. Rather, he maintained that words and sentences are best understood in terms of our whole scientific discourse. This discourse tries to accommodate our experience in the world by making suitable adjustments over time. This is not accomplished by having individual terms with fixed links to the world. Rather, he proposed that we should view language metaphorically as like a fabric that only at its periphery impinges on experience. The task of human inquiry is to modify this fabric over time so that it better fits experience. Quine claims that this is a task in which there is great flexibility—we can modify in several different places as long as we make additional appropriate modifications elsewhere. As this happens, the way words are connected to each other changes and hence their meaning is altered. (For critical discussion of Quine's views, see Putnam, 1962, 1986. For discussion of the impact of Quine's attack on analyticity for philosophy of science, see Bechtel, in press b.)

Although the notion of fixed meaning for words was already under attack in Quine's challenge to the dogmas of analyticity and reduction to experience, Quine (1960) generalized the attack when he developed his thesis of the indeterminacy of translation. He focused on the activity of translating the utterances of someone else into our own words and developed the thesis that there are always a variety of ways for doing this and that there is no determinate answer to the issue of what is the appropriate translation:

> manuals for translating one language into another can be set up in divergent ways, all compatible with the totality of speech dispositions, yet incompatible with one another. In countless places they will diverge in giving, as their respective translations of a sentence of one language, sentences of the other language which stand to each other in no plausible sort of equivalence however loose. (1960, p. 27)

Quine begins his defense of this thesis by considering a case of radical translation, where we confront a language so remote from our own that no standard translation manuals have been developed. Subsequently he attempts to bring this thesis home to show that the same moral can be drawn when dealing with other speakers of our own language or indeed with our own past speech. He views the task of understanding or interpreting the words someone utters as merely an operation of translating them into our own words. In either the foreign case or the home case, his claim is that there are no scientifically acceptable grounds (i.e., ones based on empirical or sensory evidence) for insisting that one translation is more correct than another. This is a radical thesis. Quine is not merely noting that there is a lack of perfect correlation between languages so that we cannot always identify the correct way of correlating expressions in them. Rather, he is saying that there will always be alternative, radically different, interpretations of what is said, even when the language is our own. Thus, we can take a speaker (including ourself) to be saying different and inconsistent things depending on which translation we adopt and there is no answer to the question of which is correct.

Quine's argument for the indeterminacy thesis rests on two other theses, which he calls the *underdetermination of theories* and the *inscrutability of reference*. I present only the argument from the underdetermination of theories. The underdetermination thesis holds that in science one can always construct alternative theories to accord with the same empirical data and that even when all possible data have been collected, empirical evidence will not be able to decide between these theories (Quine, 1960, 1970). Quine defends this thesis on empiricist grounds. He permits only sensory evidence to settle theoretical disputes, but notes that scientific theories make claims that go beyond the evidence. The underdetermination thesis simply holds that two theories may differ only in the areas that go beyond the evidence, so that evidence cannot settle which one is correct. Quine turns the underdetermination thesis into support for the indeterminacy thesis by imagining ourselves trying to translate someone's theory of a domain for which we possess two underdetermined theories. Quine claims simply that we could translate that person's theory into either of our underdetermined theories, and nothing would count in favor of one translation over the other. Thus, we have two translations and no evidence on the basis of which we can decide that one is correct (Quine, 1970).

If the words in a person's language had specific meanings, then such indeterminacy would not arise. The conclusion that Quine draws, however, is that we have no evidence for such meanings and so we should abandon the idea that words have specific meanings. Moreover, he claims, there are no meanings or propositions in the heads of language users that determine how we should interpret their language.[5] As a result, Quine does not view language use as a peculiarly mental activity. It is, however, a phenomenon of nature that scientists should explain. (Quine, 1973, proposes a proto-scientific analysis.) This endeavor will consist simply in articulating the logical structure of the language and showing how it relates to the world in which the speaker exists (see chapter 3). On the basis of his own logical analysis, Quine argues that some forms of human discourse are not suitably structured for use in scientific inquiry. For example, he has argued that modal discourse of the sort discussed in the following section as well as indirect quotation (where we try to capture the meaning of what someone said in different words) are poorly crafted modes of discourse that we should abandon at least when we are doing science and want to develop true accounts of nature (Quine, 1960).

Although Quine proposes a philosophy of language that leaves no room for an account of meaning, Donald Davidson, a philosopher who has been significantly influenced by Quine's indeterminacy argument, has nonetheless tried to articulate a theory of meaning within the basic Quinean perspective. To do so Davidson invokes Tarski's analysis of truth for formal languages. Tarksi (1944/1952, 1967) proposed to state the truth condition for a given sentence in a formal language in terms of T-sentences such as the following:

"Snow is white" is true if and only if snow is white.

To see this statement as more than trivial, you must recognize a fundamental difference between the two occurrences of the words "snow is white." In

---

[5]Quine's conclusion depends on the particular way he interprets the indeterminacy thesis. Although Quine argues for the indeterminacy thesis on the basis of the underdetermination of theories, he insists that indeterminacy is not simply the underdetermination of linguistic theories (Quine, 1969b, 1970). Even if a scientific theory is underdetermined, we may make theoretical posits within our theory and treat it as a real account of the world. But Quine rejects the idea of treating a translation as a theory about what the language means and allowing the posit of propositions to account for a hypothesized sameness of meaning. This claim has proven quite controversial. For further discussion, see Kirk (1973), Quine (1975), and Bechtel (1978, 1980).

the first occurrence the quotation marks tell us we are naming and so referring to the sentence "snow is white," whereas in the second occurrence we
are using that sentence to designate the fact that would make this sentence
true. Technically, we speak of the second occurrence as stated in a different
language, the *object language*, from the first occurrence, which is in the *metalanguage* (a language used to talk about the first language). Tarski's T-sentences
can be interpreted as presenting a version of the "correspondence" theory
of truth, according to which a sentence is true if it corresponds to the way
things actually are. An adequate definition of truth, for Tarski, must have
as logical consequences all the T-sentences for the language. Tarksi
demonstrated that for formal languages meeting certain conditions it is possible to produce such a definition of truth, but not for ordinary languages such
as English.

Although Tarski's goal was to define truth. Davidson (1967) takes truth
as a primitive and uses Tarski's schema to account for meaning. Thus, for
Davidson, we identity the meaning of a sentence by stipulating what would
be the case if the sentence were true. If we are trying to state the meaning
for a sentence in our own language, then, as in the T-sentence just given,
we will also use our language as the metalanguage in which to state the truth
conditions. But when we are giving the meaning for sentences in a foreign
language, we will name the sentence in the foreign language and state the
truth conditions in English, as in the following example:

"Schnee ist weiss" is true in German if and only if snow is white.

The task for a *theory of meaning*, as for a definition of truth, is to generate
T-sentences for all the sentences of the language. To do this we cannot simply
state T-sentences for each sentence of the language because there will be an
infinite number of such sentences. Rather, we will need to develop a recursive procedure that shows how to construct a T-sentence for any given
sentence.

In developing this account of meaning that relies only on truth conditions,
Davidson claims that he is remaining within Quinean strictures. Moreover,
he also endorses Quine's holism about meaning. In practice we confront the
task of ascribing meaning when we need to interpret or translate what someone is saying. What we are doing is trying to figure out what would be true
if what they said was true. Davidson maintains, like Quine, that at this juncture we have no independent criterion by which to fix the meaning of their
words. To proceed, Davidson contends, we must assume that the person in
question at least most of the time is speaking what we would also take to
be the truth and so is saying what we would say. This Davidson characterizes
as a *principle of charity*—we interpret the other person as saying as many true
things as possible (Davidson, 1973, 1974a, 1975). Adopting this principle,

we try to construct a theory of interpretation that pairs the other person's sentences with sentences of our own that are equivalent in truth values. Only if we find points where our best generative theory matches sentences we take to be false with sentences the other person takes to be true do we acknowledge that the other person may believe falsehoods. A motivation for accepting this principle is that we interpret the words of another in order to acquire information. We can gain information only if we develop a scheme that construes them as speaking the truth most of the time. Davidson draws quite strong morals front this principle of charity. For example, he denies that we can understand the idea of another person having radically different conceptual schemes or ways of understanding the world from that which we use.[6] His reason is that we would not treat the person's statements as constituting a conceptual scheme unless we could interpret them, and by the principle of charity, we must interpret most of the statements as true (Davidson, 1974b).

MODAL DISCOURSE, POSSIBLE WORLD SEMANTICS, AND CAUSAL THEORIES OF REFERENCE: KRIPKE AND PUTNAM

The philosophical analyses of language I have examined so far have concentrated on extensional language, wherein terms can be treated as referring to actually existing objects and sentences can be viewed as ascribing properties or relations to these objects. In such contexts, Leibniz's Law sanctions substitution of one term for another with the same referent without changing the truth of a sentence. Quine and Davidson are two contemporary philosophers who have argued most vociferously for limiting meaningful discourse to extensional contexts and rejecting nonextensional contexts as linguistically suspect. But nonextensional contexts are common in normal speech. One such context involves use of verbs like "know" and "believe," which we have already encountered in discussing Frege and which I discuss further in later chapters. Another common class of nonextensional sentences are ones containing what are commonly called *modal* words such as "necessarily," "must," "possibly," or "may." Consider the sentence:

It was possible that Nixon might not have been president.

If we substitute the co-referential term *the 37th President* for Nixon, we get:

---

[6]Davidson is here undercutting claims such as Kuhn's contention that in major revolutions in science the new theory is so radically incommensurable with the old that the two theories cannot be discussed using the same language. Davidson would deny that we would view someone as holding a theory if we could not interpret their theory in our language. For further discussion of Kuhn's views, see Bechtel (in press b).

It was possible that the 37th President might not have been President.

Although the former sentence seems to be true, the latter does not.[7]

In ordinary English there are a variety of seemingly valid inferences involving sentences that use modal terms. These, however, are not sanctioned by the principles of ordinary predicate calculus, which are tied to extensional language. During this century a number of proposals have been advanced to modify the axiom set governing predicate calculus to accommodate these inferences (Carnap, 1956; Church, 1943). These proposals, however, were not accompanied by appropriate semantic theories to explicate the modal operators. This deficiency was remedied when Kripke (1963) developed a model-theoretic interpretation of various axiom sets for modal logic. Subsequently, Kripke (1971, 1972), Donnellan (1972), Putnam (1973, 1975b), and others have attempted to show how the formal analysis of modal statements may serve to cast light on basic issues in the philosophy of language such as the meaning of common and proper names.

The problem in understanding a modal statement like "Reagan might not have been elected President" in an extensional manner is that it is a counterfactual statement. It asks us to envision how things might have been different. Clearly, we cannot judge the truth and figure out the meaning of such statements by determining whether Reagan was elected President. A common way of representing what such statements are affirming is to invoke the idea of *possible worlds*. This idea ultimately goes back to Leibniz, who pictured God as contemplating different logical combinations of individuals and choosing this world as the largest compatible such set (thus inviting Voltaire's satirical comment that this is the best of all possible worlds). The notion of possible worlds is used to explicate modal logic by inviting us to think of alternative universes that are defined in terms of specific changes from this universe. We then consider how other things would be different under these situations. Thus we might consider the world in which Adolf Hitler had been miscarried rather than being born and then fill in the rest of the scenario for that world. If we invoke this fiction of possible worlds, we are in a position to say what makes a modal statement true or false. A claim that an object necessarily has a property is true just in case it has the property in every possible world where the object exists. Thus, Ronald Reagan was necessarily an

---

[7]The second sentence is actually ambiguous. Using what Russell termed a 'scope distinction" we can differentiate two readings of the sentence. One reading says of the person who was the 37th President, that that person might not have been President. On this reading, commonly referred to as the *de re* reading, the sentence is true. The other reading says that it is possible that the statement "The 37th President was President" might have been false. It is on this reading, referred to as the *de dicto* reading, that the modal sentence is false, because whoever was the 37th President was a president. For further discussion see Kaplan (1969), Donnellan (1972), and Linsky (1977).

actor is true if, in every is world in which Ronald Reagan exists, he is also an actor. Because there is a possible world in which he exists and is not an actor, the statement is false.

Interpreting modal claims in terms of possible worlds, Kripke advanced his argument that names are what he called *rigid designators* and not equivalent to any description we would use to pick out the referent. The argument rests on our accepting his intuition that we can envisage the possibility that the person or thing in question would not have those properties we supposedly use to identify them. For example, we may pick out Richard Nixon as the person who was the 37th President of the United States, but then we can envisage the possibility that he would never have been elected President. So, Kripke claims, the name is not identical with the description. (See Linsky, 1977, for a rebuttal to this argument.) The name picks out the person or object itself, irrespective of what properties that person might have had in the possible world under consideration. It is not necessary that there was a person Richard Nixon, but in any world in which Nixon exists, the rigid designator "Richard Nixon" picks out that person.

What Kripke's thesis amounts to is the claim that proper names do not have a Fregean sense, but only a referent. This was a view that was held even prior to Frege by J. S. Mill (1846) and in itself may not seem terribly striking. But Kripke and others who advance this approach to understanding modal contexts also advance a similar thesis about common nouns referring to "natural kinds" like *carbon* or *gold*. These terms likewise function as rigid designators, picking out particular objects without regard to properties we use to identify them, and so they too lack senses and possess only referents. The argument for this thesis is much the same as it was for proper names. Because it is possible that the object in question might not have the property we associate with the name (e.g., gold might not be yellow in some possible world), the property cannot determine the reference. It may only be a crutch used in this world to convey the reference to someone else, but once the reference is fixed, the property no longer figures as part of the meaning of the name.

Having rejected the view that either proper or common nouns are associated with properties that serve to pick out their referents, Kripke and other advocates of modal approaches have had to offer a different conception of how these names are linked to their referents. They advance what is called a *causal* theory of names. The idea is that names are linked to their referents through a causal chain. For example, at a baptismal ceremony a name might have been assigned to a person. All subsequent use of that name for that person is traced back to the original naming. Similarly, when someone first encounters an instance of a natural kind such as a piece of gold, they might assign the name "gold" to that kind. Subsequent use of the name for substances of that kind will then be tied to it through that causal chain. (It is not relevant to the *meaning* of the term, according to theorists in this tradition, that in order to identify subsequent instances of the natural kind we will need to rely on identification procedures.)

The causal theory is viewed by its proponents as a direct challenge to a variety of traditional views about meaning. In particular, it is a challenge to the Fregean idea that terms have both sense and reference and that sense determines reference. It is also viewed as a challenge to the Wittgensteinian alternative to the Fregean idea. Wittgenstein (as discussed previously) proposed that although there may be no defining features shared by all the objects referred to by a term, there may be a family resemblance amongst the items. Causal theorists deny that there is any such set of properties that determine the meaning of such terms. Rather, the term applies directly to the object as the connection was set in place by the initial naming of the object.[8]

These attempts to explicate what is meant by modal sentences invite a question about how we recognize objects in possible worlds. How do we determine which entity in another possible world is Richard Nixon, or a piece of gold? Kaplan (1967) called this the problem of *transworld identity*.[9] Kripke (1972) responds that merely raising this question represents a fundamental mistake. Possible worlds are not things we first identify and then determine how their inhabitants correspond to the inhabitants of the actual world. Possible worlds are *stipulated*, not discovered. We stipulate which individuals exist in the possible world and what properties they have. Hence, we never need to raise questions as to which individual corresponds to an individual in our world. Starting with Richard Nixon, we decide whether or not he exists in the possible world we are contemplating, and if he does, then we attribute to him all of his *essential* properties (which are typically different from those we use to identify Richard Nixon) and whatever other properties we deem him to have in the possible world.

Although this approach avoids the problem of specifying transworld identity relations, it provokes another objection concerning the essential properties that must be attributed to any individual in a world in which the individual exists. The view that some of an entity's properties are essential to it so that if it lacked those properties it would not be the same entity is known as *essentialism*. To identify those properties Kripke, Donnellan, and Putnam rely heavily on their intuitions about what makes an object the object that

---

[8]Advocates of the causal theory, such as Rey (1983) have also criticized the proposals of psychologists like Rosch (1975) to characterize the reference of natural kind terms through prototypes. Following Kripke and Putnam, Rey takes the referent of a term to be fixed objectively, even if ordinary users of the language should need to rely on various identification strategies to determine whether something is an instance of a kind. For theorists in this tradition, the identification strategies are independent from the referent, as fixed by the causal theory.

[9]The problem is also developed by Lewis (1968), who denies that there can be cross-world identities, but only counterparts in one world that closely resemble individuals in another world.

it is. In the case of human beings, Kripke takes their origin to constitute their essential property. Thus, although Nixon might have become a sumo wrestler, he could not have been born of different parents. In the case of chemical elements, like gold and water, Putnam (1975b) contends that it is the molecular composition that is essential. Thus, water is H_2O in any world in which it exists, although it might differ in other properties from water here. In the case of artifacts, Kripke takes the matter they are made of to be crucial to their identity. Thus, Kripke argued that a podium actually made of a certain piece of wood could not be made of water frozen from the river Thames. Such intuitions, however, are not shared by everyone. For example, someone might claim that what seems crucial to someone being Richard Nixon is his physical appearance or being a politician. Lacking these properties, a person would simply not be Richard Nixon.

It is difficult to see how arguments could establish what is essential to something being the entity or kind of entity it in fact is. The fact that judgments of what is essential seem to rest on nothing more than the intuitions of some speakers is one reason some philosophers have found the whole enterprise of evaluating modal claims to be problematic. The argument for construing names as rigid designators without any properties or sense attached to them, though, depends heavily on these modal arguments. Thus, if you reject modal contexts and essentialism, as Quine and Davidson do, then you may also be quite content with associating names with descriptions or even doing away with names altogether, as Quine (1960) proposes. On the other hand, accepting modal discourse and devising a semantics for it seems to require a radically different conception of names and a sharp distinction between names and descriptions. (For further discussion of these issues, see Lewis, 1983b; Linsky, 1977.)

SUMMARY

We have now surveyed several different philosophical analyses of language. The referential analysis adopted by Frege and Russell has been severally criticized by Wittgenstein and the speech act theorists, who argue that to understand language we must look at how it is used. But modified versions of Frege's and Russell's referential analyses have been adopted by other contemporary philosophers. The extensional character of the referential theories has been maintained by Quine and Davidson, who have challenged other features such as Frege's introduction of senses and Russell's theory of descriptions. Quine and Davidson both reject the idea of a meaning for words in addition to reference and place the assignment of reference into a holistic perspective. Kripke and Putnam likewise attack Frege's notion of sense, but they also reject the extensionalism of the older referential account. They have proposed a causal theory through which names are causally linked to their referent and maintain this link across possible worlds.

In subsequent chapters it becomes apparent that these theories of language have implications for theories about the mind. (For two contemporary discussions of issues in philosophy of language that make explicit their implications for theories of mind, see Lycan, 1984, and Pollock, 1982.) Because of these connections between theories of language and theories of mind, in subsequent chapters there are numerous references back to the material introduced here. But now it is time to enter into discussion of an issue central to philosophy of mind, the issue of whether mental phenomena are distinguished from physical phenomena as a result of possessing a property known as *intentionality*.

3

The Problem
of Intentionality

INTRODUCTION

A typical mental state, for example a belief, is generally *about* something. You may believe that Hawaii is a beautiful place, in which case your belief is *about* Hawaii. This characteristic of being about something is what philosophers call *intentionality*.[1] Many philosophers, moreover, view intentionality as a feature that differentiates mental states from other phenomona of nature. The goal of this chapter is to introduce the phenomenon of intentionality and to discuss why some philosophers have viewed it as presenting an obstacle to developing scientific accounts of mental phenomena. In chapter 4, we turn to some strategies other philosophers have proposed to explain intentionality in a scientifically acceptable manner.

Before turning to some of the more explicit criteria that have been offered for identifying the intentionality of mental states, we can flesh out the basic idea that intentionality refers to the capacity of mental states or events to be about other objects or events. In the belief about Hawaii just mentioned, Hawaii and the putative beauty of Hawaii are the objects of your belief. They remain the objects of your belief even if you have never been to Hawaii and are now far away from it. It is relatively easy to see, at least in general terms,

---

[1]The term *intentionality* is a technical term drawn from Medieval philosophy, where it was used to refer to things in the mind or operations of the mind. Although there is a relationship between this term and the term *intentional* that is a derivative of *intend*, the two should not be confused. The term should also be distinguished from another related technical philosophical term, *intension*, which is commonly used to refer to the sense rather than the referent or extension of a term.

40

how this feature of mental states differentiates them from most other states or events in nature.[2] Ordinary states in the world, such as a lamp sitting on a table, are not about anything. The lamp may be causally affected by other objects, and can cause changes in other entities in nature, but it does not have states that are about other things in anything like the manner in which people can have beliefs about various objects. The ability to be about other states is not only true of beliefs, but of a host of other mental activities, such as wishing, fearing, doubting, hoping, planning. If you hope that you will get tenure, then your hope is *about* tenure. Through your mental activities, you are connected to other states in nature, but not in any straightforward causal sense. Thus, you can have a belief about a state of affairs (e.g., getting tenure) that is not causally produced by that state of affairs, and you can have a desire for a state of affairs without that desire leading you to take any action to produce it.

Starting from this informal characterization of intentionality, several philosophers have tried to develop more formal characterizations that also serve to show what distinguishes intentional phenomena from those that are nonintentional. Two of the most prominent of these are due to the late 19th century philosopher Franz Brentano and more recently to Roderick Chisholm.

BRENTANO'S ACCOUNT
OF INTENTIONAL INEXISTENCE

Brentano (1874/1973) focused attention on the fact that the things or events referred to in mental states need not be real. We can have beliefs or other mental states that are about nonexistent objects. For example, someone might believe that unicorns have only one horn or a child might hope that Santa Claus will bring wonderful presents. Even though unicorns and Santa Claus do not exist, Brentano claims that they are still presented to the person in the mental states. Brentano argues that every mental state—not just those that are normally taken to involve presentations (hearing a sound, seeing a colored object, feeling warmth or cold), but also judgments, recollections, inferences, opinions, and so on—involve an object or objects being presented to or appearing to the subject. He also claims that the fact that mental states involve such presentations of things constitutes their intentionality and distinguishes them from all physical phenomena:

---

[2]There are devices in some biological systems that give information *about* other states of the system, and human-made instruments like thermostats and gas gauges that perform similar tasks. Generally, the human-made instruments are thought to derive their intentionality from their makers, whereas the biological information carriers have been largely ignored in discussions of intentionality. See, however, the discussions of Dretske and Dennett in chapter 4, which do provide a perspective for considering the intentionality found in biological systems.

> Every mental phenomenon is characterized by what the Scholastics of the Middle
> Ages called the intentional (or mental) inexistence of an object, and what we
> might call, though not wholly unambiguously, reference to a content, direc-
> tion toward an object (which is not to be understood here as meaning a thing),
> or immanent objectivity. Every mental phenomenon includes something as ob-
> ject within itself, although they do not all do so in the same way. In presenta-
> tion something is presented, in judgment something is affirmed or denied, in
> love loved, in hate hated, in desire desired and so on. This intentional in-existence
> is characteristic exclusively of mental phenomena. No physical phenomenon
> exhibits anything like it. We can, therefore, define mental phenomena by say-
> ing that they are those phenomena which contain an object intentionally within
> themselves. (Brentano, 1874/1973, p. 88)

For Brentano, the intentionality of mental states not only distinguishes them
from purely physical states; it also undermines any attempt to study mental
states using the tools of physical science. Hence, Brentano's treatment of intentionality provides support for the dualist view that the mind is distinct
from the body (for more on dualism, see chapter 5).

The passage from Brentano has been the focus of considerable controversy. According to one interpretation, adopted by Brentano's student Meinong,
Brentano commits himself to the existence of a class of "objects" (i.e., objects of thought) that exist even when there are no objects in the physical
world that correspond to them. Thus, when I think of something, for example, of the perfect ice cream, there must be a particular object toward which
my thought is directed. But because there may be no real object fitting this
description, the object of my thought must be a peculiar kind of mental object.[3] To accommodate this interpretation, Meinong (1904/1960) introduced
a distinction between the *Sosein* (the being or subsistence) of an object and
its *Sein* (existence). Objects that do not actually exist, like golden mountains
and round squares, still have a subsistence. It is the subsistence of the object
that constitutes the intentional object of thought. So, if I say of the round
square that it is round, I am really talking about the subsisting round square,
and not any real object.

Although this provides a plausible interpretation of the passage quoted
from Brentano, Brentano actually disowned it, largely because he realized
that it led to serious problems. The difficulty was brought out clearly by Frege.
In the previous chapter, we noted that Frege (1892) introduced the distinction between the *sense* of an expression and its *referent*. The sense represented
the mode of presentation of the object (e.g., it would characterize the features
of the object). Although it might seem as though Frege's senses might serve
as intentional objects,[4] Frege recognized that if we took senses to be the ob-

---

[3]In the previous chapter, we saw that Meinong had an additional set of reasons for extending the range of objects beyond physical objects. There he used pure or subsisting objects to
explain the referent of terms like *unicorn* in do sentences like "unicorns do not exist" (see p. 20).

[4]Frege in fact allows the sense of an expression to serve as the referent in such contexts as
indirect discourse (see p. 21).

jects of thought when discussing nonexistent objects, then we would be committed to doing the same when discussing actual objects. The reason is that nothing in the mental state itself distinguishes cases in which we are thinking about actual objects from those in which we are thinking about nonexisting objects. This leads to the unwanted consequence that all of our discourse is about senses or intentional objects and not about objects in the world. (For further discussion of this problem and of Brentano's treatment of it, see Chisholm, 1967; Føllesdol, 1982; Husserl, 1913/1970, 1929/1960, 1950/1972.)

In pointing to the fact that mental states may be directed towards nonexisting objects or events, Brentano set a difficult task for subsequent thinkers. The fact that mental states are directed at objects, and that these objects do not always exist, makes it difficult to account for the intentionality of mental states. We seem to be committed to the inconsistent claims that, on the one hand, intentional states involve a relation to an object and that, on the other hand, the object to which we might hope to relate intentional states need not exist. A relation requires two objects and yet, for intentional states, there may be no second object.[5] Moreover, this is a tension for which there is no easy resolution because, as Richardson (1981) argued, we cannot really sacrifice either claim if we are to deal adequately with intentional phenomena:

> On the one hand, if we maintain that there are non-existent but real objects which are the objects of our thought, we are compelled to admit that none of our objects [the objects about which we have beliefs, etc.] are in the real world. We are barred from thinking of the concrete. On the other hand, if we admit that mental acts are not really relational, we are led to the conclusion that mental acts cannot really direct us to objects in the world (or out of it either). Our thinking does not relate us to the world. In either event, such acts can hardly be viewed as Intentional. (pp. 177–178)

From a modern cognitive science perspective, one might suppose that the problem of intentionality could be solved by postulating representations as the objects of mental states, and thus as the objects of thought. Although

---

[5]Brentano introduces the term *relation-like* to capture this character of intentional states:

In the case of other relations, the Fundament as well as the Terminus must be an actual existing thing. . . . If one house is larger than another house, then the second house as well as the first house must exist and have a certain size. . . . But this is not at all the case with psychical relations. If a person thinks about something, the thinker must exist but the objects of his thoughts need not exist at all. Indeed, if the thinker is denying or rejecting something, and if he is right in so doing, then the object of his thinking must not exist. Hence the thinker is the only thing that needs to exist if a psychical relation is to obtain. The Terminus of this so-called relation need not exist in reality. One may well ask, therefore, whether we are dealing with what is really a relation at all. One could say instead that we are dealing with something which is in a certain respect similar to a relation, and which, therefore, we might describe as being something that is 'relation-like' [etwas 'relativliches']. (1874, quoted in Chisholm, 1967, p. 146)

representations, as discussed later, may play an important role in explaining how intentionality is possible, they cannot play the role for which Brentano seemed to be positing intentional objects. The reason can be appreciated if we focus on veridical beliefs. In such cases, we want to say that our beliefs are *about* the actually existing object or state of affairs in the world. But if we make representations the objects of our beliefs in cases of false beliefs, parity of reasoning requires that we take representations as the objects of belief in the case of veridical beliefs. But this fails to capture the important element for which the term *intentionality* was introduced in the first place, namely, the idea that the object of our mental states are often things external to us. If we adopt the tool of mental representations, we must still explain how some of our mental states succeed in connecting to things in the world while others fail to do so. It is this connection, which may or may not occur, that makes these representations be *of* something and hence intentional.

CHISHOLM'S LINGUISTIC CRITERION
OF INTENTIONALITY

Brentano's criterion for intentionality seems to lead into a metaphysical thicket by raising questions about the status of intentional objects. Many English-speaking philosophers, particularly in the middle part of this century, have sought to avoid such metaphysical questions by focusing not on the phenomena of the world but on the language in which claims about the world are made. In particular, they have tried to show how we could clarify and resolve many scientific and philosophical problems by presenting our claims in terms of symbolic logic. Our language for describing mental states, however, seems to introduce some logical peculiarities, leading Roderick Chisholm, among others, to propose that we could identify intentional states in terms of the logical peculiarities in the sentences referring to them.

For purposes of the present discussion, there are two important aspects of modern symbolic logic that we need to keep in mind. The first of these is that logic is *truth-functional*. This means that the truth of any sentence that is composed from other sentences (e.g., "Today is Thursday or it is snowing") can be ascertained simply by knowing the truth value of the component sentences. A second important feature is that symbolic logic is *extensional*. As we saw in the previous chapter, this means that the truth of an expression only depends on what the expression *refers* to (its *extension*), not its meaning (*intension*). As we noted, extensional discourse obeys Leibniz's law, which permits substitution of one term for another term referring to the same object in a statement without altering the truth value of that statement. Thus, we can replace the term "212 degrees Fahrenheit" for the term "100 degrees Celsius" in the sentence "At sea level, ordinary water will boil at 100 degrees Celsius" and still have a true sentence.

Many sentences describing peoples' mental states fail to satisfy both of these conditions. The sentence

"Cathy believes that at sea level water boils at 100 degrees Celsius"

contains the sentence

"water boils at 100 degrees Celsius"

but the truth value of the whole sentence is not a function of the truth value of this component. The truth of the component statement does not inform us as to whether the whole statement is true. Moreover, it is easy to see that it fails the extensionality condition because this belief statement may be true and yet the sentence

"Cathy believes that at sea level water boils at 212 degrees Fahrenheit"

may be false. If Cathy does not know that 100 degrees Celsius is equivalent to 212 degrees Fahrenheit, she may not have any beliefs about the second sentence. If she believes falsely that 100 degrees Celsius is equivalent to 312 degrees Fahrenheit, she may even believe that it is false that water boils at 212 degrees Fahrenheit. (This feature of statements about mental states is referred to as the *failure of substitutivity*.)[6]

Many philosophers refer to sentences that exhibit these logical features as *intentional sentences*. To call attention to the fact that they are differentiated in terms of these logical peculiarities (which distinguish them from exten-

---

[6]There is a third respect in which sentences about mental states often deviate from the principles of logic that are adequate to handle most statements about the empirical world. Ordinary statements about the world conform to the principle of existential generalization, which allows us to infer from a claim such as

"I am sitting at a desk."

The claim

"Something exists at which I am sitting."

Some statements about mental states violate this principle. The statement

"I am thinking of a unicorn"

might be true but we could not infer

"There is something of which I am thinking."

sional statements), some philosophers use the spelling *intensional* for these sentences.[7]

Relying on logical anomalies like those just given above, Chisholm (1957, 1958) tried to reformulate Brentano's conception of intentionality so as to focus on the logical features of the language we use when talking about psychological activities:

> Let us say (1) that we do not need to use intentional language when we describe non-psychological, or "physical," phenomena; we can express all that we know, or believe, about such phenomena in language which is not intentional. And let us say (2) that, when we wish to describe certain psychological phenomena— in particular, when we wish to describe thinking, believing, perceiving, see- ing, knowing, wanting, hoping and the like—either (a) we must use language which is intentional or (b) we must use a vocabulary which we do not need to use when we describe non-psychological, or "physical," phenomena.[8] (1958, pp. 511-512)

Chisholm maintains that this way of framing the issue offers benefits lack- ing in Brentano's original. It avoids raising the issue of the ontological status of intentional objects by limiting the focus to language. Yet, it maintains a distinction between different kinds of phenomena in nature.[9]

A variety of objections have been raised against Chisholm's attempt to characterize intentionality linguistically. One such objection contends that such criteria do not cover all sentences about mental phenomena. Some sentences, such as "Jones is in pain" or "Cathy is thinking of Carol" are clearly about mental phenomena but do not fall under one of his three conditions (Cornman, 1962; Margolis, 1977). Another objection is that sentences not about intentional or psychological phenomena also meet his conditions. Any sentence about what is possible or necessary, for example, will show failure of substitutivity. To borrow an example from Quine (1953/1961b), it is true that

Nine is the number of the planets.

---

[7]This spelling may engender confusion because this meaning of *intensional* must be distinguished from the use of the word *intension* to refer to Fregean senses.

[8]The reason Chisholm adds this last condition is that he acknowledges that we may invent a nonintentional language for describing mental states. He justifies the original thesis by main- taining that in order to explain the meaning of the locutions in this nonintentional language we will have to relapse into intentional language.

[9]Chisholm sees his account of intentionality as undercutting attempts to analyze mentality in terms of physical processes and so unify the sciences of the mind with the physical sciences. The reason is that different logical principles will govern the two domains (see Aquila, 1977; Chisholm, 1967). For a different linguistic analysis of intentionality, see Anscombe (1965). She identifies sentences about intentional phenomena in terms of their grammatical features and argues that we should analyze intentionality in terms of grammatical features, not in terms of ontological differences.

It is also true that

It is necessary that nine is greater then seven.

But if we substitute co-referential terms we generate the false statement:

It is necessary that the number of the planets is greater than seven.

Various attempts have been made to resolve these difficulties and to develop an adequate linguistic criterion of intentionality (see Chisholm, 1967; Lycan, 1969), and many philosophers still allude to such a criterion (see Dennett, 1982; Rosenberg, 1980). However, some powerful arguments have been advanced for not pursuing this strategy. Searle (1981), for example, argued that the logical peculiarities found in language describing mental phenomena do not really characterize features of the mental state, but only a feature of the language used to discuss mental states. Intentionality refers to the fact that mental states have contents and that they refer to other phenomena, which are quite different features of the world than the logical peculiarities of sentences about mental phenomena. Thus, Searle contended that the search for a linguistic criterion is a red herring, because it does not get at the crucial aspects of intentionality. (For additional arguments against pursuing a linguistic criterion, see Richardson, 1981.) If one rejects the linguistic criterion, then one seems to be forced back to a criterion like Brentano's and the need to face the question about the status of intentional objects.

REPRESENTING INTENTIONAL STATES AS PROPOSITIONAL ATTITUDES

Another approach to characterizing intentionality has taken a cue from the common linguistic form of sentences using verbs like "believe," "hope," "desire," and the like. Statements using these verbs commonly take the form:

Cathy hopes that her movie receives good reviews.

In this form, the main verb is followed by the word "that" and a proposition. The verb serves to express a person's attitude toward the proposition. Hence, Russell (1940) introduced the phrase "propositional attitudes" to refer to such sentences. This has become the canonical form for representing mental states. Although sometimes we use verbs like "hope" and "believe" without a proposition (as in "Jim believes Cathy") such sentences can always be transformed into the canonical form using the word "that' by supplying a proposition (for example, "Jim believes that what Cathy said is true").

The canonical propositional attitude format is attractive because it provides us with two degreees of freedom for characterizing mental states, represented by the verb and the proposition. You can have the same attitude toward different propositions or different attitudes toward the same proposition. For example, you might both believe that Eileen will get the position and desire that she will not. This seems to be just the right structure for explaining a person's actions and making comparisons between people's mental states. First, the attitude and desire, when brought together and directed at the same proposition, can be the cause for action (e.g., working to sabotage Eileen's candidacy). Second, interpersonally, we may account for the difference in two individual's actions by noting how they differ in some of these attitudes. For instance, two people may both believe that Eileen is likely to get the position, but one desires that she does, while the other may desire that she does not get the job.

In addition to providing a useful way to characterize mental states, the framework of propositional attitudes also suggests a way of characterizing the intentionality of mental states—we use the proposition toward which the person has an attitude to identify the content of the person's mental state. The use of propositions to specify the content of metal states suggests a connection between the analyses of language and of mind. This connection has been exploited by a number of philosophers, so we need to consider briefly what propositions are. They are often invoked in philosophy of language to represent the meaning that might be shared by different sentences (e.g., sentences in different languages—see p. 21). In this capacity, a proposition is typically construed as an abstract entity, differentiated on the one hand from a particular sentence uttered or written in a language, and on the other from the mental state that led someone to utter or write the sentence. A person is said to have a proposition in mind when uttering a sentence, but the proposition itself is something separate from the speaker that the speaker grasps or understands. Those who invoke propositions in analyzing language also view them as serving other functions, such as serving as bearers of truth values ("the proposition Jones expressed was true") and as picking out the possible or actual state of affairs being referred to in the sentence.[10]

When propositions are also invoked to explicate propositional attitude discourse used to characterize mental states, they enable us to explicate an important ambiguity. When you and I both believe that we will eat dinner at home tonight, our beliefs are directed at the proposition "I will eat dinner

---

[10]Many philosophers, including ordinary langauge philosophers, and nominalists like Quine (see p. 50f.), have argued against the attempt to analyze language in terms of propositions. However, there has been a resurgence of interest in propositions, largely in response to attempts by Carnap, Kripke, and Montague to analyze the semantics of modal logics. For a variety of contemporary analyses of propositions, see Harman (1973, 1977), Donnellan (1974), Kaplan (1978), Perry (1979), and Stalnaker (1976).

at home tonight." Do we have the same belief when we share the same propositional attitude toward this proposition? The correct answer seems to be in one respect, yes, and in another respect, no. The ambiguity arises from the fact that "home" may refer to some particular place (e.g., my house), or to whatever counts as home for the believer in question. When it refers to whatever we count as home, we capture the respect in which you and I both believe the same thing when each of use believes that we will eat dinner at home tonight. Yet, there is also a respect in which we believe something quite different, for I believe I will eat dinner at my house in Atlanta, whereas you believe that you will be eating at a different residence, probably in a different city. This reading is accounted for by the fact that I take "home" to refer to my house, whereas you take it to refer to your house. Invoking Frege's distinction between the *sense* and *referent* of a term, in the first case it was the sense of "home" that mattered, whereas in the second it was the referent. The sense–reference distinction developed in Frege's analysis of language thus allows us to explicate the ambiguity that arises in propositional attitude characterizations of mental states. (For further discussion, see Dennett, 1982; Perry, 1977.)

The framework of propositions and propositional attitudes thus provides a convenient way to characterize mental states. It also serves to locate the problem of intentionality because the purpose of citing the proposition is to specify the content of someone's mental state. As we see in chapter 4, the Computational Theory of Mind tries to capitalize on these advantages. There is, however, a serious danger that arises when we use propositional attitude forms to represent intentional states. This form seems to offer an explanation of how intentionality arises, but it does not. The propositional attitude form suggests that the object of the propositional attitude is the proposition itself so that, for example, one's belief is *about* the proposition. This move encounters the same problem as I noted in discussing Meinong's attempt to postulate intentional objects as the objects of mental states. The problem is that if we treat propositions as the objects of intentional attitudes, then all of our mental states are about these propositions and not *about* the objects of the world. The intentionality of mental states, however, is just their ability to be *about* events in the world. When we invoke propositional attitude forms, we must be careful to remember that propositions are to be the *bearers* of intentionality, not the objects that intentional states are about. In ascribing a propositional attitude such as

Sam believes that the cat is fierce

the proposition

the cat is fierce

states what is believed, but the belief is *about* the cat and its putative ferocity, not merely the proposition. This does not count against the attempts by some cognitive scientists to use the resources of the propositional attitude structure in developing accounts of mental processing. It does mean, however, that the critical work of explaining intentionality is not done by postulating the proposition or representation. The task of explaining how propositions or representations are *about* objects or events in the world, some of which do not actually exist, remains to be carried out.

THE ATTEMPT TO DENY
THE REALITY OF INTENTIONALITY

The use of the propositional attitude to represent mental states has also led philosophers like Quine, who question the legitimacy of propositions as tools in the analysis of language, to question as well whether intentionality is a real phenomenon that our science should try to account for. Quine's arguments against propositions generally are based on his thesis of the indeterminacy of translation. This thesis, discussed in chapter 2, maintains that there is no determinate meaning to terms in a language because we can always set up alternative manuals to translate terms of Language 1 into those of Language 2. These alternative manuals will equate the same terms in the first language with different terms in the second language. According to Quine, no evidence can show us that one translation is correct. Quine viewed this argument as proving that it is a mistake to posit determinate propositions to represent the meaning of a sentence because the possibility of alternative translations show there is no unique meaning. Further, he claimed that it is a mistake to assume that speakers have definite meanings in mind when they utter sentences, because nothing prevents us from employing a different translation and hence making a different assignment of meaning.

It is the mistaken view that there are propositions, Quine maintains, that results in a mentalistic view of meaning and what he refers to as "the myth of the museum" (Quine, 1969c). This myth holds that there are specific mental states, for example, ideas or thoughts, that we express when we use language. Quine claims this is a mistake because, just as we can translate sentences in another language differently depending on which translation manual we choose, we can interpret the sentence we use to specify the content of a propositional attitude differently depending on which interpretation manual we choose. (Interpretation, for Quine, is logically comparable to translation. In both cases we are equating one set of words with another.) Imagine that someone tries to tell us that he or she believes that evolution occurred by natural selection. Because Quine claims that we can give alternative interpretations, in our own words, of the sentence representing what is believed, he denies that there is anything determinate that the person believes. Because we can apply the indeterminancy thesis to our own inner discourse by translating our own words into different words in our language, Quine further denies that there is something determinate that we believe.

Quine views his indeterminacy thesis as showing the mistake of thinking people have mental states that exhibit intentionality. In fact, he explicitly relates his indeterminacy thesis to Brentano's thesis that mental states are characterized by intentionality, but he draws the opposite conclusion from Brentano. Although Brentano held that we must recognize a special status for intentional phenomena, Quine (1960) claims that we must purge intentional terms like *belief* from our science, including our science of human behavior:

> Brentano's thesis of the irreducibility of intentional idioms is of a piece with the thesis of indeterminacy of translation.
>   One may accept the Brentano thesis either as showing the indispensability of intentional idioms and the importance of an autonomous science of intentional, or as showing the baselessness of intentional idioms and the emptiness of a science of intention. My attitude, unlike Brentano's, is the second. To accept intentional usage at face value is, we saw, to postulate translation in principle relative to the totality of speech dispositions. Such postulation promises little gain in scientific insight if there is no better ground for it than that the supposed translation relations are presupposed by the vernacular of semantics and intention. (p. 221)

In the place of a science of intentionality, Quine proposes the development of a thoroughly behavioristic analysis of human behavior. He acknowledges that we do use intentional idioms like *believes* in daily life to describe ourselves and others, but, because such terms are groundless, they must be dispensed with when we turn to science: "If we are limning the true and ultimate structure of reality, the canonical scheme for us is the austere scheme that knows no quotation but direct quotation and no propositional attitudes but only the physical constitution and behavior of organisms" (1960, p. 221).

Quine's attack on the notion of meaning has been accepted, with modifications, by a number of philosophers. Donald Davidson (1974a), for example, holds that any ascription of content to the statements or mental states of other people is a matter of interpretation, not discovery. Putnam (1983) draws a similar moral, maintaining that interpretation of the language or thought of another is essentially a holistic enterprise carried on by an interpreting agent. It is not a matter of discovering anything going on in the person.[11]

---

[11]A related position is defended by Alexander Rosenberg. He treats the logical peculiarities of intentional sentences as sufficient for repudiating intentional phenomena from science. He maintains that there is an unbridgeable chasm between intentional talk and scientific analysis and attributes our inability to formulate true laws in intentional terms to these logical peculiarities. He observes, however, that intentional language is used quite freely in other domains such as molecular biology and sociobiology. One speaks, for example, of an enzyme recognizing a substrate. But he contends that in such contexts these terms have, at least implicitly, clear behavioral definitions. Once similar behavioral definitions are in place, he thinks psychology will be able to advance. Hence, he recommends invoking the frameworks of both sociobiology and behavioral molecular biology in order to develop real explanations of human behavior. These will replace the failed attempts to develop intentional explanations (Rosenberg, 1980, 1986).

Others, however, have resisted Quine's conclusions. Some have challenged Quine's account of the significance of the indeterminacy thesis itself by arguing that a decision to adopt a determinate translation manual and develop a theory of meaning for language within it is no different than the decision to accept a particular theory in a scientific discipline and work within it. Even though, as Quine maintains, there will be other theories empirically equivalent to the one we use, he allows that we are entitled in physics to accept one theory and work within it. If we treat the activities of translation and interpretation in a similar manner to theorizing in physics, then we should view postulating mental states to account for intentional phenomena as on a par with developing a theory in physics. The measure of adequacy of a mentalistic theory will be whether it serves our scientific purposes (e.g. , explaining behavior). If it turns out that treating humans as having intentional states facilitates these ends, then countenancing such states will accord well with adopting a scientific attitude (see Bechtel, 1978; Chomsky, 1969).

Quine, however, has steadfastly resisted this approach, arguing that the indeterminacy thesis establishes more than that mentalistic theories manifest the usual underdetermination true of all scientific theories (Quine, 1969b). He claims that such theories are simply vacuous. Whether these theories are in fact vacuous, however, would seem to depend on their explanatory power. Although the final verdict is not yet in, the success of mentalistic theories that have been developed in cognitive science and the corresponding limitations of behaviorist approaches (Brewer, 1974) would seem to be evidence that these theories have explanatory power in the same manner as other scientific theories and so should be treated in the same light (see McCauley, 1987a; Palmer & Kimchi, 1986). It is then incumbent upon us to explain how the intentionality of these mental states arises. In chapter 4 I consider various theories that philosophers have advanced to account for the intentionality of mental states.

PRELIMINARY CONCLUSIONS
ABOUT INTENTIONALITY

In this chapter I have introduced what philosophers refer to as the *intentionality* of mental states—their capacity to be about things in the world. I have also examined two views about how this feature of mental states seems to distinguish them from other, purely physical states. I have also shown how we can capture the intentionality of mental states by describing them in terms of propositional attitudes, wherein the propositions state the content of mental states. But this does not yet solve the problem of intentionality, because we must still show how the propositions relate to the states in the world that mental states are said to be *about*. One approach to this problem is simply to deny that intentional mental states exist. Thus, Quine has tried to deny the reality of intentionality and show that we should limit ourselves to a behavioristic psychology that does not countenance mental states. Many have found this solution too radical. Cognitive science seems to be in the process of developing powerful explanatory theories that postulate intentional mental states. So we seem to be faced with the challenge to see if we cannot explain the intentionality of mental states. In chapter 4, I describe various strategies philosophers have pursued in attempting to do just that.

4

Philosophical Strategies for Explaining Intentionality

INTRODUCTION

In chapter 3, I discussed various conceptions of what intentionality is and how it is thought to mark a distinction between mental and nonmental phenomena. We saw how some philosophers, like Brentano, viewed intentionality as creating a gulf between nonmental and mental phenomena that prohibited the development of a science of mental phenomena comparable to the sciences of purely physical phenomena. We also saw how other philosophers, like Quine, reject the reality of intentional phenomena and propose that psychology focus not on mental phenomena at all, but strictly on the behavior of humans and other organisms. Most cognitive scientists find both of these positions inadequate. In this chapter, I describe a variety of other philosophical positions that take intentionality to be a real feature of mental phenomena but try to explain how a science that is continuous with the physical sciences can account for intentionality.

THE COMPUTATIONAL THEORY OF MIND (HIGH CHURCH COMPUTATIONALISM)

The first approach I consider takes the propositional attitude framework that we use to describe people's mental states as the basis for a scientific account of how the mind actually operates. Instead of repudiating propositions, this approach treats them as structures in the mind that serve as the content of a person's mental attitudes. Contemporary interest in this view has been inspired by the development of computers. By one interpretation, propositions can be thought of as symbols in a modern digital computer, and the attitudes toward these propositions as the ways in which configurations of these symbols are stored in the memory of the computer. For example, storing the symbol or symbols corresponding to the proposition that it is raining in the "belief bin" would constitute the propositional attitude of believing that it is raining. This account is extended from computers to humans by treating the mind as a symbol processing computer in which symbols are stored and manipulated. Jerry Fodor (1980) referred to this view as the "Computational Theory of Mind," whereas Daniel Dennett (1986) termed it "high church computationalism."

Fodor has been the foremost contemporary proponent of the Computational Theory of Mind,[1] whose basic tenet is that psychology is concerned with the formal structure of symbols in the mind and the way in which they are manipulated. Because the symbols assume the role of propositions in propositional attitude discourse, and so serve to represent the phenomena about which one is thinking, they are commonly called *mental representations*. Fodor proposed that the mind possesses a set of rules that determine what operations are performed on these representations. These rules correspond to the modes of inference we attribute to people in propositional attitude discourse. Thus, where we would describe someone as inferring the proposition "the picnic is cancelled" from the proposition "it is raining," the Computational Theory posits formal manipulations of representational symbols (e.g., moving them into various registers). Given the roles rules and representations play in such computational accounts, these accounts are sometimes referred to as "rules-and-representations accounts."

Fodor (1975) spoke of these mental representations as constituting "a language of thought." He held that psychology can only explain human behavior if it assumes that humans reason using such an internal language. To defend this claim, Fodor pointed to three kinds of phenomena. The first was rational behavior. Any explanation of rational behavior must allow for organisms to consider the consequences of the actions they are contemplating. This requires "that agents have means for representing their behaviors to themselves; indeed, means for representing their behaviors as having certain properties and not having others" (1975, p. 30). For example, only if I represent to myself that a consequence of not paying my taxes is that I will go

---

[1]Dreyfus (1982) shows that this view predates both Fodor and computers. Husserl, a student of Brentano, developed the view that mental activity consists in a variety of mental acts performed on abstract forms he called *noemata*. Husserl's approach is distinguishable from the modern computational one in that he took the *noemata* to be objects that one could consciously examine in what he referred to as the "phenomenological reduction," whereas the modern computational theory is not committed to any capacity of people to be aware of the symbols existing in their minds.

to jail will I be able to take that consequence into account in deciding whether to pay my taxes. The second phenomenon Fodor considered was concept learning. Fodor argued that we could only learn a new concept by proposing a hypothesis about what the concept might mean and then testing its adequacy.[2] For example, we learn the concept "car" by hypothesizing that it refers to objects that meet certain specifications, and then test whether, in fact, all objects meeting those specifications count as cars. This requires that we already possess a linguistic medium in which we can state such hypotheses (see Churchland, 1986, p. 389 for a rebuttal). The final phenomenon to which Fodor pointed was perception. In accord with the Empiricist tradition, he treated perception as a problem-solving activity in which the perceiver must determine what he or she is seeing on the basis of limited sensory input. Perception, like concept learning, requires the perceiver to test hypotheses (Fodor, 1975, p. 44). We must advance an hypothesis about what we are seeing (e.g., that it is a dog) before we can evaluate evidence for and against the hypothesis.

These arguments, according to Fodor, all point to the conclusion that cognitive agents must have a language-like system in which to carry out cognitive activities. An ordinary natural language like English might seem to be one candidate for this language system, but Fodor maintained that they will not suffice. Instead he proposed that the language of thought is an innate, inner language, which he called "Mentalese." Fodor offered a variety of arguments for Mentalese. First, organisms lacking a natural language can still perform many of the cognitive activities just described. They at least must be supposed to have an internal language for manipulating representations. (Patricia Churchland, 1978, responded that this reduces Fodor's position to the absurd.) Second, learning a natural language itself requires a process of hypothesis formation and testing. At least the initial hypotheses about the natural language cannot themselves be represented in the not-yet-known natural langauge and so must be represented in a more basic language.[3]

Fodor viewed the process of thinking using a language of thought as involving only syntactic processing. The mind manipulates symbols without any consideration as to what is represented by these symbols. This leads Fodor to endorse a view Putnam (1975b) called "methodological solipsism"—the view that from the perspective of mentalistic psychology what is in the world

---

[2]The reason we cannot simply learn concepts by induction and must form and test hypotheses is that concepts serve to group objects into classes, and there are an infinite number of ways of doing so (see Goodman, 1955). We must therefore specify in a hypothesis the criteria for belonging to the class. (Fodor, 1975, p. 36).

[3]For a radically different view of the mental language of computation, see Maloney (1984, in preparation). For perception, Maloney proposes to let the objects in the world serve as the representations. This solves one part of the problem of intentionality, because the representations are now self-referential. But it does not lend itself so readily to mentalistic psychology as Fodor's account of the language of thought for it is less clear how we are able to perform computations over these objects.

does not matter. For Putnam methodological solipsism revealed the incompatibility of propositional attitude psychology and computational accounts of psychology. To show the incompatibility, he told a science fiction tale about a possible world, Twin Earth, which is exactly like our planet except for one thing. In place of water, it has another substance, XYZ, which behaves just like water and is indistinguishable from it. On Twin Earth each of us has a duplicate, a Doppelgänger, who is identical to us in all respects except that he or she has molecules of XYZ everywhere we have molecules of H_2O. Because we are alike in all respects, it follows that my Doppelgänger and I must have all the same psychological states. In particular, we both affirm the sentence "I am drinking water." Despite the fact that my Doppelgänger and I are in the same psychological states, however, we mean different things by these words. My statement is about H_2O, whereas my Doppelgänger's is about XYZ. The moral Putnam drew from this tale is that meanings are not in the head: What determines the referent of my term *water* does not solely depend solely on my psychological state but also on what things I am causally connected to. Because one of the classical functions of propositions was to provide the meanings of sentences and determine their extensions, Putnam contends that the representations taken to be in the head by the computationalist account of psychology are not the same as the propositions of propositional attitude psychology. (See Burge, 1979, 1982; Stich, 1978, 1983 for related arguments.)

For Putnam, computationalist accounts of psychology are solipsistic insofar as they cannot deal with that aspect of meaning that depends on the world. Putnam saw this as a liability, but Fodor (1980) drew a different moral. The proper approach, according to Fodor, is for psychology to employ the same propositions as figure in propositional attitude psychology in order to develop an account of what happens in the mind. If something of the meaning of these propositions is lost by treating them as structures in the head, then psychology must make do with the syntactic structures that could be in the head. In defense of this view, he claims first that the only thing that can influence our behavior is what is formally represented inside the system. Whether we exist in a world of H_2O or in a world of XYZ does not affect our behavior unless it affects our internal structures: "[I]t's what the agent has in mind that causes his behavior," not what these mental states refer to (Fodor, 1980, p. 67). Second, Fodor claims that it is fortunate that psychology is limited to using these formal structures in explaining behavior because otherwise we would have to discover lawlike connections between representations and external objects. But these are not possible unless we can identify the right natural kinds that serve as the referents for our mental representations.[4] We will only possess such knowledge once all the other sciences

---

[4]Philosophers use the term *natural kind* to refer to sets of objects which figure in scientific laws and have defining conditions, as, for example, gold is defined by its atomic number.

have completed their work and discovered the true natural kinds.[5] (See Field, 1978, for additional arguments on behalf of the Computational Theory.)

One of the attractive features of the Computational Theory is that it can readily explain such logical peculiarities of discourse about mental states as the failure of substitutivity of co-referential expressions (see chapter 3). The Computational Theory holds that the cognitive system can only perform those manipulations sanctioned by the rules and representations it has. When it lacks a rule or appropriate information, it will not be able to make appropriate substitutions. Consider how a computational account of Oedipus might work. Early in the play *Oedipus Rex*, Oedipus learns that Jocasta is the Queen and desires to marry her. But unbeknowst to Oedipus, Jocasta is also his mother. In the computational model, Oedipus would store the proposition

I am married to Jocasta

in his belief bin. The model possesses a rule permitting it to substitute one name for another when it knows that they are co-referential. But at this stage the system does not know that "Jocasta" and "my mother" are co-referential and does not carry out the substitution. When Oedipus learns this information later in the play, it is formally represented in the model. Now, in a purely formal fashion, the model infers the new sentence

I am married to my mother.

Although the Computational Theory can thus explain the failure of substitutivity of co-referential expressions in descriptions of Oedipus' mental states, it does not so clearly address the issue of how these mental states can be *about* something. The representations the Computational Theory attributes to the mind are assumed to have a referential function, but the theory does not explain how they perform this function. Thus, Richardson (1981) objects that the Computational Theory, like any theory positing intentional objects, simply postpones the problem of explaining intentionality. To explain the intentionality of mental states, we must explain how representations connect with objects in the world. If we cannot account for this, we are left in the position

---

[5]This argument seems quite unsound, for it assumes that scientists cannot begin to articulate laws until natural kinds are discovered. But it is only through the search for lawlike regularities that they will be discovered. There are difficulties in identifying environmental factors that control various behaviors and cognitions, but it is the endeavor to find such regularities that will allow us to pick out the natural kinds. Investigators can propose and test such laws even knowing that further investigation in psychology or other disciplines may force their revision. Maloney (1985a) also argued that if Fodor is right that we must await the discovery of natural kinds, that counts against his solipsistic psychology as well. Fodor's injunction against the possibility of such laws does not seem as compelling as his case for needing a computational psychology.

of treating thinking activities as totally removed from the natural world. Fodor (1987) has developed an alternative strategy for attacking this problem. It explains how mental representations are about features of the world in terms of their causal connections to external states in the world. Any such approach as this, however, must overcome a serious obstacle that we noted at the outset. One of the distinguishing features of the intentionality of mental states is that they can distort the real situation in the world and be about things that do not exist. A causal account runs the risk of connecting every mental state to an external state and so making it impossible to misrepresent states in the world and impossible to refer to nonexistent entities.

REPRESENTATIONS WITHOUT COMPUTATIONS

The Computational Theory is not just a speculative philosophical proposal. Many researchers in artificial intelligence (AI) likewise view cognitive sytems as formal symbol manipulators. They attempt to develop formal symbol structures that can produce intelligent behavior.[6] However, numerous philosophers have criticized the Computational Theory of Mind, either as defended by Fodor or as it figures in AI. Most of those who reject it do accept the view that cognitive systems represent things and hence are intentional systems. What they deny is that this requires specific states within cognitive systems that are employed as *representations* and are manipulated by formal *rules*. All that is required, they maintain, is that there be activity of some sort in the system that explains how it has mental states that are about things. In this section, I describe a variety of arguments against the computational account. Specific proposals as to how the mind can be representational, and hence intentional, without performing computations upon representations are discussed in subsequent sections.

The first objection against the Computational Theory is that it is empirically implausible as an account of human cognition. Dennett (1977) raised this objection in his review of Fodor's *Language of Thought:*

> Fodor seems to suppose that the only structures that could guarantee and explain the predictive power of our Intentionalistic calculations *must* mirror the syntax of those calculations. This is either trivially true (because the 'syntactic' structure of events or states is defined simply by their function) or an empirical claim that is very interesting, not entirely implausible, and as yet not demon-

---

[6]Many AI researchers would probably not endorse some features of Fodor's account of the language of thought, such as the claim that the language of thought must be innate. Fodor, however, would maintain that this is simply a logical consequence of the formal symbol manipulating view they do endorse.

strated or even argued for, so far as I can tell. For instance, suppose hamsters are interpretable as good Bayesians when it comes to the decisions they make. Must we in principle be able to find some saliencies in the hamsters' controls that are interpretable as tokens of formulae in some Bayesian calculus? If that is Fodor's conclusion I don't see that he has given it the support it needs, and I confess to disbelieving it utterly. (p. 279)

More recently, Dennett (1986) claimed "that a computational symbol manipulating brain seems profoundly unbiological" (p. 66). Similarly skeptical is P. S. Churchland, who contends that "sentence-crunching seems insensitive to evolutionary considerations" (1986, p. 388; see also P. S. Churchland, 1980a). She poses an evolutionary dilemma for the defender of a language of thought: Either we must view sentence processing as arising early in phylogeny, or we must claim that sentence processing procedures employed in human cognition have no roots in the mental processes of other organisms. The second option is unsatisfactory because nonlinguistic humans as well as nonlinguistic members of other species seem eminently capable of rational planning, and so seem to participate in the same sort of cognitive actions as we do. On the other hand, the assumption that nonlinguistic and prelinguistic organisms that manifest cognition all possess a complete language of thought strikes her as wildly implausible (see Kitcher, 1984, for a response).

The computational account of cognition seems empirically problematic in other respects. Because the system is to operate with purely formal or syntactic rules for manipulating representations, every aspect of the meaning of the symbol that is to affect psychological processing must be encoded formally. Working totally according to syntactic principles, the system will not have access to the contexts that, in natural language, serve to disambiguate different meanings of terms. In analyzing natural languages, Searle (1979) has argued that it is hopeless to develop formal or syntactic accounts of the meanings of expressions because these expressions frequently take on different meanings in different contexts. But this is exactly what is required by the Computational Theory. This objection actually predates the modern computational theories of Fodor and AI. Much earlier in the century, Husserl proposed an account of cognition in terms of the manipulation of stored propositions.[7] Martin Heidegger (1949/1962) opposed Husserl's program on the grounds that the variability in the information we deal with could not be adequately expressed by fixed propositions. Heidegger proposed that the way to overcome this problem is to recognize that some of the information we employ is not represented in the mind, but is found in such things as cultivated skills and our social nexus. Herbert Dreyfus (1979) has further developed Heidegger's objections in his own criticisms of AI and concludes that AI is misguided when it tries to represent all information a cognitive

---

[7]See footnote 1.

system uses in terms of syntactic symbols stored in the head (see chapter 7 for further discussion of Dreyfus's position).

A further objection to the Computational Theory focuses on the number of such mental sentences each of us must possess if the account is correct. If every mental state is to be understood as some form of storage or processing of a sentence in the language of thought, each of us will need to have an infinite number of such sentences stored in our mind/brain. The reason is that we have an infinite number of beliefs, many of which we never actively consider consciously. For example, most of us believe that zebras do not wear overcoats, although it is doubtful that many of us consciously considered this proposition until Dennett introduced it as an example. Similarly, most of us believe that bears are less than n feet tall for every n greater than seven (see P. S. Churchland, 1986). Critics of the computational view claim that such an infinite set of mental sentences could not be stored in the mind/brain.[8]

The computational theory's claim that all knowledge is to be represented syntactically generates still other problems. One concerns how we identify information relevant to a particular task. Those designing artificial intelligence systems already face such a problem with systems which have relatively little stored information. Dennett (1984a) illustrated this problem, commonly known as the "frame problem" (McCarthy & Hayes, 1969), in terms of a story in which a robot is told its power supply is in a room where a bomb is set to go off. The robot must decide how to save its power supply by summoning up relevant information and making appropriate inferences. The problem is to provide it the right set of rules for doing this. Such a robot must respond to various contingencies, each of which makes different information relevant to its task. It cannot search all information without getting caught in an endless process of reasoning. As even more information is stored in formal representations, this task becomes even more difficult (see also Dreyfus, 1985).

A final objection to the computational view focuses on the difficulty of ever determining the actual character of the formal representations of the language of thought. Dennett (1982) claimed that if we posit such a syntactic symbol system as Fodor's language of thought, we should be able to address the question of whether all of us have the same language of thought, or different ones. Differences in our languages of thought could explain cognitive differences, but because we have no independent way to identify

---

[8]Ortony (personal communication, May, 1987) suggested that this objection can be countered if we distinguish between represented beliefs and those that are deducible from the represented beliefs. The plausibility of this response depends on the plausibility of developing an axiom set from which beliefs like those mentioned by Dennett and Churchland can be derived. It is not clear that it will be possible to develop consistent axiom sets for each person that will generate just the right set of sentences to which they will affirm their belief when queried.

differences in our languages of thought, any such explanation becomes circular. Moreover, we know from natural languages that different messages can be carried in the same language and different languages can carry the same message. So we cannot infer similarities or differences in languages simply from similarities or differences in the way they are used. We are left positing a language of thought about which we can seemingly learn nothing.

If we find arguments[9] such as these reason enough to reject the Computational Theory, we are left with a challenge of showing how a cognitive system represents things and so is intentional. One of the chief virtues of the computational approach was that it was designed to capture the way we ordinarily describe mental states in terms of propositional attitudes and so acquired all the benefits of that approach. Dennett claimed, however, that we can employ the propositional attitude framework to describe people without equating propositions with formal symbols in the mind. To do so, we need an alternative account of what is involved when someone "grasps" a proposition. Dennett (1982) proposed the following: "Propositions are graspable if and only if predicates of propositional attitude are projectable, predictive, well-behaved predicates of psychological theory" (p. 10). All this requires is that our theoretical ascriptions of propositional attitude co-vary with predictions about behavior. It does not require in addition that what goes on within the mind be computation over propositions.

P.M. Churchland also defended using propositional attitudes without invoking the Computational Theory. He compared the predications made in propositional attitude discourse with predications made in the physical sciences, many of which do not have any special ontological entailments:

> The irony is that when we examine the logical structure of our folk conceptions here, we find not differences, but some very deep *similarities* between the structure of folk psychology and the structure of paradigmatically physical theories. Let us begin by comparing the elements of the following two lists:
>
> | *Propositional attitudes* | *Numerical attitudes* |
> |---|---|
> | . . . believes that P | . . . has a length$_m$ of n |
> | . . . desires that P | . . . has a velocity$_{m/s}$ of n |
> | . . . fears that P | . . . has a temperature$_k$ of n |
> | . . . sees that P | . . . has a charge$_c$ of n |
> | . . . suspects that P. | . . . has a kinetic enegy$_j$ of n |
> | . | |
> | . | |
> | . | |
>
> Where folk psychology displays *propositional* attitudes, mathematical physics displays *numerical* attitudes.(Churchland, 1984, p. 64).

---

[9]For further discussion of these and other arguments against the Computational Theory, see Amundson (1987), Bailey (1986), Harman (1978), Haroutunian (1983), Hatfield (1986), and Sher (1975).

Churchland contended that we can develop laws that refer to propositional attitudes just as we can develop laws referring to numerical attitudes. Just as talk of numerical attitudes does not commit us to positing a special entity—velocity$_{m/s}$—neither does talk of propositional attitudes commit us to treating representations as entities.[10]

Although Dennett and Churchland claim that we can still employ the propositional attitude account without endorsing the Computational Theory, Fodor can still object that they have not told us what activities in a person's head enable the person to represent his or her environment. Fodor claims that it is a virtue of the Computational Theory that it is able to do so. Consider the argument he makes for a language of thought (Fodor, 1975):

1. The only psychological models of cognitive processes that seem even remotely plausible represent such processes as computational.
2. Computation presupposes a medium of computation: a representational system.
3. Remotely plausible theories are better than no theories at all.
4. We are thus provisionally committed to attributing a representational system to organisms. (p. 27)

The third premise in Fodor's argument seems entirely reasonable, and it imposes a burden on anyone taking issue with his conclusion. One must either present models of cognition that are not computational or show that computation does not presuppose a representational system.

Stich (1983), in defending what he referred to as the syntactic theory of mind, rejected the second premise in Fodor's argument, arguing that although the operations within the mind can be construed as formal or syntactic operations like those of a syntactic theory (in linguistics), the objects upon which these syntactic operations are performed need not be viewed as representations—that is, as units to which content can be assigned. Stich claimed that much of the work in both artificial intelligence and cognitive psychology has this character. Researchers in these fields postulate syntactic procedures in order to explain behavior, but then do not require that all the syntactic objects used in producing the output be interpreted as representing anything (see Von Eckardt, 1984, for a related argument.) Stich's approach is thus computational but does not hold that the entities being manipulated are representations. This seems to have been the approach of many practicing researchers in cognitive science, Fodor's claims to the contrary not withstanding (see, however, McCauley, 1987).

---

[10]See also Churchland (1979), where he suggested that we might think of propositional attitude ascriptions as adverbial modifications of the way we characterize people. They will thus function in much the same way as "quickly" does in "X moves quickly."

More recently, however, a number of practitioners of cognitive science have proposed a program that rejects Fodor's first premise (that the only remotely plausible psychological models are computational). Advocates of "connectionist" or "parallel distributed processing" (PDP) models have proposed ways to model cognitive phenomena that are not computational in the sense used here. They do not perform operations upon stored symbols in the manner of a von Neumann computer. In brief, what these researchers are doing is exploring the capacities of a class of systems designed on the model of neural networks. The systems consist of nodes, each of which has a determinate degree of activation at any time and is connected to a number of other nodes to which it sends inhibitory or excitatory stimuli. When given an initial pattern of activation, the excitations and inhibitions passing through the system will alter the activation states of the nodes until a stable pattern is achieved. The strengths of excitatory and inhibitory connections can be designed to change as a result of local activity in the system. When systems are so designed, they can learn to respond in new ways with the result that they will settle into different states on subsequent occasions. What is of interest is that researchers have employed such systems (as simulated on von Neumann computers) to model certain cognitive functions. On tasks like pattern recognition their performance is much more human-like than that of rule-processing machines. In these simulations, the researchers interpret the activity of the system and so treat the system as representational, but the system does not operate by performing computations on representations. Connectionist models provide one example of how it is possible to develop a representational theory without a Computational Theory.[11]

The advent of connectionist models gives support to those who endorse the Representational Theory of Mind but reject the Computational Theory. Yet, the Representational Theory of Mind does not yet account for intentionality because it does not explain how the mind is capable of representing things. Three different philosophical theories have recently emerged, each of which has tried to explain how the mind/brain can represent things and so be intentional: (a) the information theoretical approach, (b) the biological reduction approach, and (c) the intentional stance approach. These are discussed in the remaining four sections.

---

[11]For discussion of this class of cognitive models, see Rumelhart and McClelland (1986) and McClelland and Rumelhart (1986). It is interesting to note that in advocating this new class of models, Rumelhart (1984) made remarks that echo those given by philosophical critics of the computational approach. He commented on the futility of constantly developing more complex rule-based accounts of cognition to handle apparent anomalies in the behavior of actual cognizers. He advocated PDP accounts because they are capable of explaining both behaviors that accord with rules and behaviors that violate them within a common framework. For an introduction to the philosophical questions raised by connectionist models, see Bechtel (in press c). For a set of criticisms of connectionist models as alternatives to computational models, see Fodor and Pylyshyn (1987).

THE INFORMATION THEORETIC APPROACH

Because intentional states are states that bear information about other states, some philosophers have sought to explain intentionality by an appeal to the mathematical theory of information advanced by Shannon and Weaver (1949). Appeals to mathematical information theory have often been rejected on the grounds that information theory is concerned with the capacity of channels to convey information, not with the particular information they carry. Fred Dretske (1981, see also 1983 and the commentaries following), however, argued that there is a useful insight in information theory that can be exploited. This is the idea that one state carries information about another just to the degree that it is lawfully dependent on that other state. Dretske proposed that if there is a deterministic and lawful relationship so that I can infer from the signal that it had a particular cause, then the signal gives me information *about* that cause. The lawful relationship between cause and signal accounts, he maintained, for the signal being *about* the cause. Thus, *aboutness* is not a unique feature of mental states, but is found in all causal relationships:

> *Any* physical system, then, whose internal states are lawfully dependent, in some statistically significant way, on the value of an external magnitude (in the way a properly connected measuring instrument is sensitive to the value of the quantity it is designed to measure) qualifies as an intentional system. (Dretske, 1980, p. 286)

The challenge, as Dretske saw it, is not to explain how something could manifest intentionality, but to explain how something could exhibit the right kind of intentionality to be a mind. What is characteristic of our mental states is not that they have content, but the specific contents they have. A typical measuring instrument generally carries much more information than we, the users, acquire from it. It carries information about every step in the causal aetiology of the instrument's reading. Our cognitive states distinguish between different contents that are indiscriminately recorded by typical measuring instruments. The contents of the mental state are the properties measured; not all the causally necessary intermediate states. To capture this difference, Dretske (1983) distinguished between what he calls "digital" and "analog" information in perception:

> In passing from the sensory to the cognitive representation (from seeing the apple to realizing that it is an apple), there is a systematic stripping away of components of information (relating to size, color, orientation, surroundings), which makes the experience of the apple the phenomenally rich thing we know it to be, in order to feature *one* component of this information—the information that it is an apple. Digitalization (of, for example, the information that *s* is an apple) is a process whereby a piece of information is taken from a richer

matrix of information in the sensory representation (where it is held in what I call "analog" form) and featured to the exclusion of all else. (p. 61)

Dretske reversed the normal way we think about intentionality. His causal analysis makes almost every state intentional and so, rather than asking how some states come to have the unique characteristic of intentionality, Dretske's task is to explain how some status have focused and limited intentionality. In his analysis, Dretske emphasized the relational side of intentionality (see p. 43), and this raises the question of whether Dretske can account for intentional states that fail to refer to anything real. The problem can be recognized by viewing Dretske's account in the manner he intends—as part of an epistemological project designed to explain what knowledge is and how it is possible. In epistemology, too, Dretske reversed the normal strategy, which is to start with belief and to ask under what conditions a belief counts as knowledge. In Dretske's account, all informational states automatically carry knowledge; the challenge is to show how we could come to have false beliefs. This involves showing how the extraction process can go wrong and so misrepresent things in the world.

Many commentators on Dretske's account claim that his treatment of false beliefs and failures of reference as due to distortions of otherwise veridical knowledge and referential information is misguided. An implication of Dretske's approach would seem to be that in order to possess knowledge we simply need to remove the errors induced by our cognitive system. Then we can regain the Eden in which we possessed uncorrupted information (see Churchland & Churchland, 1983). This seems to denigrate the mind by viewing it as a distorting agency, both as regarding knowledge and intentionality. Such a view is at odds with an evolutionary perspective, which would construe the minds of higher organisms as improving the organism's ability to gain information, not imposing distortion.[12]

Although many philosophers (e.g., Fodor, 1984) maintain that Dretske has approached intentionality in the wrong manner, his approach certainly has an allure. It makes the "aboutness" aspect of intentionality totally natural insofar as it emerges as an aspect of ordinary causal relationships. This approach would be particularly attractive if it did not seem to reduce mental states to potentially distorted products of reliable input states. John Heil (1983) developed an account that is similar in some respects to Dretske's, but that

---

[12]Another philosopher, Sayre (1986), attempted to combine the mathematical theory of information with an evolutionary perspective in order to account for the intentionality of perception. The main contribution of the perceptual system, for Sayre, is to focus on and track specific sources of information in the environment so that the resulting states in the brain provide the organism with information *about* relevant parts of the environment. An evolutionary perspective figures in Sayre's account because he considered how organisms have evolved the ability to acquire focused, relevant information from their environment. For discussion, see the commentaries that follow Sayre's paper and his response.

introduces cognitive components in a more constitutive manner. He agreed with Dretske and with the psychologist J. J. Gibson (1979) in treating information as something that is present in our environment and available to be "picked up" by cognitive agents. Like Dretske and Gibson, Heil treated the pickup of information as causally generating mental states of the cognizer. However, he differs from both in characterizing these mental states in a neo-Kantian fashion (chapter 1), maintaining that mental states result only once perceptual experience is conceptualized using concepts supplied by the agent. The position is not totally Kantian, however, in that he insists that the process of conceptualization is not inferential, but causal. Given both the perceptual apparatus of the cognizer and his or her conceptual framework, the information in the sensory stimulus causes beliefs in the person. Thus, Heil disagrees with Dretske when Heil holds that the information in the environment is not intentional because it is not conceptualized. Yet, for Heil also, information figures centrally in explaining the intentionality of mental states. It serves to connect states of the agent to features of an environment. In the last part of this chapter I discuss how a related view of the relationship between organism and environment can figure in an analysis of intentionality.

THE BIOLOGICAL REDUCTION APPROACH

Although Dretske's analysis tries to show that intentionality is a feature of nature generally, John Searle has argued that it is a feature found only in certain biological systems and so requires a biological, not cognitive science, explanation. In defending a biological analysis, Searle does not tell us what features of biological systems make them intentional (indeed, I argue later that it is a peculiar feature of Searle's position that he cannot logically attempt this). Rather, he simply maintains that only a biological theory could explain intentionality.

Searle characterizes intentionality by drawing upon the analysis of speech acts which he had developed previously (Searle, 1969, 1979; see chapter 2, this volume). The intentionality of both speech acts and intentional states, for Searle, consists in what he called their "directionality of fit." Some speech acts and mental states are supposed to correspond to the way the world is, whereas others impose a burden on the world to correspond to them. A belief, for example, is supposed to correspond to the way the world is, but a command imposes a burden on the world to correspond to it. In many mental states there is a causal connection as well as the semantic relation between the intentional state and the world. Thus, perceptual experiences depend causally on things in the world while commands may cause certain effects in the world. Searle (1981) portrayed these causal connections as reversing the direction of fit relations:

perceptual experiences have the mind-to-world direction of fit and the world-to-mind direction of causation (roughly, that means that they are satisfied only if the world is as it perceptually seems to be and if its being that way causes its perceptually seeming that way), whereas intentions in action are exactly opposite in both direction of fit and direction of causation. They have world-to-mind direction of fit and mind-to-world direction of causation (that means that they are satisfied only if the world comes to be the way one tries to make it be and if its coming to be that way is caused by one's trying to make it that way. (p. 729)

Although he treated the analysis of speech acts as providing a useful model for developing the analysis of intentionality, Searle insisted that intentionality of mental states is more basic. Language does not have what Searle termed "intrinsic intentionality" but only "derived intentionality," which it acquires from the underlying mental state. Searle does not offer a positive account of what intrinsic intentionality is, but settled for showing us what lacks it. Like speech acts, Searle maintained that computers only have derived intentionality. He rejected the Computational Theory of Mind because he maintained that computational processes are insufficient to account for intrinsic intentionality.

Searle argued for these claims by presenting a *Gedankenexperiment* (thought experiment) in which he imagined himself playing the role of a computer that is programmed to answer questions about a story (here I simplify a bit[13]). The crucial element in Searle's account is that both the story, the questions, and Searle's output are all in Chinese, a language he does not understand. He was able to "answer" the questions only because, along with the Chinese symbols that contain the story and the questions, he received rules stated in English that told him how to produce new strings of symbols depending on the strings he found in the story and question lists. The whole arrangement is so cleverly designed that while Searle believed he was only manipulating symbols and did not know that he was answering questions in Chinese about a story in Chinese, he was in fact producing perfectly coherent output that native speakers of Chinese would find authentic. Searle contended that because he did not understand what he was doing, his symbol manipulating activities could not be counted as intentional in the sense of being about

---

[13]Searle's *Gedankenexperiment* is intended to replicate the structure of Schank and Abelson's (1977) design for story understanding programs. Schank proposed that we, as well as computer programs, could understand stories by using "scripts," which are structures for representing information in terms of general features of certain types of events. The useful thing about scripts is that they contain default information about what would happen in certain kinds of episodes. We can use this information to supplement what we are actually told in the story. The fact we or a program use scripts in understanding a story is supposed to explain how we are able to answer questions about a story where the information was never explicitly stated in the story. For simplicity I have left the scripts out of Searle's *Gedankenexperiment*.

what the story is about (as it would be if the story and questions had been presented in English). Because he was executing all the formal symbol manipulation posited by a computational analysis and yet did not understand, the computational analysis is inadequate:

> In the Chinese case I have everything that artificial intelligence can put into me by way of a program, and I understand nothing; in the English case I understand everything, and there is so far no reason at all to suppose that my understanding has anything to do with computer programs—i.e., with computational operations on purely formally specified elements. As long as the program is defined in terms of computational operations on purely formally defined elements, what the example suggests is that these by themselves have no interesting connections with understanding. They are certainly not sufficient conditions, and not the slightest reason has been given to suppose that they are necessary conditions or even that they make a significant contribution to understanding. (Searle, 1980/1981, p. 286)

This argument is intended to undercut the claim that cognitive scientists who try to understand cognition by analyzing the program used by the mind are able to explain the intentionality of mental states. Searle defended his interpretation of the Chinese Room *Gedankenexperiment* against a number of possible objections. Because one of these objections is particularly likely to occur to readers, it is worth briefly considering. The objection is that while Searle did not know Chinese, he, together with the rules for processing the questions to produce the answers, does. Searle responded that having the rules external to him is incidental—he could perfectly well memorize them. He would still not understand Chinese. He would only behave like someone who understood Chinese. Searle's intuition seems sound—most people would not claim to understand Chinese or mean their answers to be *about* things if they operated in this fashion. But perhaps this is because Searle's *Gedankenexperiment* falsely represents the kinds of rules needed to understand language. He required a separate rule for each question and story for which an answer is to be given. Such a set of rules could not, in principle, provide answers to the infinite variety of questions and stories that a Chinese person could answer. If we were dealing with a set of rules that might actually suffice for carrying on the kind of conversation Searle imagined, it is far from clear that Searle could convince us that the system does not understand Chinese. The rules might just encode what is required to understand Chinese![14]

Although Searle's case is intended to count against the adequacy of the Computational Theory of Mind, his claim that a formal system is insufficient to account for intentionality is not really that contentious. We already

---

[14]See Harnad, 1987; for other responses to Searle's Chinese Room example, see Bynum (1985), Carleton (1984), Rey (1986), Russow (1984), and Thagard (1985).

saw that the Computational Theory left the question of the intentionality of the formal symbols totally unexplained. What is more surprising is Searle's claim that computational theories do not play any role in explaining intentional behavior. Computational theories are intended to characterize the kind of internal processes occurring within a system that enable it to behave in the appropriate way. If computational accounts are incorrect, some account of what it is that enables certain sorts of systems to show intentionality seems called for. Searle's response to this issue is to claim that by default it must be the biology of a system that equips it to exhibit intentionality:

> It is not because I am the instantiation of a computer program that I am able to understand English and have other forms of intentionality (I am, I suppose, the instantiation of any number of computer programs), but as far as we know it is because I am a certain sort of organism with a certain biological (i.e., chemical and physical) structure, and this structure under certain conditions is causally capable of producing perception, action, understanding, learning and other intentional phenomena. And part of the point of the present argument is that only something that had those causal powers could have that intentionality. Perhaps other physical and chemical processes could produce exactly these effects; perhaps, for example, Martians also have intentionality, but their brains are made of different stuff. That is an empirical question, rather like the question whether photosynthesis can be done by something with a chemistry different from that of chlorophyll. (1980/1981, p. 299; see also Searle, 1984)

The analogy between intentionality and photosynthesis actually undercuts Searle's position. We could not inquire as to whether a substance other than chlorophyll could produce photosynthesis unless we knew what causal capacities enabled chlorophyll to do so. Searle would seem obliged to acknowledge that some account will be developed of what interactive capacities the brain must possess to exhibit intentionality. If someone could develop an analysis of the causal processes involved in producing intentionality, it would provide the basis for construction of a program-like theory that described these processes. Searle, therefore, must simply settle for asserting that intentional phenomena are biological and not attempt to explain how biology produces intentionality in the same manner as we can explain chemically how photosynthesis occurs. Intentionality, therefore, remains a mystery on Searle's analysis.

THE INTENTIONAL STANCE APPROACH

Dennett (1971/1978) adopted an approach to intentionality that is radically different from those we have examined so far. He contended that when we characterize a system, either natural or artificial, in terms of beliefs and desires, we adopt what he called "the intentional stance." This is the perspective from which we typically view people in daily life, and Dennett maintained that it will sometimes prove useful to view other systems in a like manner. This perspective is not only convenient when we are trying to predict how a person or other system might behave, but it can also be useful when we want to explain why such a system behaved as it did. To develop the explanation, however, we must change perspectives and adopt what Dennett referred to as the "design stance." From the design stance we describe the mechanical activities in the system that enable it to perform as an intentional system. (In discussing Homuncular Functionalism in Chapter 7 I describe Dennett's strategy for going from the intentional stance to the design stance in greater detail.)

Although maintaining that the intentional stance in which we characterize systems in terms of beliefs and desires is often useful to us, Dennett also contended that no systems, ourselves included, are *really* intentional. The view that the entities we posit are fictitious and do not really exist is commonly called "instrumentalism." Although Dennett thus seems to be an instrumentalist about intentional attributions of beliefs and desires, he only reluctantly accepted this label. He is reluctant because he maintained that we cannot do without the intentional stance, either in practice or in principle. From the intentional stance, he claimed, we acquire information that would not be available otherwise. Moreover, this information is about "something perfectly objective: the *patterns* in human behavior that are described from the intentional stance, and only from that stance, and which support generalizations and predictions" (Dennett, 1981c, p. 64).

One aspect of Dennett's discussion of the intentional stance makes it appear nearly vacuous. Dennett said that we can adopt the intentional stance toward almost anything. For example, we can attribute to a bookcase the desire to keep books in a convenient place and the belief that staying just as it is will accomplish this. This use of the intentional stance imparts no useful information. But Dennett contended that when dealing with systems like human beings, attributions of belief and desire are not nearly so trivial and the intentional stance provides important theoretical information. It tells us how the system is related to its environment—what information it has acquired and what actions it is disposed to perform. This leads us to say "that the organism continuously *mirrors* the environment, or that there is a *representation* of the environment in—or implicit in—the organization of the system" (Dennett, 1981c, p. 70). In order for a system to stand in such a relation to its environment, it must have sufficient internal resources and hence the "apparently shallow and instrumentalistic criterion of belief puts a severe constraint on the internal constitution of a genuine believer, and thus yields a robust version of belief after all" (p. 68).

Given that he takes intentional ascriptions to be useful, it would seem that

Dennett should treat beliefs and desires to be real. (See Richardson, 1980, for reasons why Dennett should be a realist about the intentional stance.) Dennett, however, cited a number of reasons for not being a realist. One of the most important draws upon Putnam's Twin Earth argument, which we discussed previously. As that argument tried to show, the way in which we interpret the content of the mental states of a system may depend on things external to it. For Dennett, this shows that intentional ascriptions are environment-relative and so are not intrinsic characterizations of a system. This suggests that what Dennett is actually opposed to is not the reality of intentional states like beliefs and desires, but the view that these are internal states of the system. In fact, Dennett said that "belief is a perfectly objective phenomenon." What he denied was that it is a "perfectly objective *internal* matter of fact" (Dennett, 1981c, p. 55). It is computational theories like Fodor's that treat intentional states as internal states, and so it is the computational view that Dennett seems to be opposing in rejecting realism toward intentional states. This is brought out clearly in a passage in Dennett's (1977) review of Fodor's *Language of Thought*:

> In a recent conversation with the designer of a chess–playing programme I heard the following criticism of a rival programme: 'It thinks it should get its queen out early'. This ascribes a propositional attitude to the programme in a very useful and predictive way, for as the designer went on to say, one can usually count on chasing that queen around the board. But for all the many levels of explicit representation to be found in that programme, nowhere is anything roughly synonymous with 'I should get my queen out early' explicitly tokened. The level of analysis to which the designer's remark belongs describes features of the programme that are, in an entirely innocent way, emergent properties of the computational processes that have 'engineering reality'. I see no reason to believe that the relationship between belief-talk and psychological process talk will be more direct. (p. 279)

What else could intentional states be if they are not internal states of a system? As I have argued elsewhere (Bechtel, 1985a), Dennett's argument that intentional attributions depend on the system's environment suggests an answer. We could construe beliefs and other intentional states as relational states holding between a system and its environment. Attributions of beliefs and desires would not then describe internal states of a system, but describe how it relates to an environment. A system would have a belief about water if it stood in the appropriate relationship to water.

This proposal, however, must be qualified. In discussing Brentano (chapter 3 this volume) we noted that a relational view of intentionality is problematic because one of the important features of intentional states is that they can represent nonexistent phenomena. A system could not possibly stand in a relation to something that does not exist. Although this would seem to doom the approach I have just suggested, it does not. To avoid this obstacle we must first adopt a holistic, not an atomistic, interpretation of mental states (in the spirit of Quine and Davidson—see chapter 2). It is only the whole set of a person's cognitive states that we should try to relate to the environment. Next, we can appeal to a concept of a notional world that Dennett (1982) has introduced. Dennett introduces this notion in order to specify what is represented in a person's mental state. A notional world is not the actual world, but a possible world (see chapter 2) in which all the beliefs a person had would be true and all of his or her desires would be reasonable. To identify such worlds, Dennett proposed that we start with the actual world and consider how we could modify it in order to render a person's false beliefs true and his or her unreasonable desires reasonable. The modified worlds that meet these conditions are the person's notional worlds.

Notional worlds allow us to characterize a person's intentional states relationally without having to relate all of them to the actual world. To see how this is done it will be useful to view a person's mental states as comparable to biological traits. Just as we evaluate biological traits in terms of how adaptive they make an organism to an environment, so we can evaluate beliefs in terms of how adapted they make the system to its environment. Just as some biological traits are well suited to the organism's environment, so some beliefs will be appropriate to the system's environment because the objects actually exist in the manner specified. In this case the relational account can be applied without difficulty. Some biological traits are not well adapted and yet we can determine what kind of environment they would be adapted to. We do the comparable thing for false beliefs when we posit a notional world. Although there are not states in the world to which these beliefs relate, we can say what kinds of possible states they would relate to and how these differ from the states that do exist.[15]

The tool of notional worlds thus provides a way to construe Dennett's

---

[15]Dennett also offered two additional arguments for an instrumentalistic treatment of intentional states, both of which can also be handled by the kind of account sketched here. One argument relies on the fact that no actual system is fully rational, whereas the intentional stance assumes full rationality. This, however, can be answered by treating our initial intentional ascriptions as idealizations, much like the idealized gas laws used in physics. In a realistic account, these would be modified as necessary to describe a person's actual mental life in much the way psychologists of reasoning have proposed theories of how we reason that account for deviations from normative logic (see Kahneman, Slovic, & Tversky, 1982). For a different critical response to this argument of Dennett and general doubts about using the rationality assumption to ground intentional interpretations, see Stich (1981) and Dennett (1981b) for a reply. Dennett's other argument pointed out that belief ascriptions are sometimes quite indefinite so that we may describe two people as believing the same thing (Dennett and a chemist both believe salt is sodium chloride) even though there may be major differences in how their belief relates to other beliefs (e.g., Dennett cannot use this belief to solve chemical problems whereas the chemist can). This problem, however, is dealt with using the tool of notional worlds which reveal differences in the range of worlds to which the people are adapted.

postulation of an intentional stance in a realist, noninstrumentalist fashion. Beliefs and desires generally characterize people in terms of how they relate to features of their environment, and we account for the differences by noting how their notional worlds differ from the actual one. (I developed this analysis further in Bechtel, 1985a.) In this account of Dennett, I have compared intentional properties to adaptive biological properties of organisms. This suggests that we might incorporate an analysis of intentionality within a generalized evolutionary framework.[16] Although this marks a clear departure from Dennett's instrumentalism, it is well within the spirit of other features of his view. Dennett (1978b), for example, rejects B. F. Skinner's behaviorist strictures against postulating intelligent mental operations within the mind, claiming that postulating intelligent activities in the mind is acceptable as long as one can give an evolutionary explanation of how the mind came to acquire these intelligent processes. He also argues that the classical behaviorist law of effect (that behavior can be modified according to whether it is rewarded or punished) is simply an internalized form of natural selection that itself is the product of natural selection[17] (Dennett, 1975/1978).

Treating intentional ascriptions of beliefs and desires to a system as characterizing the relation between the cognitive system and its environment has some important consequences for cognitive science. It argues for (a) differentiating our intentional characterizations of cognitive systems from internal processing models, but also (b) for understanding cognition in its environmental and phylogenetic context. I briefly develop these points here.

The first consequence is one we already noted in distinguishing the Representational Theory of Mind from the Computational Theory. Now we can see more clearly why intentional ascriptions of beliefs and desires should

---

[16]Sayre (1986) offered an alternative approach to embedding an account of intentionality within an evolutionary perspective (see footnote 12).

[17]When Dennett adopted an evolutionary perspective (see Dennett, 1983) he committed himself to both an adaptationist account of evolution and an optimizing view of natural selection. An adaptationist view holds that it is appropriate to explain each trait as being selected because of its contribution to the organism's fitness, whereas the optimizing interpretation sees natural selection as producing optimally adapted organisms. These interpretations fit with Dennett's account of the intentional stance, which views it as a normative or ideal perspective. However, they have been severely criticized within evolutionary biology. Gould and Lewontin (1979; Lewontin, 1978) argue against adaptationism by noting that not all traits of organisms are the product of natural selection. To show that something is the product of natural selection it is necessary to demonstrate in an engineering fashion how selection actually promoted the trait. Furthermore, evolutionists generally view natural selection as a *satisficing process*, to use Simon's (1955/1979) term. Selection promotes any available traits that contribute to fitness and does not select only the most adaptive. In developing a realist perspective on the intentional stance we need to take these evolutionary considerations into account. This requires us to surrender both the adaptationist view and the optimizing view and focus on how our cognitive states actually equip us to deal with the environment and how they occasionally render us maladaptive.

be distinguished from internal processing models. Propositional attitudes are a way of characterizing the cognitive system *vis a vis* its environment, but it is not uncommon in science to use different accounts to describe the behavior of a system and to describe the internal processes that make the behavior possible. For example, a yeast cell performing fermentation is described physiologically as metabolizing sugar to produce alcohol, whereas in biochemistry the reaction is explained in terms of networks of enzymes and cofactors which together make it possible for a cell to metabolize the sugar. Similarly, we can view the characterization of how a system relates to its environment as different from the processing model that explains how it is able to accomplish this. When we actually try to develop a processing model, there are several different types we might consider, including the computational model as articulated by Fodor and employed in traditional AI, a syntactic model as described by Stich and employed in much traditional work in information processing psychology, or a connectionist model as advocated by some recent theorists and investigated in recent AI. The adequacy of the processing model is determined by whether it correctly describes the processes that operate in real cognitive systems, not by whether it invokes the formal structure of intentional accounts which describe the behavior of the cognitive system in its environment.

Although we can thus distinguish the task of developing intentional accounts that invoke propositional attitudes from that of developing processing accounts, this perspective on intentionality also suggests ways in which the two frameworks need to be related. It is important for those working on processing accounts to attend to the intentional perspective, in which the behavior of a cognitive system is characterized in terms of its beliefs and desires about the environment. It is this intentional perspective that identifies what aspects of the behavior of a system need to be explained by the processing account. (What is required is what Darden & Maull, 1977, referred to as an "interfield theory." See Bechtel, in press b, chapter 6 for more details on interfield theories.)

From this perspective we can make sense of calls by psychologists like J. J. Gibson (1979) and Ulric Neisser (1975, 1982) for adopting an ecological perspective in psychology. They object to an overemphasis on laboratory research in psychology (e.g., memory studies with nonsense syllables or vision studies using tachistoscopically presented stimuli), which they view as not focusing on the really important features of cognitive systems. Both Gibson and Neisser argue that in their natural habitats organisms respond not to the simple stimuli used in laboratory research but to coherent sets of stimuli that have both spatial extension and temporal duration. Gibson called these stimuli "affordances" because they present information that afford action to organisms.

The intentional perspective is similar to Gibson's and Neisser's ecological perspective insofar as it focuses on environmental information to which the system is responding. But, if we recall Dennett's account of the relation between the intentional stance and the design stance, we can also see how the intentional perspective would relate to information processing accounts at the design level. We do not need to take the additional step Gibson took when he coupled his call for an ecological approach with a repudiation of information processing approach. (See Fodor & Pylyshyn, 1981, and Hamilyn, 1977, for arguments that the information processing is still required even if we accept certain aspects of Gibson's position.) There are internal processes that enable a cognitive system to have intentional states, and laboratory research is needed to identify these. What the intentional stance does is provide a perspective for identifying how the system relates to its environment. Starting from this perspective, that laboratory research can identify what internal processes enable it to so relate. (See Glotzbach & Heft, 1982, for a related argument.)

Dennett (1983) proposes that the intentional stance provides a framework for cognitive ethology, a discipline that seeks to identify the cognitive capacities of particular organisms (and by extension, perhaps, artificial systems) that are relevant in their natural habitats. Cognitive ethology can generate what Anderson (1986) referred to as a "cognitive profile" for a species. This profile provides a description of the different kinds of information an organism is sensitive to, the kinds of things it can remember, and the ways it can use that information. It thereby offers a perspective on the organism that lies between specific accounts of how the organism behaves in the environment and the internal processing that produces the behavior. The information collected in the cognitive profile then tells the researcher trying to develop the internal processing models what capacities need to be explained in the processing account.

Adopting the view that intentional ascriptions characterize organisms in terms of their beliefs and desires about their environments also allows us to place our analysis of particular systems in phylogenetic perspective. We can examine different ways in which organisms have evolved to relate cognitively to their environment. In the case of humans, language clearly plays a major role in how we encode our beliefs about our environment and represent our desires. This raises the question of the extent to which the intentionality of mental states depends on the availability of language as a vehicle for communication. Philosophers have offered a variety of perspectives on the question of whether language is a prerequisite for intentionality or makes use of prior intentionality (for examples, see Bennett, 1976; Chisholm, 1984; Gauker, 1987; McDowell, 1980; Sellars, 1963a; Tennant, 1984); psychologists have also sometimes provided relevant evidence (e.g., Furth, 1966).

Interest in whether intentionality of mental states is more basic than that of language has been stimulated by recent work on animal communication, especially language research carried out with apes. Although this work has certainly been controversial, investigations by the Gardners (Gardner & Gardner, 1969) and others suggested that chimpanzees could use linguistic items intentionally. This finding could be interpreted as evidence for the claim that the capacity for intentionality exists prior to language learning. However, a common objection to the early ape language projects was that intense behavioral shaping was required before the animals could use the linguistic symbols, and it was not clear that the chimpanzees were really using the symbols with meaning. This would undercut the claim that the animals already possessed intentionality. Savage-Rumbaugh (1986) however, provides quite compelling evidence that the chimpanzees are using their symbols intentionally. Moreover, she is now engaged in pioneering research with pygmy chimpanzees (*Pan paniscus*), which demonstrates that members of this rare species, when provided a suitable environment, are capable of acquiring the use of symbols with specific meanings without a regimen of specific reinforcement and even from simply observing use by humans (Savage-Rumbaugh, McDonald, Sevcik, Hopkins, & Rupert, 1986).

The question of whether this indicates prior intentionality remains complex, however, because pygmy chimpanzees also exhibit a reasonably large set of vocalizations when in their native habitat. These vocalizations may already be intentional modes of communication and provide the basis for the animal's ability to use more complex languages in experimental settings. On the other hand, other researchers, such as Carolyn Ristau (1983, 1987), have tried to demonstrate that intentional behavior is found in animals, such as shore birds, that are clearly nonlinguistic. Although there are fundamental questions to be addressed about how we assess the intentionality of such animals, this research suggests that we may be able to examine the development of intentionality phylogenetically by looking at how different organisms have developed different capacities to deal with information in their environment. One benefit of such a comparative perspective is that understanding the kinds of cognitive capacities from which our abilities develop can both help us to characterize accurately our own cognitive capacities, and provide guidance when we try to explain what internal processing makes these cognitive capacities possible.

SUMMARY OF PHILOSOPHICAL APPROACHES
TO INTENTIONALITY

These last two chapters have focused on what many take to be the defining feature of mental states—their intentionality. In the previous chapter I presented several different attempts of philosophers to say what is distinctive about intentionality and why intentionality rendered scientific accounts of mental states impossible. In this chapter I have presented a variety of proposals philosophers have advanced to explain intentionality within a framework of natural science. I began with the Computational Theory of Mind, which seeks to use the propositional attitude format for describing mental states as the basis for generating an account of internal processing. Thus, Fodor proposes a theory of psychological activities which postulates that people actually perform inferences in a language of thought. This approach is common in AI, but it does not explain intentionality. I then presented the Representational Theory of Mind as a position that maintained that the mind was intentional and appropriately described in terms of propositional attitudes but rejected the idea that internal processing involved computation of these propositions.

I discussed three ways philosophers have tried to explain the representational capacities of mind—Dretske's information theoretic approach, Searle's biological reduction, and Dennett's intentional stance approach. Dretske's approach used the mathematical theory of information to explain how one state could be about another. It had the virtue of making intentionality into a natural phenomenon but seemed problematic insofar as it treated cognitive capacities principally as introducing distortions into an otherwise veridical process for knowledge acquisition. An evolutionary perspective would suggest that mental states play a more positive role in generating intentionality. Searle's approach linked intentionality to our biological constitution, but it seemed to make intentionality mysterious. It claimed that intentionality was a biological phenomenon, but denied that we could explain what makes certain biological states intentional. Dennett's intentional stance perspective made the intentional perspective something we adopt with respect to certain systems. What seemed most problematic about his approach was his instrumentalism with regard to intentional attributions, but I have suggested how we might develop a version of Dennett's approach that views intentional states realistically. It does this by treating them as states of the system that are adaptive to features of the system's environment.

Brentano thought that the intentionality of mental states had implications for what kind of entity we took minds to be. Minds, he claimed, could not be physical bodies because physical objects lacked intentionality. Many of the philosophers discussed in this chapter, however, have tried to show how intentional states might arise in physical systems. But this points to a fundamental question: What is the relation between minds and physical objects? That is the focus of the next two chapters.

5

The Mind–Body Problem: Dualism and Philosophical Behaviorism

INTRODUCTION

For three centuries philosophical inquiry has focused particularly on two questions about minds: What kind of things are minds? and How do minds relate to bodies? In this chapter and in chapter 6, I explore the major positions philosophers have advanced to answer these questions. My discussion generally follows the historical order in which these positions were developed because later positions were often put forward to overcome difficulties thought to confront earlier positions. One should not conclude from this that the positions discussed earlier are of only historical interest, however, because each position still has active advocates both amongst philosophers and practitioners of various of the cognitive sciences. I begin this chapter with a discussion of mind–body dualism, which has served as a major foil for those developing alternative positions. I also examine philosophical behaviorism, which constitutes one of the earliest attempts to avoid dualism and integrate mental phenomena into the physical universe.

DUALISM

The term *dualism* is generally applied to positions that view mental phenomena as somehow outside the framework of natural science. We need to distinguish two broad kinds of dualism: substance dualism and property dualism. *Substance dualism* considers the mind to be a nonphysical entity separated from the body. *Property dualism* is a more modest position that does not postulate nonphysical entities but that maintains that some of the properties these objects possess constitute a distinct class of mental properties. Substance dualism is the better known position and will be the principal form I discuss in this section.

The very question of whether the mind is a different substance from the physical body is a legacy of Descartes. By now the Cartesian perspective is so entrenched in our general culture that many people find it difficult to conceive of an alternative where the question would not arise. However, the differentiation of mind and body was quite foreign to the Aristotelian perspective that preceded Descartes. The Aristotelian approach characterized and classified objects in terms of what they did rather than in terms of their intrinsic character. This is perhaps a subtle difference, but it leads to radically different forms of inquiry. As we saw in chapter 1, Aristotle distinguished between the *matter* and *Form* of an object, but held that any object consisted of matter organized according to a particular Form. Aristotle's focus was on Form, not matter, for it was in terms of its Form that an object was characterized. This applied not only to inanimate objects but to animate ones as well. Aristotle spoke of the Form of living things as their *psyche* or *soul*. But Aristotle did not think of the soul as a discrete part of the living organism. Rather, he viewed it as the defining character of the organism.

For Aristotle, the Form of both animate and inanimate objects is discovered by observing the kind of activities they perform. Aristotle distinguished three classes of organisms in terms of the activities they are capable of performing and hence identified three different kinds of souls. Plants are capable of taking in nutrients and reproducing and these functions define the vegetative soul. Animals are not only capable of these activities, but of sensing things in their environment and of moving about in their environment, and these functions define the animal soul. Finally, humans are able to reason, which is the distinctive function of their souls (see *De Anima* in McKeon, 1941).

Within Aristotelian thinking, there is virtually no temptation to think of the soul as a distinctive thing that might be separated from the rest of the organism. (The qualifier "virtually" must be added because Aristotle seems, at least, to play with the idea that the reasoning soul might be capable of surviving the dissolution of the body.) The scientific revolution of the 16th and 17th centuries resulted in the rejection of Aristotle's account of nature in terms of matter and Form and this ultimately led to a different perspective on mental activity. Basic to the new physics was a conception of matter as passive and inert, subject to the forces that impinged on it from without. The task for physics was to develop laws governing the ways objects affected each other, either by striking them or exerting forces upon them. The question arose whether this view should be extended to the activities of animals and humans as well. Many investigators thought it should be. The 17th century English philosopher Thomas Hobbes is perhaps the best known of those who pressed for a complete account of human activity, including thinking, in the same terms as nonanimate physical objects. Even Descartes was strongly attracted to this prospect. He was fascinated by the behavior of hydraulic systems and viewed them as possible models of the physiological processes in humans and other animals. Harvey's work on the circulation of the blood, involving a pump pushing fluid through a series of channels, was a readily available model for Descartes. Descartes advocated a similar view of the nervous system, construing it as a set of channels through which animal spirits were circulated. This circulation, he thought, mechanically produced the physical behavior of living systems.

Descartes, however, contended that this attempt to explain behavior in physical terms reached an inevitable limit in those human endeavors involving the use of language and reasoning. He found these human activities to be so different in kind from those found in the rest of nature that he did not think they could be explained in the same way. He did not deny that mechanical systems or other animals (which he took simply to be mechanical systems) could utter words, but he claimed "it never happens that it [a non-human animal] arranges its speech in various ways in order to reply appropriately to everything that may be said in its presence, as even the lowest type of man can do" (Descartes, 1637/1970, p. 116). With regard to reasoning, he thought that although machines or animals might behave appropriately in many specific contexts, they would not exhibit the kind of general rationality that humans exhibit. These differences between humans and other animals, Descartes thought, could only be explained if we posited a special kind of substance in human beings—mental substance.

A substance for Descartes is characterized by that basic property that it cannot lack and still be the same substance. For physical substance, this property is extension (i.e., the occupation of space). Descartes claimed that although we can imagine that other characteristics of physical objects are radically changed or eliminated, we must always construe them as occupying some amount of space. In contrast to physical substance, Descartes considered the defining property of mental substance to be thinking. Descartes construed thinking generically, so as to include believing, supposing, hoping, and so on. (Descartes here includes the same class of activities that we would describe in propositional attitude discourse and which Brentano would describe as intentional. See chapter 3.) Descartes maintained that thinking and extension define two different classes of objects. The radical nature of the split Descartes envisioned is made clear in his *Meditations on First Philosophy*. After casting doubt over as many of his beliefs as possible, Descartes concluded initially that only his belief that he exists as a thinking thing is beyond doubt. Although he was able to doubt that he had a body, he was not able to doubt that he was a mind. Because Descartes could imagine his mind existing without his body, he concluded that the two are totally separate kinds of entities.

Descartes' dualism has been the object of many objections. One of the most serious of these focuses on the interaction of mind and body. If the two substances are so different, it seems hard to explain how they can interact with one another—how could thoughts cause physical motions of the body? Descartes proposed a solution. He claimed that at a central location in the brain—the pineal gland—the mind could alter the movements of the animal spirits flowing through the nerve channels, thereby influencing the activity of the body. Although subsequent inquiry has discredited Descartes' animal spirit theory and has identified a different function for the pineal gland, these are not the most serious problems with Descartes's proposed solution. There remains the more basic problem of explaining how two substances whose properties differ so radically could affect each other. Gassendi posed the objection as follows:

> [It] still remains to be explained how that union and apparent intermingling [of mind and body] . . . can be found in you, if you are incorporeal, unextended and indivisible. . . . How, at least, can you be united with the brain, or some minute part in it, which (as has been said) must yet have some magnitude or extension, however small it be? If you are wholly without parts how can you mix or appear to mix with its minute subdivisions? For there is no mixture unless each of the things to be mixed has parts that can mix with one another. (Gassendi, 1641/1970, p. 201)

The same question was put to Descartes by Princess Elizabeth in 1643: "How can the soul of man, being only a thinking substance, determine his bodily spirits to perform voluntary actions?" (Kenny, 1970, p. 135).

Descartes maintained that such objections were illegitimate. First, they assumed that the interaction of mind and body would follow the common pattern of causal interaction, when it really involves a different sort of interaction altogether. Second, he contended that "the human mind is [not] capable of conceiving at the same time the distinction and the union between body and soul, because for this it is necessary to conceive them as a single thing and at the same time to conceive them as two things; and this is absurd" (Kenny, 1970, p. 142). Most commentators find Descartes' responses inadequate. Richardson (1982), however, maintained that they are logically sufficient. He claimed that in his first response Descartes was noting that ultimately any explanation in terms of forces must stop with some forces that are taken to be basic, and so contending that we must stop the search for explanation of interaction by positing the existence of a mode of causal interaction between mind and body. To explicate the second response, Richardson appealed to Descartes' repeated denial that the relation between mind and body is comparable to that of a pilot to a ship. Rather, he viewed the relation as much more intimate. Richardson proposed that Descartes treats some states as states of the joint substances (thus entities with two natures) and not of either alone. He quotes as evidence the following passage from Descartes:

> there are . . . certain things which we experience in ourselves and which should be attributed neither to the mind nor body alone, but to the close and intimate union that exists between the body and the mind. . . . Such are the appetites of hunger, thirst, etc., and also the emotions or passions of the mind which do not subsist in mind or thought alone . . . and finally all the sensations. (Descartes, 1644/1970, p. 238)

If these states are states of a joint substance, then insofar as they are in part states of a physical substance, they can interact with physical substances in the ordinary manner. Likewise, insofar as they are states of a mental substance, they can interact with other mental states in the manner appropriate to mental states. Although this makes Descartes' response appear more coherent than it has generally been thought to be, there still remains a great mystery in explaining how the two natures can combine to form one entity. Thus, the debate over how interaction between mind and body could occur continues.

Although Descartes is often viewed as the paradigmatic dualist, there have been many others since Descartes. Brentano and William James were two prominent dualists in the 19th century. In our own day, the philosopher Karl Popper and the neurophysiologist John Eccles have jointly advanced a version of dualism (actually, tri-ism) which they prefer to speak of as "interactionism" (Popper & Eccles, 1977). Like Descartes, they focus on aspects of mental activity which they claim could not be accomplished by physical bodies. One such aspect is the ability of mental activities to generate abstract objects of thought, which assume a life of their own. These include mathematical objects, scientific theories, and works of literature. Popper[1] characterized these objects as constituting a distinct realm that he called "World 3." World 3 is distinguished from World 1—the world of physical objects—and World 2—the world of mental activity—by the fact that it is governed by normative principles such as the rules of logic. Popper insisted that principles of logic have an objective validity whether or not anyone ever follows them and so postulates that they have objective existence in a realm separate from the physical world or the world of thought.

The argument that mental activities are distinct from physical activities follows from the need for an intermediary that can apply information from World 3 to the physical World 1. Popper claimed that no purely physical system can grasp the abstract contents of World 3. Hence, there must be mental activities that grasp World 3 objects and then causally interact with events in World 1. Critics have taken issue with Popper's claim that no World 1

---

[1]In what follows I focus particularly on the portions of Popper and Eccle's joint book that were written by Popper.

objects can interact with abstract objects. Nondualists maintain that there is nothing problematic in physical objects grasping abstract objects. Even such clearly physical systems as computers can be so designed as to follow rules of logic and to reason about scientific theories or works of literature. The key to their being able to do so is their design, but this design is found in their physical existence and is not something distinct (see P. S. Churchland, 1986, p. 340).[2]

To press his position, Popper developed an additional argument that is intended to show that only interactionism can give the *proper* account of how World 3 principles regulate World 1 activities. The term *proper* is critical in this context, because Popper allows that World 3 objects are frequently instantiated in World 1 objects (e.g., a novel is instantiated in the paper and ink of a book) and hence can affect other World 1 objects in the way World 1 objects normally affect other World 1 objects (e.g., by holding down papers on which it is placed, etc.). The mode of interaction with which Popper is concerned involves World 3 objects affecting World 1 objects not because of their instantiation but because of their content. This argument is presented as part of a criticism of physicalist theories discussed in the following chapter. He maintained that such theories must either deny that there are mental events or render them inefficacious:

> We can divide those who uphold the doctrine that men are machines, or a similar doctrine, into two categories: those who deny the existence of mental events, or personal experiences, or of consciousness; . . . and those who admit the existence of mental events, but assert that they are "epiphenomena"—that everything can be explained without them, since the material world is causally closed. (Popper & Eccles, 1977, p. 5)

Because it is implausible to deny the occurrence of mental events altogether, the only plausible position for a physicalist, according to Popper, is epiphenomenalism. *Epiphenomenalism* holds that mental states are paired with brain states, but that there are no causal relations between them. Only brain states have causal efficacy and so mental states are mute.

---

[2]Popper denies that the performance of logical operations by computers affects his arguments, maintaining that because they are the product of human design, "both the computer and the laws of logic belong emphatically to what is here called World 3" (Popper & Eccles, 1977, p. 76). Churchland, however, shows how this response fails:

> Does the computer, which is a physical machine, interact with World 3 or not? If it does, then why not brains? Or does Popper perhaps mean that the functional states of computers really are not physical states after all? His reply misses entirely the point of the functionalist theory [see chapter 7], which is that mental states are states described at a high level of functional organization and implemented in brains. If a frankly physical system such as a computer can follow rules and procedures: can conform to mathematical laws, and can deduce conclusions never before deduced by man or machine, then it is plain that one need not hypothesize nonphysical mechanisms merely on the strength of a system's capacity to follow rules and logical laws. (1986, p. 341)

Having construed physicalism as a form of epiphenomenalism, Popper contends that epiphenomenalism is inconsistent with evolutionary theory because, according to Popper, evolutionary theory is committed to explaining all traits of species in terms of natural selection. But natural selection can only explain the emergence of a trait by showing how possession of the trait systematically provides individuals of the species with the instruments for survival (Popper & Eccles, 1977, p. 73). Because epiphenomenalism renders mental activity inefficacious and so useless as an instrument for survival, evolutionary theory cannot explain the origin of mental activity. Because he takes evolutionary theory as giving the only plausible account of how traits could emerge, he contends that the physicalist position is untenable.

This argument is seriously flawed. As I discuss in the next chapter, most physicalists, especially proponents of the Identity Theory, would reject Popper's treatment of their position as entailing epiphenomenalism. They maintain that mental states simply are physical states and as such provide whatever benefit the physical states do (Mortensen, 1978). But even if we grant Popper's interpretation of physicalism, his argument fails. Evolutionary theorists have proposed mechanisms other than natural selection to explain evolutionary change (Gould & Lewontin, 1979). Moreover, even if we restrict ourselves to natural selection, the argument fails. Natural selection permits a trait that is linked to advantageous traits to be favored even if it is nonadvantageous itself. A simple biological case illustrates this point. We explain why plants are green not by showing any advantage to being green but by showing that the allele responsible for chlorophyll in plants is also responsible for their green color and showing that possessing chlorophyll is advantageous. We do not require evolutionary theory to explain both why plants are green and why they have chlorophyll, or even why chlorophyll causes plants to be green. We turn to biochemistry to explain that connection; all evolutionary theory is required to do is explain why having chlorophyll benefited plants (see Bechtel & Richardson, 1983). Thus, even if mental states are epiphenomenal to certain kinds of brain states, they could be favored by selection if those brain states aided organisms in their quest for survival. Hence, physicalism is not inconsistent with evolutionary theory and we are not forced to adopt interactionism as the only alternative.

Descartes' and Popper's arguments are two of the most common arguments for dualism, but a number of others (e.g., Polten, 1973) have also been put forward. Many people are led to dualism by asking: How could the features of mind we observe in introspection be explained in terms of physical processes? By introspection, we notice the qualitative character of our mental life—that it seems to be filled with images, feelings, and so forth. It also seems to be characterized by intrinsic intentionality (see discussion of Searle in the previous chapter). These characteristics appear alien to the physical universe so that there is an incommensurability between what we recognize in ourselves when we perceive an object and the neural activities that are occurring in our brain. Equally, there seems to be an incommensurability between another person making reference to a dog and the pattern of neural activity in that person's brain.

Nondualists commonly respond to such claims by pointing to other incommensurabilities in nature, such as that between living and nonliving phenomena. They contend that although it once seemed inconceivable that inert matter could manifest the characteristics of life, that gap has been bridged by modern biology. Furthermore, introspection may not reliably tell us how things are. Just as we know that our perceptual mechanisms do not reveal the essential nature of the external world, it is possible that introspection does not reveal the real nature of inner experience. Progress in building machines that simulate human behavior may also lead us to understand what is really involved when we introspect on our experience.

It is worth noting at this juncture that some people draw their support for dualism from a quite different sphere. They see a dualist perspective as essential to our understanding of the moral and religious status of human beings. For many people, our moral perspective requires that human agents be free because moral judgments only make sense if agents are free to choose actions according to their own volitions. Insofar as any form of physicalism would seem to be deterministic in placing human beings under control of causal forces in nature, physicalism seems to undercut the potential for human freedom and thus our moral perspective. Our system of moral judgment, therefore, seems to require dualism.

A variety of responses have been offered to this kind of argument. One response is simply to reject the claim that our moral perspectives depend on human freedom, as B. F. Skinner (1948, 1971) does. Another is to argue that the form of freedom which is fundamental to our moral perspective is not incompatible with physicalism. Indeed, there is a philosophical position known as *weak determinism* that holds that free will and determinism are compatible. This position maintains that the form of freedom necessary for morality is sufficient freedom from external constraints that we are able to do what we choose to do (whether or not our choice was determined). When that condition is met, we can be held morally accountable for our actions. It is not necessary in addition that the procedure whereby we arrive at our choice be free. (For a recent philosophical exploration of this issue, see Dennett, 1984b, 1984c.)

So far in this section I have focused on substance dualism, but, as I noted at the beginning, a weaker form of dualism exists—property dualism. Property dualism holds that some objects have mental properties in addition to their physical properties. Drawing this distinction between mental and physical properties allows the property dualist to capture an intuition shared by most dualists—that there is a distinctive character to mental phenomena—

and yet reject the object dualist's claim that we must posit a separate substance in order to capture this difference. Property dualists only insist that mental properties are differentiable from physical properties. The same object, however, is able to possess both kinds of properties.

There are actually a variety of versions of property dualism that differ from one another in their account of how mental properties relate to physical properties. One version holds simply that each instance of an entity instantiating a mental property is an instance of an entity instantiating a physical property, without there being any other connection. This view is closely related to the position of the Token Identity Theory, which is discussed in chapter 6. A more classical version of property dualism, the dual aspect theory advanced by Huxley in the 19th century, holds that some events have two aspects. Generally, this view embraced epiphenomenalism and maintained that the mental aspect of the event had no effect on the physical aspect, although it was sometimes held that the physical aspect caused the mental aspect. According to this view, mental properties have the same relative relation to the operations in a person as displays on a CRT have to the operations going on within the computer—they simply relate what is happening without influencing the course of events. In its time, this epiphenomenalist position seemed to possess an important virtue: Because mental properties were only caused by physiological properties but did not figure in the chain of physiological events, psychology could develop in its domain in relative autonomy from physiology. However, more recently this position has attracted little interest because it renders mental properties inefficacious.

Property dualism has recently been revived in a different guise by Kim (1982a; see also 1978, 1982b). He described the relationship between mental properties and physical properties as one of *supervenience*. The concept of supervenience was originally developed to account for the relationship between moral properties and physical properties. Twentieth century moral philosophers like G. E. Moore and R. M. Hare argued against any definition of moral properties in nonmoral terms but recognized that it would be preposterous to allow that two individuals could behave in the same manner in the same circumstances and one of them be deemed good and the other evil. The principle of supervenience was introduced to block this possibility. It holds that if two individuals or acts are alike in all their physical properties, then they are also alike in their moral properties. For Kim, the attractive feature of the supervenience model is that it offers a way of explaining how mental properties of events might relate to physical properties of events. He proposed, however, strengthening the classical concept of supervenience, introducing the concept of "strong supervenience," which holds that if individuals share the same physical properties, then they *must* share the same mental properties.

Kim contended that the supervenience thesis avoids the problem of rendering the mind causally inefficacious. In his view, mental properties have all the causal effects of the physical properties upon which they supervene. To explicate this point, Kim (1979) compared the supervenience of mental properties on physical properties to the supervenience of the ordinary observable properties of physical objects on their physical microstructures. The microstructure determines the causal behavior of an object, but we can attribute the causality equally to the microstructure and the observable properties. Likewise, supervenient mental properties have all the causal properties associated with their underlying physical properties. Thus, through the supervenience theory we can recognize the difference between mental properties and physical ones, allow for the causal efficacy of mental properties, and not have to explain the interaction of mental and physical.

The most common kind of objection raised against dualism of either the object or property sort is that it is metaphysically extravagant. It is construed as violating *Occam's razor*, the principle that we should be parsimonious in our ontological assumptions and only postulate those entities necessary for our science. If we can account for all phenomena without postulating additional mental entities or properties, we should do so. One reason for adhering to Occam's razor with regard to the mind is that if the mind or mental properties are so radically different from physical objects or properties, then we may have a difficult time studying them through natural science. The techniques of scientific research generally, including those of cognitive science, assume that we are dealing with physical mechanisms working in accord with ordinary physical principles. For this reason even Popper agreed that research should be grounded on physicalist assumptions. He presented dualism as simply a position that we will be led to accept as a result of the failures of physical research to explain mental phenomena, not a position that should guide our research. Given this apparent fruitlessness of dualism as a foundation for science, we need to begin to consider the various non-Dualistic theories that have been advanced to replace it.

PHILOSOPHICAL BEHAVIORISM

One of the first alternatives to dualism that was carefully worked out was a position known as *philosophical behaviorism*. It was popular during much the same period as psychological behaviorism dominated psychology. Although philosophical behaviorism and psychological behaviorism are aligned in rejecting dualism, *behaviorism* means something quite different for proponents of these two positions. For psychologists, behaviorism is an empirical research program that endeavors to discover laws that can explain behavior of humans and other organisms in terms of occurrent stimuli and an organism's past history of conditioning. Its distinctive character is that it rejects appeals to mental events in order to explain behavior. Whereas psychological behaviorism is an empirical research program, philosophical behaviorism is primarily concerned with the semantics of our common mentalistic vocabulary. It seeks to explain the meaning of mental terms like *belief* without having to treat them as referring to some mental substance. The goal is to translate terms that purport to refer to mental activity into terms that speak only of behaviors or propensities to behave in certain ways. Thus, the philosophical behaviorist does not eliminate mental discourse, but offers a way to legitimize it. Despite these different objectives, philosophical behaviorists and psychological behaviorists have often viewed each other as allies. Skinner (1945), for example, offered behavioral analyses of mental terms. Philosophical behaviorism and psychological behaviorism have especially been allied in rejecting the view (central to cognitivism) that mental events are processes internal to the mind which cause behavior. In this section, I focus on the position of philosophical behaviorism and simply note the similarities between it and psychological behaviorism.

Philosophical behaviorism traces its origins to two broader philosophical movements discussed in chapter 2. One was Logical Positivism, which proposed to explicate the meaning of sentences used in a science in terms of the conditions that would verify their truth. One of the goals of the Positivists was unifying all science. They proposed that if we could reduce discussion of mental phenomena to discussion of behavior and propensities to behave, we would both secure the meaning of mental terms and take the first step toward unifying psychology with physics. Then the remaining task would be to reduce discussion of behavior to more basic theories in the physical sciences.

The second philosophical movement that gave rise to philosophical behaviorism was Wittgenstein's analysis of ordinary language. Wittgenstein construed many philosophical issues, such as the mind–body problem, as resulting from linguistic confusion. He proposed to do away with such confusion by attending carefully to the ways our language, including our mental idioms, is used in ordinary discourse.

The *locus classicus* of philosophical behaviorism is Gilbert Ryle's 1949 monograph *The Concept of Mind*. In that work Ryle presents philosophical behaviorism not simply as an alternative to the traditional views of dualism and materialism, but as doing away altogether with the question of the relation of mind and body, which he characterized as the issue of "the ghost in the machine." Ryle characterized the mind–body problem as resulting from what he labelled a "category mistake" because it "represents the facts of mental life as if they belonged to one logical type or category (or range of types or categories), when they actually belong to another" (1949, p. 16). Ryle used an example to explicate the notion of a category mistake. Imagine a person who, having been shown the buildings, faculty, and so on, of a university, now asks to see the university. The person assumes that it is another entity comparable to those already exhibited. Because the term *university* does not refer to items in the same category as the terms *building* and *faculty*, the person commits a category mistake in looking for the university to be something of the same kind. Similarly, Ryle claimed that a category mistake is committed when we look for the mind as a separate component of the body in addition to its various physical parts, or when we try to identify the mind with some physical part of the body.

The alternative, according to Ryle, is to recognize that mental and physical vocabularies belong to different logical types and follow different rules. Mental vocabulary, according to Ryle, does not attempt to describe behavior in anything like the way physiological vocabulary describes processes occurring inside of people. Rather, according to Ryle, we use mental vocabulary to speak about how someone behaves or is likely to behave. Ryle illustrated this by considering a variety of mental idioms and showing how they can be accommodated within the general approach he outlines. For example, we can explicate what we mean when we say that someone believes that it will rain by pointing to various behavioral propensities, such as the propensity to carry an umbrella, to cancel plans for a picnic, and the like.[3]

Wittgenstein (1953), and Malcolm's interpretations of Wittgenstein (see Malcolm, 1984), represent further developments of philosophical behaviorism. Like Ryle, Wittgenstein and Malcolm traced the commonly held view that the mind must be a special entity to the propensity of philosophers and others to misuse ordinary language. The corrective for this is careful analysis of the way language ordinarily functions. One way we misuse language is when we treat mental terms as referring to events which we then maintain are, by definition, private (e.g., pains or beliefs). Our ability to use language at all depends on our using it intersubjectively. When used intersubjectively, other people can ascertain whether a particular speaker is using it correctly. This check on accuracy would be lost if mental idioms really referred to private events. Hence, Wittgenstein and Malcolm maintain that we should reject the idea that these idioms refer to such private events. (For a recent attack on this argument, see Chomsky, 1986.)

Wittgenstein and his followers also maintained that we can discover some of the constraints on the proper use of mental terms by attending to the way in which they are learned. A dualist might hold that we learn terms like believe and hope by first recognizing through introspection the states in us that correspond to believing something or hoping for something and then learning to apply the appropriate labels to those states. Philosophical behaviorists question how we could teach another person to connect a term to a state that

---

[3]Ryle offers a different kind of analysis of what might be called *mental occurrences*—events like experiencing a certain feeling or thinking a particular thought. He proposes to treat events like thinking as analogous to events like speaking: thinking is talking to oneself.

only that person can experience. We lack any way of testing to see whether the person applied the term correctly. The alternative they propose is that mental terms, such as *pain*, are learned in a public context where, for example, we see people getting hurt. It is such public phenomena that provide the criteria for the correct use of mental vocabulary.[4]

The philosophical behaviorist also rejects the view that mental terms characterize states of the person that possess causal efficacy (e.g., that we do things because of beliefs). Such mental terms as *belief* characterize dispositions and, according to Ryle (1949), "to possess a dispositional property is not to be in a particular state, or to undergo a change" (p. 43). For example, when we attribute brittleness to an object we are not claiming that it is in a particular internal state that causes it to break, but only saying that it is such that it would break easily. Similarly, in attributing a belief to someone we are not making a claim about the person's internal states but simply characterizing the person in terms of what he or she might do in particular circumstances. The philosophical behaviorist claims that it is wrong to treat mental states as causes of behavior. We cannot identify the mental states independently of behavioral states, and so cannot treat them as causes of behavior (see Malcolm, 1984).

In rejecting internal mental states, philosophical behaviorism is clearly incompatible with the cognitive science program of explaining behavior in terms of processing models. For Ryle, talk of internal processing adds nothing to what we understand about a person when we know his or her propensities to behave in specific ways. For Wittgenstein, experimental psychology is a misguided effort to bring psychological talk within experimental science. His proposal is that instead we should to try to understand psychological phenomena by examining how language has evolved to deal with human behavior.

Like psychological behaviorism, philosophical behaviorism has lost popularity in recent years. This is largely due to the recognition of apparently serious difficulties with the position. It is obvious that we cannot simply translate mental terms into descriptions of behaviors because mental states such as beliefs do not always manifest themselves in behavior. Philosophical behaviorists tried to equate mental terms with terms ascribing *dispositions* or *propensities* to behave in certain ways under appropriate stimuli. For example, my belief that I have an appointment at 10:00 a.m. might be iden-

---

[4]A commonly proposed alternative view is that we see things happening to others that are similar to things that happen to us and then infer that the other person is feeling as we have felt in like circumstances. Wittgenstein explicitly rejected this view on the grounds that even if there were an internal state in us, we would have no grounds for re-identifying it later as the same state. The reason is that if the state is not public, there is no check on whether we are in fact re-identifying the same state. We might actually forget how we used the word before and identify another state.

tified not with some behavior I am now doing, but with the propensities I have to behave in particular ways. For example, if I have this belief, then if I notice that my watch reads 9:59, I will suddenly get up and dash out of the office.

The dispositional analysis does not avoid all problems, however. First, individual mental states cannot generally be equated with distinct behavioral dispositions. My belief that I have a 10:00 a.m. appointment will be associated with a wide variety of dispositions. In fact, this set may be unlimited and will include a number of dispositions that we would be unlikely to consider until they arose. For example, if I am detained in the Dean's office at 9:59 a.m., I may not get up and dash out, but may request to make a telephone call.[5] There seems to be no end to the variety of such possibilities. The philosophical behaviorist seems committed to analyzing beliefs in terms of potentially infinitely long lists of conditional sentences, which introduces further problems. One of the purported virtues of philosophical behaviorism was its account of how we learn to use mental terms through experience. However, the proposal that mental terms are to be equated with potentially infinite lists of conditional statements renders that claim dubious, because we would have to learn this potentially infinite list in order to learn mental terms.

There is a second problem that is more serious. The conditional sentences that are supposed to give the meaning equivalences of mental terms almost inevitably employ mental terms themselves. In the example of my belief that I have a 10:00 a.m. appointment, I used a conditional sentence about what would happen if I noticed the time on my watch. The term *noticed* is also a mental term, which must in turn be given a translation into conditional sentences. This suggests that we are caught in a circle of mental terms in which the behavioral correlates of one term can only be stated by using other mental terms. Critics have argued that we can never get out of this circle because all purported behavioral translations of mental terms would themselves employ mental terms. (See Chisholm, 1957; Geach, 1957.)

A third problem concerns the ways in which we could go about assigning dispositions to agents. We cannot ascribe dispositions except on the basis of behavior already performed. But, as Armstrong (1968) objects, previous behavior always underdetermines dispositions. We can always impute a variety of dispositions to account for any particular behavior. If we take mental terms to ascribe particular dispositions to agents, then we must assume that something about the agent fixes what disposition is to be ascribed. This only

---

[5]There is a further problem in that this same action, asking to make a phone call, may be the result of quite different mental states (e.g., believing that the Dean wanted me to acquire certain information). The same behavioral disposition may thus be linked to an indefinite number of mental states.

seems possible if we treat mental terms as referring to determinate inner states whose character fixes the disposition involved. This, however, violates the strictures imposed by philosophical behaviorism.

One of the foundations upon which philosophical behaviorism was built, the verificationist theory of meaning, has also been challenged in recent years. Quine (1953/1961a) criticized as a dogma of empiricism the assumption that we could logically define theoretical terms observationally and increasingly philosophers of science have come to acknowledge that we might have to accept terms into our scientific vocabulary that cannot be logically reduced to observational terms. If we give up verificationism in general, there would seem to be no reason not to do so in the case of mental discourse as well. Doing so permits the mental terms to be introduced within psychological discourse in much the same manner as theoretical terms are introduced into a science (see Fodor, 1968; Geach, 1957; Sellars, 1963b). This, of course, leaves open the question of what these theoretical terms refer to. In chapter 6 I discuss some alternative attempts to explicate the reference of mental terms within a generally physicalistic framework.

INTERMEDIATE SUMMARY
OF THE MIND–BODY PROBLEM

In this chapter I have examined two philosophical views of the relationship of mind and brain that have been very influential in shaping discussions of this issue. Descartes differentiated mind and brain and he and others have tried to show in what respects the mind is a different kind of entity from physical objects like the brain. Dualism has encountered a number of problems in explaining the relation between mind and body and has been accused of inflating our ontology unnecessarily. Philosophical behaviorism avoids dualism by denying that mental states are internal states of people. Instead it tries to analyze mental states in terms of behavioral dispositions, a move that encounters a number of problems. Both of these views have thus faced severe criticism so that, while some philosophers still maintain them, most have pursued other options. Some of these are considered in the next chapter.

6

The Mind–Body Problem: Versions of Materialism

INTRODUCTION

In the previous chapter I introduced the mind–body problem and discussed two philosophical answers to it. Another traditional answer holds that mental states are states of the brain. This view, which commonly goes by the names *materialism* and *physicalism*, can be traced back at least to Hobbes and was further developed by Gassendi and LaMettrie in the 17th and 18th centuries. Most contemporary philosophers and probably most cognitive scientists endorse materialism. Since the 1950s, however, philosophers have tried to state the thesis of materialism more precisely. As a result, they have developed a variety of different versions of materialism. I examine three contemporary versions in this chapter, each of which has a quite different set of consequences for cognitive science.

MIND–BRAIN TYPE IDENTITY THEORY

The phrase "Identity Theory" properly refers to the approach developed in the 1950s by U.T. Place (1956/1970), Herbert Feigl (1958/1967, 1960/1970), and J. J. C. Smart (1959/1971) and advocated by a number of philosophers in the following decade. These theories proposed that mental states were identical with states of the brain. The qualifying expression "type" has been introduced more recently to distinguish this view from a weaker view that attained prominence in the 1970s and 1980s, known as the "Token Identity Theory," which is taken up in a later section. The type/token distinction refers to the difference between a class of events (the type) and a specific member of the class (a token). The term *chair* identifies a type of object, whereas my desk chair is a token of that type. The Type Identity Theory holds that all instances of a particular type of mental state (e.g., experiencing a certain kind of pain or seeing a certain color) are identical to instances of a correlated type of neural event (e.g., a certain pattern of neural firings).

One of the chief inspirations for the Type Identity Theory was work by neurophysiologists such as Köhler, Penfield, and Hebb, which was seen as pointing to an isomorphism of phenomenal reports with specific neuroprocesses. Feigl construed the philosophers task to be to provide "logical and epistemological clarification of the concepts by means of which we may formulate and/or interpret those correlations" (1960/1970, p. 35). Epiphenomenalist views such as we discussed in the previous chapter provide one way of interpreting these results. According to epiphenomenalism, the complete causal analysis of behavior will focus on the interaction of brain events, but there will be a second set of causal relations according to which some brain states will produce phenomenal states. Feigl rejects epiphenomenalism, characterizing its treatment of mental states as positing "purely mental 'danglers'," which Feigl called a "very queer solution": "These correspondence laws are peculiar in that they may be said to postulate 'effects' (mental states as dependent variables) which by themselves do not function, or at least do not seem to be needed, as 'causes' (independent variables) for any observable behavior" (p. 37). The alternative Feigl advanced is that mental terms refer to exactly the same states as do the physical terms even though they describe the states differently: "Utilising Frege's distinction between *Sinn* ('meaning', 'sense', 'intension') and *Bedeutung* ('referent', '*denotation*', 'extension'), we may say that neurophysiological terms and the corresponding phenomenal terms, though widely differing in *sense*, and hence in the modes of confirmation of statements containing them, do have identical *referents*" (p. 38). Identity theorists thus invoke Frege's analysis of identity states (see chapter 2) to explicate how mental states and physical states can be identical: Mental idioms and physical idioms are different descriptions of the same states.

One issue discussed in the early literature on the Identity Theory was the range of mental states to which this account should apply. Place was the first to propose the Identity Theory but he accepted the philosophical behaviorist's identification of some mental states with dispositions. He contended only that some other mental concepts could not refer to dispositions—he held that there was "an intractable residue of concepts clustering about the notions of consciousness, experience, sensation, and mental imagery, where some sort of inner process story is unavoidable" (1956/1970, p. 43, see also 1988). These inner processes would be processes in the brain.

Other proponents of the Identity Theory generalized it, however, so as to hold that all mental terms, including those that the philosophical behaviorist had analyzed as referring to dispositions, really referred to brain states. The extension was very natural. In other disciplines, disposition statements are often reduced to statements about the internal constitution of the object possessing the disposition. The brittleness of glass, for example, is identified with its physical structure. Similarly, identity theorists proposed that it is the state of the brain that accounts for a person being in a certain mental state such as having a particular belief (see Armstrong, 1968).

The most difficult problem confronting early proponents of the Identity Theory was to make clear what the claim that mental states are identical to brain states means. The Identity Theorist is committed to what Smart (1959/ 1971) called identity in the "strict sense," not mere correlation. (Popper, as I discussed in the previous chapter, misconstrued the Identity Theorist's position as one of correlation.) Many critics have found the idea of a strict identity of mental and physical states to be either unintelligible or obviously false because mental terms and physical terms differ so greatly in their meanings. The following objection is fairly typical:

> To say that consciousness *is* a form of matter or of motion is to use words without meaning. The identification of consciousness and motion indeed can never be refuted; but only because he who does not see the absurdity of such a statement can never be made to see anything. . . . If he cannot see that, though consciousness and motion may be *related* as intimately as you please, we *mean* different things by the two words, that though consciousness may be *caused* by motion, it *is* not what we mean by motion anymore than it is green cheese—if he cannot see this there is no arguing with him. (Pratt, 1922/1957, p. 266)

Objections to the Identity Theory are often presented in terms of *Leibniz's Law* that, as we saw in chapter 2, holds that if two terms refer to the same object, then any property that is truly predicated of the object referred to by the first term must also be truly predicated of the object when referred to by the second term and vice versa. Critics claim to find a number of properties that could be attributed either to physical events or to mental events, but not both. One such property is intentionality (see chapters 3 and 4), which is thought to apply only to mental events and not to physical events. If it is true that mental events exhibit intentionality and brain events do not, then brain events and mental events are not identical. Shaffer (1965) raises this objection:

> when I report that I suddenly remembered that Henry was sick, the intentionality of this report, i.e., that it is about Henry and his sickness, is an essential part of it. This intentional feature is lost if we simply report that a particular neural event had suddenly occurred; such a report would not be about Henry at all, only about a brain event. Of course we could always give these new functions to brain-events, but that would be to redefine physicalistic expressions, instead of redefining mentalistic expressions, leaving us where we began. (p. 95)

There are a number of other properties that seem to behave similarly. For example, when we experience an after-image we seem to experience something with a particular color and shape. Because there is no object with that color and shape that we actually see, it is common to say that the object exists in our mind. But we would not say that an object of that color and shape existed in our brain. Hence, there are objects in the mind that are not in the brain.

Physical events also have properties that mental events seem to lack. For example, all physical events have spatial coordinates—they occur at some location. But, as Shaffer (1965) claims:

> so far as thoughts are concerned, it makes no sense to talk about a thought's being located in some place or places in the body. If I report having suddenly thought something, the question where in my body that thought occurred would be utterly senseless. (p. 97)

So, Shaffer and others have concluded, mental events cannot be brain events.

Another common objection to the Identity Theory holds that mental events and physical events cannot be the same since we are acquainted with them in different ways. It is claimed that we are directly aware of mental states—we do not need to perform investigations to find out about them. We have what is termed *privileged access* to our mental life. However, we can only find out about the states of our brains very indirectly, if at all. Because we have privileged access to our mental events but lack such privileged access to brain events, critics charge that the two cannot be the same.

Smart's (1959/1971) classic paper in defense of the Identity Theory consists largely of attempts to rebut objections of this sort by clarifying what is involved in a claim of identity. To begin with, he maintained, identity claims are not claims of logical necessity that can be established by analyzing how we use language. Rather, they are contingent claims that could turn out to be false. The identity theorist is willing to contemplate the possibility that mental events could be something other than brain events, but contends that in us they are brain events. Hence, objections that mental terms and physical terms have different meanings does not count against the identity thesis. Smart countered the contention that most people do not know about their brain processes, whereas they know about their phenomenal state, by claiming that the Identity Theory does not depend on how people understand the concepts used to express the claim, but only on whether both terms in fact refer to the same thing. He contended that "there can be contingent statements of the form 'A is identical with B', and a person may well know that something is an A without knowing that it is a B. An illiterate peasant might well be able to talk about his sensations without knowing about his brain processes, just as he can talk about lightning though he knows nothing of electricity" (Smart, 1959/1971, p. 58).

In response to the objection that most people ascribe different properties to mental experiences than to physical experiences, Smart maintains that this is simply a feature of our current language use. In the future, we might revise our language to permit predications of intentionality, for example, to brain states. Smart himself, in fact, advocated one revision in our language. To counter the objection that our phenomenal discourse seems to refer to phenomenal properties (e.g., color properties) that are distinct from physical properties, Smart proposed what he called "topic-neutral" terminology. Thus, he recommended translating "I see a yellowish-orange after-image" into *"There is something going on which is like what is going on when* I have my eyes open, am awake, and there is an orange illuminated in good light in front of me, that is, when I really see an orange" (Smart, 1959/1971, p. 61). The point of translating reports into topic-neutral form is to avoid the assumption that these reports are reports about peculiarly mental properties that could not be identified with physical properties. Smart's proposal also deals with the after-image objection. After-image talk suggests that there is an object corresponding to the image in the mind, but Smart's topic-neutral rendering does away with any temptation to say that there is a phenomenal object present when we see after images. Rather, it leads us to say that what is occurring are simply events like those which occur when we see real, external objects. Smart's proposal of topic-neutral translations has been controversial. For sample criticisms, see Cornman (1962/1971) and Margolis (1978).

As I noted earlier, many of the objections to the Identity Theory have relied on Leibniz's Law. Implicitly, what Smart was doing was trying to show that the demands of Leibniz's Law can actually be met by appropriate linguistic maneuvers. Other defenders of the Identity Theory have adopted a different strategy that denies the applicability of Leibniz's Law to these contexts. Cornman (1962), for example, maintains that, Leibniz's Law is not violated when mental predicates are found to be inapplicable to physical states or vice versa. We would only have a violation if one predication had a different truth value than the other. But in this case the inapplicable predication is neither true or false. He took this as showing that we are confronted with a case of a category mistake such as Ryle described. Cornman, however, drew a different lesson than Ryle. He maintained that it is legitimate to posit cross-category identities and that in such cases Leibniz's Law is simply inapplicable. He supported this analysis by considering another case:

> We talk of the temperature of a gas as being identical with the mean kinetic energy of the gas molecules. But although we can say that the temperature of a certain gas is 80° Centigrade, it is surely in some sense a mistake to say that the mean kinetic energy of the gas molecules is 80° Centigrade. If this mistake is what I have called a category mistake, then this is a case of cross-category identity. If it is also a category mistake to talk of a fading or dim brain process, then we have some grounds for thinking that the identity of mind and body

would be a cross-category identity, and, therefore, that the Identity Theory need not involve conceptual difficulties. (Cornman, 1962/1971)

As just noted above, the defenders of the Identity Theory construed the identity of mental events and physical events as something that is true but could have been false. Such statements are referred to as *contingent*. Relying on his analysis of modal statements (see chapter 2), Saul Kripke (1972) has argued that contingent identities are impossible. As we saw, Kripke held that necessary statements are true in all possible worlds, and that a *rigid designator* is a term that picks out the same entity in any possible world in which the entity exists. A *nonrigid designator* is a term that changes its referent across possible worlds. (For example, "Jimmy Carter" is a rigid designator. It picks out the same person in any world in which Carter exists. The term "39th President of the United States," however, is not a rigid designator because another person could have been elected in 1976.) Kripke argued that proper identity claims must equate terms that are rigid designators. This entails that all identity claims are necessary, not contingent because both names will pick out the same object in each possible world. Having construed all identity claims as necessary, Kripke argued that mental states cannot be identical to physical states. He maintained that terms referring to mental states and to brain states are rigid designators. Because we can stipulate a possible world in which terms referring to mental states would not refer to the same things as terms referring to brain states, these rigid designators cannot pick out the same objects. Hence, they cannot stand in an identity relations.

Although Kripke's arguments are sophisticated, many philosophers and probably most empirical researchers find them to be beside the point when addressing empirical issues. Part of the difficulty stems from the question of how we determine what are the possible worlds. Kripke's answer, as we saw earlier, is that we stipulate possible worlds—we determine what features of the current world to alter to arrive at the possible world. This treatment of possible worlds, however, has the unfortunate consequence of making the evaluation of claims about what is possible depend on our ability to imagine certain situations. But it is clear that we may think something is possible and later discover that it is not. People thought the Evening Star could cease to exist and the Morning Star remain in existence, but we now know that is not possible. Similarly, although we might conceive of brain states existing without concomitant mental states, that may not actually be possible. Linguistic legislation cannot settle that issue. Thus, even if we grant Kripke the claim that all identities must be necessary identities (a contentious claim in itself), the rejection of the Identity Theory does not follow. (For other philosophical criticisms of Kripke's arguments, see Barnette, 1977; Feldman, 1974, 1980; Kirk, 1982; Lycan, 1974; Maxwell, 1978; and Sher, 1977.)

I noted at the beginning of this discussion that proponents of the identity thesis have viewed themselves as giving a logical exposition of research advances in neuroscience. But neuroscience research, as many critics have noted, could never establish anything more than a correlation between mental events and brain events. Whether we adopt a correlation claim (which even dualists can accept) or an identity claim seems to be an issue that goes beyond the empirical evidence. Proponents of the Identity Theory often appeal to Occam's razor to support their position. Occam's razor calls upon us to accept a theory that posits fewer entities rather than one that posits more entities with no gain in explanatory power. Feigl implicitly was using Occam's Razor in the passage quoted earlier in which he commented on the peculiar character of epiphenomenalism. Smart (1959/1971) referred to it directly in his defense of the Identity Theory:

> Why do I wish to resist [parallelism]? Mainly because of Occam's razor. It seems to me that science is increasingly giving us a viewpoint whereby organisms are able to be seen as physico-chemical mechanisms: it seems that even the behavior of man himself will one day be explicable in mechanistic terms. There does seem to be, so far as science is concerned, nothing in the world but increasingly complex arrangements of physical constituents. All except for one place: consciousness. . . . That everything should be explicable in terms of physics except the occurrence of sensations seems to me to be frankly unbelievable. (p. 54)

However, critics of the Identity Theory object that we cannot do with fewer entities in this case. Mental and physical properties appear differently to us and we need to explain this difference. This requires positing at least dual properties if not dual objects.

The debates between identity theorists and their critics seem to result in a stalemate, with neither side able to convince the other. (For further discussion of the Type Identity Theory, see Enc, 1983; Hill, 1984.) Dennett (1979) commented on how the issue polarizes people:

> The Identity Theory's defining claim that mental events are not merely parallel to, coincident with, caused by, or accompaniments of brain events, but *are* (strictly identical with) brain events, divides people in a curious fashion. To some people it seems obviously true (though it may take a little fussing with details to get it properly expressed), and to others it seems just as obviously false. The former tend to view all attempts to resist the Identity Theory as motivated by an irrational fear of the advance of the physical sciences, a kind of humanistic hylephobia, while the latter tend to dismiss identity-theorists as blinded by misplaced science-worship to the manifest preposterousness of the identity claim. (p. 252)

Deciding between the identity claim and parallelism may be impossible if we appeal only to how we describe mental and physical states and people's intuitions as to whether a brain state could possess mental properties and vice versa. An alternative approach is to construe identity claims as claims made in the course of scientific research and to consider how scientists typically evaluate such claims.

Generally, identity claims are made at the outset of scientific research, not at the end of research. Moreover, Leibniz's Law is not used to evaluate the correctness of an identity claim, but to generate new empirical hypotheses to be investigated. Identity claims often are advanced when investigators think that there might be an identity between entities previously investigated separately in different research fields. Leibniz's Law becomes relevant when researchers try to use what one field knows about the entity to deal with problems that originally arose in the other domain. For example, Mendel (1865) initially posited factors (later called *genes*) that he took to be responsible for the inheritance of traits between parents and offspring. Chromosomes, on the other hand, were identified in cytological research, where the elaborate procedures involved in meiosis and mitosis suggested that they must play some important role in inheritance from one cell to the next. Boveri (1905) and Sutton (1903), on the basis of evidence that abnormal chromosome distribution led to abnormal development, proposed that chromosomes were the units of heredity. This generated the identity claim that Mendelian factors were units on the chromosomes, which then led to the extremely fruitful research program of the Morgan school. Information that was known about chromosomes was applied to genes and vice versa. The fruitfulness of the identity claim was something that could only be evaluated as a result of the research that resulted from it, not at the time it was advanced (see Bechtel, in press b, chapters 5 & 6; Churchland, 1986; Darden & Maull, 1977; Wimsatt, 1976). To apply the same perspective to the mind–brain case would require treating the Identity Theory as a working hypothesis to be further investigated. If, on the basis of psychophysical identity claims we can use what is known about mental events to advance our understanding of neural processes and vice versa, then an identity claim rather than a correlation claim will have been justified.

In countenancing inner states as causal factors that can be used in explaining behavior, the Identity Theory is certainly more compatible with endeavors in current cognitive science than was philosophical behaviorism. But the Identity Theory only licenses appeal to internal events by assuming that types of mental events are identical with types of neural events. Hence, cognitive theories are limited to ways of classifying mental events that map unto those used in neuroscience. Such a connection may undercut the endeavors of cognitivists because the most fruitful way to classify events for cognitive purposes may not correspond to those required for neuroscience (see Fodor, 1974, and p. 109, this volume). Moreover, insofar as the Identity Theory was inspired by work in neuroscience, there is at least the suggestion that cognitive theories should parallel neuroscience theories. Thus, the Identity Theory seems to give primacy to the neurosciences over the investigations of cognitive science. At best, cognitive theories might describe in cognitive terms the same processes neuroscience describes in more physical vocabulary.

One topic on which many recent materialists have taken issue with the Type Identity Theory has been the assumed correlation of mental events with physical events. These materialists, however, have disagreed on the proper response. *Eliminative materialists* view this as a reason for eliminating mental talk from our language in favor of talk about our brain whereas advocates of the Token Identity Theory propose that we should continue to talk about mental phenomena, but recognize that it is only individual mental events that can be identified with physical events. They deny that we can correlate types of mental events with types of physical events. I turn to these positions in the two sections that follow.

ELIMINATIVE MATERIALISM

Eliminative Materialists begin by claiming that neuroscience research does not demonstrate the correlation of brain processes with mental processes claimed by the Type Identity Theory and argue that this as a reason to replace mental talk with talk about brain states. More pointedly, they contend that there are no mental phenomena and that those who thought there were were mistaken.[1]

In part, Eliminativists see themselves as more thorough-going materialists than Identity Theorists. Feigl, in a postscript he added 10 years after he wrote an essay in which he advocated the Identity Theory, repudiated it in favor of Eliminativism. He did so because he concluded that mental phenomena could not be identified precisely with brain activities. He proposed that rather than trying to force a tighter integration of mental concepts with physical concepts, we could begin to use the physical concepts as replacements for the mental concepts. He predicted that once neuroscience is sufficiently developed we will no longer need to speak of other people as experiencing feelings of pleasure and the like, but will instead use the new concepts of neuroscience (Feigl, 1958/1967, pp. 141–142).

Paul Feyerabend reached the same conclusion somewhat earlier. Feyerabend (1963/1970) maintained that in the very formulation of statements of

---

[1]It is useful to compare Eliminativists with Dualists. Both criticize the Identity Theory by noting that the things we say about mental events are radically different from the things we say about brain events. Dualists appeal to Leibniz's Law at this juncture to contend that therefore mental events cannot be identical to brain events. Eliminative materialists, on the other hand, see these differences as showing that our mental talk committed us to saying things that were literally false and that we should therefore abandon mental discourse in favor of discourse about the brain.

psychophysical identity, the Identity Theorist seemed to be committed to nonreducible psychological properties. He endorsed basically the same remedy as Feigl, proposing that we should abandon mentalistic language just as we abandoned language about devil possession once the modern theory of epilepsy was developed. We should replace mentalistic terminology with new terminology drawn from neuroscience. Feyerabend recognized that many people would not be able to accept the suggestion that our ordinary mentalistic discourse might be radically wrong. To illustrate the kind of objection he expected, he quoted J. L. Austin's (1955-1957/1960) defense of ordinary language:

> Our common stock of words embodies all the distinctions men have found worth drawing, and the connections they have found worth marking, in the lifetime of many generations: these surely are likely to be more numerous, more sound, since they have stood up to the long test of the survival of the fittest, and more subtle . . . than any that you or I am likely to think up. (p. 182)

Feyerabend (1963/1970) however, is unimpressed by such claims about ordinary language:

> First of all, such idioms [of ordinary language] are adapted not to *facts*, but to *beliefs*. If these beliefs are widely accepted; if they are intimately connected with the fears and the hopes of the community in which they occur; if they are defended, and reinforced with the help of powerful institutions; if one's whole life is somehow carried out in accordance with them—then the language representing them will be regarded as most successful. At the same time the question of the truth of the beliefs has not been touched.
>
> The second reason why the success of a 'common' idiom is not at all on the same level as is the success of a scientific theory lies in the fact that the use of such an idiom, *even in concrete observational situations*, can hardly ever be regarded as a *test*. There is no attempt, as there is in the sciences, to conquer new fields and to try the theory in them. (p. 144)

Besides this global repudiation of the privileged status of our ordinary mental talk, Feyerabend also rejected Descartes' claim that mental discourse is infallible in such a manner that if we think we are in a certain mental state, no other evidence could establish that we were not. In contrast, Feyerabend contended that reports of mental states rely on linguistic idioms and that we may need to revise these idioms. Moreover, he contended that our mentalistic idioms are not theory neutral but encode a theory about private mental events. Although this theory is deeply entrenched, it may be wrong. If it is, our continued use of mentalistic discourse perpetuates a myth.

Rorty, in his early writings, concurred with the basic thrust of Feyerabend's position. More so than Feyerabend, however, Rorty focused on the point of connection between old frameworks and new frameworks and defended identifying objects specified in the old framework with those specified in the new framework. He thus advocated what he called the "disappearance form" of the Identity Theory, which maintains that as science advances we introduce new vocabulary to talk about that for which we previously used another vocabulary. When we do so we recognize that the old vocabulary is inadequate so that:

> the relation in question is not strict identity, but rather the sort of relation which obtains between, to put it crudely, existent entities and non-existent entities when reference to the latter once served (some of) the purposes presently served by reference to the former—the sort of relations that holds, e.g., between "quantity of caloric fluid" and "mean kinetic energy of molecules". There is an obvious sense of "same" in which what used to be called "a quantity of caloric fluid" is *the same thing* as what is now called a certain mean kinetic energy of molecules, but there is no reason to think that all features truly predicated of the one may be sensibly predicated of the other. (Rorty,1965/1971, p. 176)

Rorty also tried to diagnosis why people commonly resist attempts to get rid of mentalistic vocabulary. He attributed it to the impracticality of surrendering the old idiom in favor of a new scientific vocabulary.[2] A number of critics, however, were unsatisfied with this reply. Cornman (1968) and Bernstein (1968/1971) contended that because sensation talk is used in observational reports, the language that replaces it will inevitably take over its very function, and so nothing will actually be eliminated. The new discourse will still pick out the same mentalistic phenomena; it will simply employ new words. Rorty rejected this claim. He maintained that the content of what we report is actually a function of our language and so will change if we change to a new language: "if we got in the habit of using neurological terms in place of 'intense,' 'sharp,' and 'throbbing,' then our experience would be of things having those neurological properties, and not of anything, e.g., intense" (Rorty, 1970/1971, p. 228).

More recently, Rorty (1979) has attempted to differentiate his position from Feyerabend's by focusing on how we know about mental states, not what they are. He takes as his primary target the claim that mental phenomena are phenomena to which we have privileged access. He maintained that it is this idea of privileged access to our minds that makes people think that there is an essential nature to human beings. Rorty denied that we have such

---

[2]The inconvenience of ceasing to talk about sensations would be so great that only a fanatical materialist would think it worth the trouble to cease referring to sensations. If the Identity Theorist is taken to be predicting that some day "sensation," "pain," "mental image," and the like will drop out of our vocabulary, he is almost certainly wrong. But if he is saying simply that, at no greater cost than an inconvenient linguistic reform, we *could* drop such terms, he is entirely justified. And I take this latter claim to be all that traditional materialism has ever desired. (Rorty, 1965/1971, p. 185)

privileged access into what it is to be human. The language we use to describe our mental states incorporates our theories about what it is to be human, and these theories represent culturally based decisions. Different cultures may make different decisions as to what a person is, and will encode these in their language. Neither philosophy nor science can answer the question of what it is to be a person and thus settle what language we ought to use. It is one task of philosophy, according to Rorty, to expose the fact that our mentalistic idioms encode the decisions made in our culture and do not directly describe the reality of mental life.

Eliminative Materialism has never been a highly popular position, but it still retains prominent proponents. Stephen Stich (1983) construed his syntactic theory of the mind (see chapter 4) as an eliminativist position insofar as it proposes to develop scientific psychology without any reliance on intentionalist folk psychology. Patricia and Paul Churchland, in advancing their claims for cognitive neuroscience as our best hope for developing a viable science of the mind, often make claims reminiscent of Feyerabend and Rorty. They have maintained that by continuing to characterize mental events in terms of propositional attitudes we may hinder our efforts to really understand mental states. Through inquiry into how the brain works, they claimed, we may learn better ways to describe our mental states. Paul Churchland in particular has argued that through understanding the neuroprocesses occurring in the brain we may enrich our mental life by, for example, distinguishing musical sounds that we conflate at present. (See P. M. Churchland, 1981a, 1985, 1986; P. S. Churchland, 1980b, 1983, 1986; Churchland & Churchland, 1981. I discuss the Churchlands' views more fully in Bechtel, in press b.)[3]

Insofar as it recommends replacing mentalistic accounts with neuroscience ones, Eliminative Materialism has negative implications for much work in cognitive science. Much theorizing in cognitive science employs a clearly mentalistic perspective (Palmer & Kimchi , 1986), which Eliminative Materialism maintains is probably mistaken. If Eliminative Materialism is correct, we should abandon cognitive inquiries and redirect resources to neuroscience, which has the best hope of explaining how the mind/brain operates.

The basic reason why Eliminativism has not achieved wider acceptance is that mentalistic arguments play such a central role in our ordinary thinking about ourselves as well as in the theories of the social sciences that it seems impossible to do without them. Kim (1985), for example, pointed to some of the critical ways in which we employ this mentalistic perspective:

The intentional psychological scheme—that is, the framework of belief, desire,

---

[3] A position closely related to Eliminative Materialism—sociobiology—advocates eliminating the mentalistic approach in favor of one drawn from evolutionary biology (see Rosenberg, 1980).

and will—is one within which we deliberate about ends and means, and assess the rationality of actions and decisions. It is the framework that makes our normative and evaluative activities possible. No purely descriptive framework such as those of neurophysiology or physics, no matter how theoretically comprehensive and predictively powerful, can replace it. As long as we can think of ourselves as reflective agents capable of deliberation and evaluation—that is, as long as we regard ourselves as agents capable of acting in accordance with a norm—we shall not be able to dispense with the intentional framework of beliefs, wants, and volitions. (p. 386)

Defenders of Eliminative Materialism maintain that such claims on behalf of our mentalistic idioms are simply guesses about what direction science and society will follow. What Kim makes clear, however, is that in offering a replacement for our mentalistic framework, the Eliminativist must show not only how we can do psychology without mentalism but also how the social sciences can function without it and how humans can conduct their lives and determine courses of action without it. Although a scenario in which we give up our basic mentalistic conception of human beings and adopt the conceptual framework of neuroscience is certainly possible, it strikes most as profoundly implausible. (For further discussion, see McCauley, 1986.)

There is, moreover, something problematic about the way the Eliminativist construes the issue. The Eliminativist makes it an either/or matter—either we maintain our mentalistic perspective or adopt the neuroscience one, but not both. This, however, may be to conflate issues. It may be that neuroscience explanations, and even the language of neuroscience, focus at a different level then common sense psychological discourse. Consider again Dennett's distinction (discussed in chapter 4) between intentional psychology and design-level and physical-level psychology. Following Dennett, I argued that intentional psychology played a different role than design-stance psychology. Although the latter sought to develop internal processing models of cognition, intentional psychology figured in explaining how an individual dealt with his or her environment, including other cognitive agents. Much the same point may be applicable to the controversy over Eliminativism. It may be that we can both preserve mentalism and develop a neuroscience perspective even if the two fail to mesh perfectly. The two perspectives will serve different purposes. The final position considered in this chapter, Token Identity Theory, attempts to show how the two perspectives can both be accepted even though they differ.

TOKEN IDENTITY THEORIES

Like Eliminative Materialists, Token Identity Theorists are skeptical of the Type Identity Theory's claim that research will support a correlation between types of phenomena described mentally and types characterized physically, but they draw a different inference than do Eliminativists. Rather than repudiating mental discourse, Token Identity Theorists sanction its continued use by advocating a weaker version of the Identity Theory. They maintain that every token of a mental event is a token of a neural event, but do not require that types of mental events be equated with types of neural events. Thus, the Token Identity Theory holds that (a) every time I am in a particular mental state, that mental state is identical to a brain state, but (b) on other occasions when I am in the same mental state I may be in a different brain state.

Donald Davidson's position, Anomalous Monism, has been one of the more controversial versions of the Token Identity Theory. The position holds that the same event may be both mental and physical (hence, monism), but that there are no laws relating the mental description with the physical one (hence, anomalous). Davidson (1970/1980, see also 1973, 1975) put forward Anomalous Monism as a way to reconcile the following three theses, all of which he took to be compelling, but which seem inconsistent:

1. *The Principle of Causal Interaction*, which asserts that "at least some mental events interact causally with physical events."

2. *The Principle of the Nomological Character of Causality*, which states that "where there is causality, there must be a law: events related as cause and effect fall under strict deterministic law."

3. *The Anomalism of the Mental*, which claims that "there are no strict deterministic laws on the basis of which mental events can be predicted and explained." (Davidson, 1970/1980, pp. 80-81)

Davidson's monism held that mental activities are each identical with some physical activity (generally neurological activities). This is the critical identity claim that allows Davidson to satisfy the first two theses. Because all mental events are physical events, they can interact causally with other physical events and these interactions can be characterized through deterministic physical laws. The claim that there are no laws relating mental descriptions of events with their physical descriptions has the consequence that we cannot infer mental descriptions of events from their physical descriptions.

Davidson's resolution of the supposed incompatibility between the three theses has inspired a number of criticisms. Some critics have objected that Davidson cannot defend his monism claim because we cannot establish the identity of mental and physical without being able to correlate types. Davidson, however, is not concerned to argue for the identity; he simply posited it as necessary if we are to accommodate theses 1 and 2. His concern, rather, is to argue for the lack of laws relating mental and physical descriptions.

In arguing for anomalism Davidson does not deny argue that we might develop generalizations linking events described mentally with events described physically. He simply contended (Davidson, 1970/1980) that these generalizations will not have the character of law:

> The thesis is that the mental is nomologically irreducible: there may be true general statements relating the mental and the physical, statements that have the logical form of a law; but they are not *lawlike* (in a strong sense to be described). If by absurdly remote chance we were to stumble on a non-stochastic true psychophysical generalization, we would have no reason to believe it more than roughly true. (p. 90)

The reason that the statement would not be lawlike is that the predicates would be drawn from two different vocabularies that cannot be merged in a law. Davidson contended that "nomological statements bring together predicates that we know are made for each other" (p. 93). This only occurs when they are drawn "from a theory with strong constitutive elements" (p. 94). This claim does not itself establish the anomalism of the mental for we might think that there are strong constitutive elements linking mental and physical predicates or that these could be developed. The essential claim in Davidson's argument is that such connections are impossible. He maintained that such divergent principles govern our use of mental and physical vocabulary that we could not integrate them into one theory. Our system of mental attributions is governed by the principle of rationality, that is, we ascribe beliefs and desires in such a way as to make other people appear rational. To do this, we must be free continually to reassess our attributions of mental predicates and so we cannot tie them strongly to physical properties.[4]

Davidson's argument against the possibility of developing constitutive principles linking psychological and physical vocabularies seems to place demands on such principles that we would not accept in other areas. In contexts where scientists have tried to unite the vocabularies of two different domains (e.g., the term *gene* from genetics and the term *chromosome* from cytology), they have recognized that their proposals were fallible and might have to be revised as new evidence became available. There may be cases where we want the theories of one discipline only to answer to the demands of that discipline without being constrained by the demands of other disciplines (see Abrahamsen, 1987; McCauley, 1987b). But there are other occasions when the constraint imposed by remaining consistent with the theoretical commitments of related disciplines may be an advantage. Such constraints may help show which of two competing theories within one

---

[4]According to Davidson (1970/1980): The point is . . . that when we use the concepts of belief, desire, and the rest, we must stand prepared, as the evidence accumulates, to adjust our theory in the light of considerations of overall cogency: the constitutive ideal of rationality partly controls each phase in the evolution of what must be an evolving theory. An arbitrary choice of translation scheme would preclude such opportunistic tampering of theory. (p. 98)

discipline is more likely to be true. Moreover, such constraints may force us to modify theoretical commitments in one of the disciplines. This, in fact, is one of the beneficial products of crossing disciplinary boundaries and consulting work in another discipline (see Bechtel, in press b, chapter 6; also McCauley, 1986). Davidson's proscription removed psychological theorizing from any such benefit.

The reason for Davidson's strong opposition to principles bridging psychology and neuroscience lies in his commitment to the principle of rationality as the sole foundation of our attempts to interpret agents in psychological terms (see Davidson, 1973). Behind Davidson's position lies a particular conception of what psychological discourse involves, a conception that discounts the status of psychology as a science. The principles of psychology are not to be the basis for predicting or explaining behavior (which would require laws), but for developing rational accounts of behavior by interpreting agents in terms of coherent sets of beliefs and desires. (See Lycan, 1981b, for critical discussion.)

Davidson's contention that rationality provides the sole criterion for judging psychological accounts seems not only unnecessary but wrong. We can employ rationality as one criterion in developing psychological explanations without requiring that it be the absolute criterion. We do recognize that both we and other people are sometimes irrational, but this does not undercut our ability to develop accounts that interpret our behavior as generally rational. An important strategy in science is to try to identify entities in multiple ways so that judgments based on one way of identifying the entities can be tested using other ways. The principles that emerge are more robust and hence more credible when this is possible (Campbell, 1966; Cook & Campbell, 1979; Wimsatt, 1981). Davidson's reliance on rationality alone as a basis for fixing mental interpretations forecloses that option. If we reject relying on rationality alone, however we also undercut Davidson's case for anomalous monism.

Davidson's version of the Token Identity Theory leaves a place for cognitive theories, but at the expense of rendering cognitive accounts nonscientific. However, other philosophers who have offered different arguments for favoring Token Identity Theory over Type Identity Theory present a version of Token Identity Theory that is far more friendly to cognitive science. Fodor (1974) and Putnam (1975b) have offered reasons to think that the relationship between mental types and physical types is such that the same mental event may, under different circumstances, be realized in quite different physical events. Fodor appealed to the fact that we classify things differently for different purposes. For example, we may classify objects by color or by shape, and there is no reason to think the two classifications will correspond. Similarly, the classifications useful in psychology may be quite different than those useful for neuroscience. For example, it may be useful in social psychology to classify activities of promise making, which is an activity that can be performed through many different physical activities that are not likely to form one physical type.[5]

Putnam offered a related argument for the claim that a given mental type of mental event may be realized by different physical events. He appealed to the fact that although there are modest differences in the constitution of our own brains over time and between the brains of different people, we ascribe the same psychological states to them. Furthermore, comparative psychologists are quite prepared to ascribe the same psychological states to members of different species, whose brains are even more different from one another, and we can imagine ascribing the same states to aliens with totally different brains. Putnam (1978, 1983) also contemplated the possibility that the same neurological states may underlie different psychological properties. He contended that psychological interpretation depends on considerations external to the system so that the very same system in different environments will be interpreted differently. Although Putnam's approach, which makes psychological ascriptions depend on environmental circumstances, is certainly controversial, it brings to the fore one of the central factors that has motivated the development of the Token Identity Theory—the fact that although psychology and neuroscience may both be characterizing the same states, they may have different criteria for grouping them into classes.

Token Identity Theory, as developed by Fodor and Putnam, provides an account of the relation of mind and brain that is more congenial to the endeavors of current cognitive science than other versions of materialism because it allows an autonomous domain for cognitive theorizing. This autonomy, however, can also be dangerous if it entails, as some Token Identity theorists maintain it does, that cognitive theories are incommensurable with neuroscience theories so that cognitive science cannot learn from neuroscience or give guidance to neuroscience. A strategy for relating cognitive science and neuroscience that yet allows some autonomy for cognitive science is discussed in Bechtel (in press b, chapter 6).

SUMMARY OF VIEWS
ON THE MIND–BODY PROBLEM

In this chapter and in chapter 5, I have surveyed the major philosophical positions on the relation of mind and body and have explored their significance

---

[5] In discussing dualism in the previous chapter, I noted that property dualism would turn out to be in many respects quite similar to the Token Identity Theory. We can now appreciate the similarity. Property dualism maintains that mental properties constitute a distinct class of properties that will be true of the same events as physical properties. According to the Token Identity Theory, events may be classified as mental events or as physical events depending on what properties are attributed to them. This enables us to view the Token Identity Theory as positing distinct sets of mental and physical properties, which might both be instantiated in the same individual. Hence, Token Identity Theory is quite similar to property dualism.

for cognitive science. Object dualism treats minds as radically different kinds of objects than physical bodies like the brain, and so puts study of mental activity outside the limits of physical science. The other positions, in contrast, all bring mental phenomena within the domain of physical science, but differ in how they do so. Philosophical behaviorism argues that mental discourse should be construed as referring to behavior or dispositions to behave, and not to internal events in the brain. In denying internal processing, it rejects the kinds of explanation advanced in contemporary cognitive science.

The versions of materialism considered in this chapter all recognize some form of internal processing and in that respect are more consistent with research in cognitive science. The Type Identity Theory, however, equates mental events with physical events occurring within the brain. Although the identification of mental states with physical states assures the reality of mental states that cognitive science might study, Type Identity Theory would also entail that the internal processes employed in cognitive accounts would be isomorphic to the ones used in neuroscience. This gives primacy to neuroscience over cognitive science. Eliminative Materialism similarly focuses on the neurological processes occurring in the brain, but maintains that because these neural accounts are inconsistent with cognitive accounts, we should forego cognitive accounts in favor of neural ones. Thus, Eliminative Materialism would advocate abandoning cognitive science for neuroscience.

Token Identity Theory claims that there can be alternative, incompatible accounts of the internal activities of cognitive systems—one neural and one cognitive. Thus, of all the philosophical positions on the mind–body problem, Token Identity Theory is most compatible with the programs of cognitive science. The Token Identity Theory does raise the question of how mental events are to be categorized if this categorization is to be different from the categorization applied to brain events. Advocates of the Token Identity Theory have proposed that mental events be advocated functionally. The philosophical program known as *Functionalism* has attempted to explain what this involves. Hence, the next chapter is devoted to examining Functionalism more closely.

7

Functionalism

INTRODUCTION

Functionalism represents a philosophical attempt to explicate a critical part of the research program of cognitive science—the way in which mental events are recognized and classified. Functionalism maintains that mental events are classified in terms of their causal roles. Thus, a mental event would be described in terms of its role in the mental system just as a cam shaft is characterized in terms of its causal role of controlling the opening and closing of valves in a car engine. An important aspect of this approach is the claim that mental events can be recognized and classified independently of their physical constitution. For this reason, Functionalism is often viewed as incompatible with the Type Identity Theory.[1] The position on the

---

[1] Australian functionalists, such as Smart and Armstrong, as well as some Americans such as Lewis and Lycan, however, do not differentiate their position from the Type Identity Theory. Smart's topic neutral characterization of mental states is, in fact, a paradigmatically functional characterization. These philosophers, moreover, maintain that the one-to-one correspondence of mental states and physical states was not a critical part of their position. What was critical was that the work performed by the mental state be understood as performed by some physical states. Thus Lewis (1966/1971 and 1972/1980) construed functional identification of mental states as providing the basis for subsequent determination of what physical states instantiated them. When we find a physical state that instantiates the role characterized functionally, then we have established that it is the same as the functionally identified state. Lewis (1969/1980) further contended that to accuse the Identity Theorist of holding a one-to-one type identification of mental states and physical states is to construct a strawperson. He maintained that the Identity Theorist always acknowledged context relativity in terms of what instantiated the mental state. The examples used by early identity theorists may have suggested a commitment to a one-to-one relationship, but that simply reflects a first attempt to formulate the materialist view. It was to be expected that the account would become more complex as the Identity Theory matured. The Churchlands have also criticized Functionalists such as Fodor who regard Functionalism as opposed to reductionistic forms of materialism. See P. M. Churchland (1981b).

mind–body problem with which Functionalism is most often coupled is the Token Identity Theory, which likewise dissociates mental event descriptions from those applying to physical events.

Using the term *Functionalism* for this mode of classifying mental events is prone to cause confusion for social and behavioral scientists. In psychology, for example, the term was applied to the research program developed at the turn of the century, most notably at the University of Chicago in the work of Dewey and Angell. Key to this approach was an evolutionary perspective that directed psychologists to attend to the use to which an organism put its cognitive capacities. This evolutionary orientation has been manifest in many 20th century approaches to psychology, including behaviorism. The evolutionary perspective of psychological functionalism has not played a major role in the philosophical program that goes under the same name. However, in the last part of this chapter I sketch a version of philosophical Functionalism that does introduce an evolutionary perspective.

There are actually a variety of different versions of philosophical Functionalism current today. I survey four of these in the first section. Although Functionalism of one form or another has attracted a broad spectrum of adherents, it has also aroused a number of criticisms. Thus, in the second section I present some of the major objections to Functionalism and the answers Functionalists have offered in response. In the last section, I develop the alternative version previously mentioned.

VARIETIES OF PHILOSOPHICAL FUNCTIONALISM

The fact that there are a variety of forms of Functionalism is not always recognized, and people tend to conflate the various versions. This situation can be particularly confusing since proponents of one version often criticize other versions (and sometimes present their criticisms as criticism of Functionalism generally). Although all versions of Functionalism agree that mental states are to be identified primarily in terms of their interactions with one another, they differ mainly over how these interactions are to be specified. I begin with a view that identifies these interactions in terms of our ordinary mental discourse and then turn to views that draw their inspiration from contemporary research endeavors in cognitive science.

Folk Psychological Functionalism

Folk Psychological Functionalism interprets the conceptual framework assumed in propositional attitude discourse (see chapter 3) as incorporating a theory about the causal factors governing human behavior. (This theory is called a *folk theory* because it is supposed to reflect common knowledge, not scientific knowledge.) David Lewis (1972/1980), suggested that mental terms like *desire* and *believe* are defined in terms of this theory. To show that there is really a theory underlying propositional attitudes, it is necessary to codify it. Lewis proposed that this can be done by articulating a number of platitudes of the folk psychology captured in propositional attitude discourse:

> Think of commonsense psychology as a term-introducing scientific theory, though one invented long before there was any such institution as professional science. Collect all the platitudes you can think of regarding the causal relations of mental states, sensory stimuli, and motor responses. Perhaps we can think of them as having the form:
>
> > When someone is in so-and-so combination of mental states and receives sensory stimulation of so-and-so kind, he tends with so-and-so probability to be caused thereby to go into so-and-so mental states and produce so-and-so motor processes. (p. 212)

Lewis viewed this theory as determining the meanings of our mental terms in much the same manner as theories in other disciplines determine the meanings of their component terms. For example, in Newtonian mechanics, the meanings of terms like *mass* and *force* are specified in term of laws like "force = mass x acceleration."[2]

One problem with Lewis' approach is that if this theory turns out to be wrong, our whole discourse about mental events will turn out to be vacuous and nonreferring. (See Wilkes, 1981, who developed this and other criticisms.) Armstrong (1968, 1984) developed a variation on this approach that avoids appeal to any implicit theory. He appealed instead to an analysis of our ordinary mentalistic vocabulary to define mental terms. He claimed that the meanings of various mental terms affirm certain causal relations in the same way as the meanings of terms like "elastic" and "brittle" specify causal physical contingencies. Part of what we mean when we ascribe to a person the general belief that "all F are G," for example, is the expectation that if the person learns that *a* is F, that would causally generate the belief that *a* is G. These causal relationships define what it is to have a mental state for Armstrong.

One of the major goals of this form of Functionalism is to show how we understand the meaning of ordinary mental terms without appealing to philosophical behaviorism and without knowing the nature of the underlying brain states. These terms specify a nexus of causal agents which we in-

---

[2]To bring out the abstract character of this kind of theory, Lewis proposed using the Ramsified version of the theory that results from replacing the theoretical terms of the theory with variables bound by existential quantifiers. The point of this is to de-mystify the theoretical terms and show that their role in the theory is fully characterizable in terms of the interactions described by the theory and not any intrinsic properties.

voke to explain the behavior of cognitive agents.[3] Folk Psychological Functionalism does seem to perform this task successfully. The deeper question, however, is whether these analyses will be of any use in developing scientific accounts of how cognitive systems operate. Some philosophers, such as Fodor, view folk psychology as a starting point for developing such scientific theories. But to develop these analyses as scientific endeavors it is necessary to go beyond analyses of ordinary psychological vocabulary. We need to develop new theoretical perspectives that can be tested empirically. In developing such scientific theories, functional analyses may play a different role, suggesting how such theories are to be structured. The following three versions of Functionalism were developed in that spirit.

Machine Table Functionalism

Machine Table Functionalism is one of the earliest versions of Functionalism, developed primarily by Putnam (1960). A Turing Machine (see Turing, 1937) is a simple device that consists of:

1. a potentially infinitely-long tape containing a linear sequence of squares, on each of which one of a finite set of symbols can be written,
2. an execution unit, which can be in one of a finite number of internal states, and
3. an indicator that points to one of the squares on the tape.

The activities of the execution unit are directed by a finite set of conditional rules that specify an action to be performed, given the particular symbol that appears in the indicated square and the internal state of the execution unit. The action consists of writing the same or different symbol in the square, moving to an adjoining square, and maintaining or changing the internal state of the execution unit (see Fig. 7.1). If the machine has no instruction for its current state and number on the tape, it stops. The total operating capacity

---

[3] Lewis compared the way in which this theory is presented to a story a detective might tell about the death of a certain Mr. Body:

> X, Y and Z conspired to murder Mr. Body. Seventeen years ago, in the gold fields of Uganda, X was Body's partner. . . . Last week, Y and Z conferred in a bar in Reading. . . . Tuesday night at 11:17, Y went to the attic and set a time bomb. . . . Seventeen minutes later, X met Z in the billiard room and gave him the lead pipe. . . . Just when the bomb went off in the attic, X fired three shots into the study through the French windows. (Lewis, 1972, p. 208)

Just as we can follow this story without knowing who X, Y, and Z are, Lewis contended that we can follow ordinary discourse about the causal relation of mental events without knowing what neural processes bring them about.

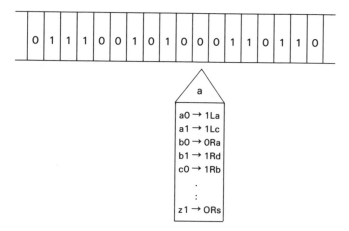

FIG. 7.1   A simple Turing Machine. On each square of the potentially infinitely long tape appears either a *0* or a *1*. The pointer of the execution unit is pointed at a square containing a *0*. The *a* in the triangular part of the execution unit indicates that the execution unit is in state *a*. The conditional rules which govern the activity of the execution unit are stated in the boxed part of the execution unit. The letter and number before the arrow specify the conditions under which the rule applies (e.g., when the executive is in state a and the pointer is pointing at a 0). The sequence after the arrow indicates what number the execution unit should write on the square to which it is currently pointing, whether it should move left or right, and what state it should then enter. The first rule, which applies to the situation pictured, tells the head to write a *1* on the square to which it is currently pointing, move left one square, and enter (remain in) state a.

of a particular Turing Machine can be summarized in a Machine Table that presents the conditional rules that govern the behavior of the system. A problem is given to a Turing Machine by specifying the initial symbols on the tape, and the symbols on the tape when the machine stops (if it does) represent its solution. Putnam was initially interested in Turing Machines because the relation of the program governing the operation of the Turing Machine seemed to stand in much the same relation to the physical device as the mind stands to the brain. He thought that by appealing to this analogy he could defuse much of the concern about the ontological status of the mind, because there seems to be no reason to be a Dualist with respect to a Turing Machine, and the cases seem quite comparable.

Turing Machines have taken on additional interest in discussions about the character of the mind as a result of the argument, due to Turing and Church, that as long as the processes carried out by the mind are effectively computable ones, there is a Turing Machine that will be behaviorally equivalent to the mind.[4] This suggests that we can specify the activities of the mind in a Turing Machine table and that we might identify mental states with states or disjunction of states of a machine specified by the machine table (thus the name "Machine Table Functionalism"). Putnam (1967/1980) applied the machine table analysis to pain. Rather than being a brain state, he proposed that pain is a state or set of states of a system that result from certain sorts of inputs, where the overall behavior of the system is specified by a machine table. Putnam also distinguished this proposal from philosophical behaviorism by claiming that his analysis did not require a translation of pain discourse into any dispositional discourse. Rather, pain is equated with a state in the system that, in accord with the machine table, causally produces other states within the system as well as outputs from the system.

Machine Table Functionalism has aroused a variety of objections even from those who generally count themselves as Functionalists. Block and Fodor (1972/1980) complained that there are a number of features of psychological phenomena that cannot be satisfactorily handled by Machine Table Functionalism. For example, it cannot capture the important distinction between actually occurring mental states (actually contemplating the proposition that if there are rain clouds and thunder, then rain might follow) and dispositional states (believing but not actively contemplating the proposition that if there are rain clouds and thunder, then rain might follow). This is because all states indicated in the machine table are of one kind. An additional objection is that a machine table account will individuate mental states too finely, since it will distinguish states in two automata if there is any difference in either the input conditions or the output conditions for a particular state, no matter how trivial. A further objection is that the states in the machine table must be finite, whereas the number of psychological states is potentially infinite.

Block and Fodor, however, also suggested how to overcome these problems with Machine Table Functionalism. Machine Table Functionalism treated a machine state as comparable to the whole psychological state of a person. The key to their proposal is to identify mental states with computational states inside the system, where the states are defined in terms of kinds of operations performed. The result is that we will not identify a mental state with a state of a particular machine but with an operation that could be performed in a variety of machines. Developing the analysis in this way also allows us to differentiate between procedures available in the machine (which might

---

[4] The critical claim here is Church's Thesis that any procedure that is effectively computable can be accomplished through a recursive procedure. This is only a thesis, not a proven theorem, since the notion of effective computation involved is intuitive and not formally defined. When this thesis is combined with Turing's account of a Universal Turing Machine, which could compute all such recursive functions, we obtain the claim that if the mind employs effective procedures, a Universal Turing Machine could carry out any task the mind can.

be compared with dispositional states) and those procedures actually being performed. Moreover, we can compare procedures in two machines even when other processes in the two machines differ. The two procedures count as the same if they could substitute for one another without changing other activities within the system. Fodor and Block thus advance Computational Functionalism as a replacement for Machine Table Functionalism.

Computational or AI Functionalism

This form of Functionalism is closely associated with the Computational Theory of Mind discussed in chapter 4. It views the mind as carrying out formal operations on symbols encoded within it. Haugeland (1981/1985) has characterized the resulting view of the mind as an interpreted automatic formal system. A formal system is simply one in which discrete symbols are manipulated according to a finite set of rules. These rules differentiate amongst symbols in virtue of formal features such that a specific rule will manipulate two formally equivalent symbols in the same way. An automatic system is one in which the rules governing the manipulation of symbols are incorporated into the system and do not have to be continually supplied by an external agency. Finally, an automatic formal system is interpreted when its symbols are supplied with a semantics, that is, they are taken to refer to things external to the system. Using the expression *syntax* to refer to the formal properties and *semantics* for the interpretation, Dennett (1981a) characterized this version of Functionalism as one in which the mind is viewed as a syntactic engine that emulates a semantic engine.

Computational or AI Functionalism is thus committed to characterizing mental activities in terms of symbols and rules for manipulating those symbols. In order to employ this framework to compare systems, especially to compare computers to humans, we must make the notions of symbols and rules precise so that we can determine when two systems are employing the same set of rules and symbols or representations and when they are using different sets. The reason this is necessary can be recognized by considering one proposed test for comparing humans and machines—the Turing Test (Turing, 1950/1964). This test would accept a computer as comparable to a human being in intelligence if human beings cannot distinguish the computer's performance from that of a human being. The notion of Turing Equivalence developed from this test equates two systems that produce the same output from the same input. Turing Equivalence, however, does not establish that two systems work in the same way because it considers only the output behaviors and not whether the same internal procedures (rules and symbols) are employed. A variety of computer systems can produce the same overall outputs using vastly different sequences of steps. This potential for developing different rule systems to compute the same function gives rise to a distinction that was once made between two approaches to artificial intelligence. One approach, which took the generic name *artificial intelligence*, saw its task to be simply to design machines that could perform cognitive functions, with little concern for whether they performed them in anything like the way humans do. The other, which adopted the name *cognitive simulation*, took as a major objective the development of machines that performed cognitive functions in the same way as humans do. This distinction is important for Computational Functionalism. If Computational Functionalism is to be an account of human cognition, then the goal must be a cognitive simulation where computer programs carry out the same operations as human beings.

"Carrying out the same operations" is characterized in computer parlance as following the same *algorithm*, where an algorithm simply specifies a sequence of steps, each step constituting a primitive procedure. In order to compare algorithms, however, we need a specification of the primitive procedures from which algorithms are constructed. For computer programmers these are provided by the language in which the program is written. Most computer programs are written in higher level computer languages, each instruction of which is translated, through procedures known as "compiling" and "interpreting," into a specific set of operations in a lower level language. Ultimately the instructions must be translated into machine code, whose primitive symbols direct specific physical operations within the computer. Although skilled programmers may move freely between higher level languages and the lower level languages into which the higher level is being interpreted or compiled, weaving several levels into the same algorithm, most programmers remain at the same level. For them, the programming language can be thought of as specifying the primitive operations available in the machine and so is spoken of as defining a "virtual machine."

Pylyshyn (1980, 1984) appealed to the concept of a virtual machine in developing a framework for comparing programs. The virtual machine provides the *functional architecture* of the machine. He proposed that in terms of what is specified in the functional architecture we can compare operations in different computers or those in a computer with those in a human being:

> two programs can be thought of as strongly equivalent or as different realizations of the same algorithm or the same cognitive process if they can be represented by the same program in some theoretically specified virtual machine. A simple way of stating this is to say that we individuate cognitive processes in terms of their expression in the canonical language of this virtual machine. The formal structure of the virtual machine—or what I call its *functional architecture*—thus represents the theoretical definition of, for example, the right level of specificity (or level of aggregation) at which to view mental processes, the sort of functional resources the brain makes available—what operations are primitive, how memory is organized and accessed, what sequences are allowed,

what limitations exist on the passing of arguments and on the capacities of various buffers, and so on. (Pylyshyn, 1984, p. 92)

In the case of a computer, the functional architecture is not absolute. We can change the primitive capacities of the machine by supplying an interpreter or a compiler to introduce a higher level language, or by going directly into a lower level language. But in the case of humans, Pylyshyn argued that there is a basic cognitive architecture made available by the biological constitution of the nervous system. For Pylyshyn, discovering the structure of this architecture constitutes a primary task for cognitive science. Only when we know what this architecture is will we be able to specify what the basic primitive operations are and so have a basis for comparing processes in the computer and human being.

Pylyshyn proposed two methods for discovering the functional architecture of the human mind. One involves developing simulations in which the resource demands (as measured, e.g., in processing times) for different tasks correlate with those found when human agents carry out the same tasks. Although the absolute times will differ between humans and machines, if the amounts of time required for different tasks exhibit the same ratio in the human and the computer, then it seems reasonable to assume that they are drawing upon comparable basic operations. This, however, does not directly reveal the level of the functional architecture because it is possible in both cases that the operations are interpreted or compiled into more basic ones. It only tells us that the comparison between systems is appropriate at some level. Pylyshyn's other approach is to identify the functional architecture with those operations whose performance cannot be altered by information. He speaks of these operations as "cognitively impenetrable." The idea is that if information can alter the performance, then the operation is not fixed solely by the biology.[5] The difficulty is to find operations so fixed, especially if the biological system is an adaptive one that may itself be modified in response to cognitive processing.

Although difficulties remain in establishing when a machine and a human process information in the same way, the strategy of Computational or Artificial Intelligence Functionalism is clear. Once we identify a comparable set of basic procedures that can be executed by both minds and a computer, we should try to design and implement algorithms on the computer that use the same sequence of basic operations as those followed by the human mind.

---

[5] Pylyshyn's criterion is quite similar to one Fodor (1983, 1985) used to identify modules in the mind. These modules are specialized devices for performing particular cognitive tasks. Fodor maintained that these modules will only be found for processing sensory input and producing output and that psychology will only be able to explain cognitive operations performed through these specialized modules, not those carried out by general reasoning strategies. Putnam (1984) argued for extending the notion of modules more broadly.

Computational Functionalism is thus committed to what Searle (1980/1981) spoke of as "strong AI." The computer is not simply a tool for running programs that characterize the behavior of the mind (as a computer could run a program in order to determine the trajectory of a comet without actually going through the same processes as the comet does). Computers and the mind perform equivalent procedures in producing their behaviors and these procedures are what this version of Functionalism equates with mental processes. (See Anderson, Greno, Kline, & Neves, 1981, for an attempt to satisfy the demands of strong AI. For a philosophical discussion and evaluation of attempts in artificial intelligence to model human mental activity, see Boden, 1977.)

A common objection to Computational or Artificial Intelligence Functionalism is that it seems to view the mind as comparable to contemporary von Neumann computers wherein an executive serially accesses information stored in memory and directs operations to be performed on it in order to carry out the task at hand. But it is now clear that the human nervous system is performing a great number of operations at the same time and that there may be nothing comparable to the executive function as currently incorporated into von Neumann computers. However, this objection fundamentally misconstrues what Computational Functionalism is committed to. It is not committed to the claim that the operations in the mind are comparable to those in a von Neumann computer. One reason Pylyshyn is concerned about the functional architecture of the mind is that he expects it will likely be different than that found in contemporary computers. He holds that we must discover the appropriate architecture and develop computers using that architecture (either as their basic architecture or as one compiled or interpreted onto another architecture) before serious modeling of human cognition can be accomplished. What the computational view is committed to is the claim that cognition is a symbol processing activity. This commitment, however, is also being challenged by those developing nonsymbolic models in artificial intelligence such as parallel distributed processing machines (see discussion in chapter 4). If these challenges based on non-symbolic modes prove correct, then Computational Functionalism will be jeopardized.

Homuncular Functionalism

Homuncular Functionalism takes its name from the often-ridiculed view that cognitive functions are performed by a little person (homunculus) inside one's head. The problem with that approach was that it did not actually explain anything about cognition. We must still explain how the little person performs his or her cognitive activities and we risk an infinite regress in which the little person needs its own homunculus, and so on. Homuncular Functionalism endorses the positing of homunculi inside a person, but avoids the regress objection by positing vast numbers of these, each of which is dumber than the overall system but performs a task needed by the whole system. Dennett characterizes Homuncular Functionalists as taking out and then paying back intelligence loans. The loan is taken out when we characterize the system and its homunculi as intelligent. We pay this loan back by taking out new loans, positing an internal team of homunculi within each homunculus. This constitutes progress, since each level of homunculi requires homunculi of less intelligence. We repeat the process until we reach homunculi that require so little intelligence that we can replace them with machines and the whole loan is paid back.[6]

Underlying Homuncular Functionalism is a conception of scientific explanation that Cummins (1975, 1983) called "functional explanation."[7] The goal of functional explanation is to answer the question "In virtue of what, does S have P?" Cummins suggested that the proper way to answer such a question is to "construct an analysis of S that explains S's possession of P by appeal to the properties of S's components and their mode of organization" (Cummins, 1983, p. 15). The components can be identified in two ways, either physically or in terms of their capacities to interact with other components. The latter constitutes a functional analysis that can be represented by a flow chart that shows how the overall activity of the system results from the performance of operations within the system.

So far my characterization of Homuncular Functionalism has tried to distinguish it from Computational Functionalism, but the idea of a flow chart suggests a way of relating the two views. The activities assigned to boxes in a flow chart are tasks for which programmers would try to write subroutines. Dennett (1975/1978) himself developed this comparison:

> The AI researcher *starts* with an intentionally characterized problem (e.g., how can I get a computer to *understand* questions of English?), breaks it down into sub-problems that are also intentionally characterized (e.g., how do I get the

---

[6] Lycan(1981a) vividly characterizes this process by using an analogy:

> Imagine that you are a cost-benefit analyst from Harvard Business School, hired by some corporation to lift its sagging profits. On an inspection tour you are introduced to each of the various vice-presidents who head the corporation's major divisions. You ask one of the vice-presidents how his particular division is organized; he introduces you to each of his department heads. One of the departments interests you, and you ask how *it* corporately performs its job. This process continues until at one final point you are shown a large room full of clerks, each of whom does nothing but sort numbered index cards into pigeon-holes. 'Here's the problem!' you cry. 'These people should be replaced by machines!' (pp. 28-29 n.)

[7] This account of explanation differs from the standard philosophical model, the deductive-nomological model. The deductive-nomological model views explanation as a matter of subsuming a description of an event under a general principle or law from which the event description could be derived. For more on this model, see Bechtel (in press b).

computer to *recognize* questions, *distinguish* subjects from predicates, *ignore* irrelevant parsings?) and then breaks these problems down still further until finally
he reaches problem or task descriptions that are obviously mechanistic. (p. 80)

Although there is this affinity between Homuncular Functionalism and Computational Functionalism, the focus is different. The goal of most AI researchers[8] is synthetic—to design a program to perform the overall task. The
hierarchical structure of a program is ultimately not critical, with the operations in the subroutines being of a piece with the operations in the main program. For the Homuncular Functionalist, however, the hierarchical structure becomes more important. The Homuncular Functionalist treats the boxes
in the flow charts as characterizing actual modular units which carry out their
own activities. Just as beliefs and desires are attributed to the overall system,
Homucular Functionalists like Dennett also attribute beliefs and desires to
the homunculi that make up the system. A homonculus' beliefs and desires
will be different from those ascribed to the whole system—they will be beliefs
and desires about the tasks to be performed by the homunculus (see also
Lycan, 1981a, 1981c).

In addition to proposing a hierarchical view of cognition, Homuncular
Functionalism does not insist on a single distinction between function and
structure. It compares a system to a set of Chinese nesting dolls. As we un-
pack each one we proceed to a more microlevel. The process continues in
the same manner until we are down at the neurophysiological level. Lycan
(1981a) accordingly proposes that the identity theory becomes a special case
of Homuncular Functionalism:

> if we also accept my claim that homunctional characterizations and physiological
> characterizations of states of persons reflect merely different levels of abstrac-
> tion within a surrounding functional hierarchy or continuum, then we can no
> longer distinguish the functionalist from the identity theorist in any absolute
> way. 'Neuron' , for example, may be understood *either* as a physiological term
> (denoting a kind of human cell) or as a (teleo-) functional term (denoting a relayer
> of electrical charge); on *either* construal it stands for an instantiable—if you like,
> for a role being played by a group of more fundamental objects. Thus, *even
> the identity theorist is a functionalist*—one who locates mental entities at a very
> low level of abstraction. (p. 47)

OBJECTIONS TO FUNCTIONALISM

In the previous section I described a number of versions of Functionalism.
Despite the differences between them, they share a common assumption that

---

[8] There are exceptions, including Selfidge's (1955) work on pandemonium models and Minsky's (1986) appeals to a society of minds and demons.

what defines mental states are their capacities to interact with one another. Although this perspective has been adopted by many philosophers, it has also been the object of a number of criticisms. In this section, I discuss several objections that have been raised against Functionalism and some of the replies that have been made on its behalf.

Objections to Causal and Mechanical Analyses

One type of objection to Functionalism challenges the attempt to characterize mental states causally. Philosophical behaviorists like Malcolm are one source of this objection. Philosophical behaviorists maintain not only that behavior and behavioral dispositions provide the criterion for attributing mental states to people but also that there is a logical connection between mental states and behavior. If a relationship is logical it cannot be causal, because causal relations are contingent and discovered empirically whereas logical relations are not. With any causal relationship it should at least be conceivable that the purported cause does not produce the effect. But this is not possible when the events are related logically. Thus, Malcolm (1984) claimed, for example, that a state of panic is logically related to what induced the panic. Hence, we cannot conceive of the panic occurring without that inducing circumstance and so the relationship between the inducing circumstance and the panic cannot be causal.

The Functionalist, however, rejects the claim that the relation between mental states and behavior is a matter of logic. We might use behavior to identify someone's mental state, but that identification is fallible. The one mental state will be connected with a variety of different mental states in this causal network. This opens up the possibility that we will be able to identify the mental state in a variety of different ways. Any one of these ways can be regarded as fallible, revisable if other ways of identifying mental states lead us to a different conclusion. When several different indicators point in the same direction, then our evidence for the mental state is robust and more reliable than when we must rely on only one indicator (for a discussion of the importance of robust results in the development of science, see Wimsatt, 1981). To reconsider Malcolm's example, if a variety of behavioral and physiological criteria all indicate that a person is in a state of panic, then, even without knowledge of the panic inducing state, we may conclude that the person is in panic. Conversely, even if we know that a person has experienced a circumstance that usually induces panic, if other criteria do not confirm the existence of panic, we will decide that the circumstance in question did not cause panic.

The use of the computer to try to simulate mental processes has provoked a flurry of other antimechanistic objections. These maintain that viewing cognitive processes as mechanical processes like those in a computer is dehumanizing. Boden (1981), however, argued that computer simulations are far less dehumanizing than earlier mechanical models since they postulate internal processes. These internal processes are analogues to subjective states posited in more humanistic analyses of human behavior. Insofar as possessing subjective internal states is a major aspect of our sense of ourselves as humans, the computer model and the functionalist analysis that accompanies it are humanizing rather than dehumanizing.

A common challenge to computer simulations of mind is that computers can only behave as they are programmed. But human thinking, it is asserted, is not so constrained because it is capable of creativity. There are two ways to respond to this objection. One is to question whether humans themselves might not be programmed in the relevant sense. Even the most devoted Empiricist admits that humans come equipped to process information in certain ways. These native processing procedures might constitute a program. In addition, humans are generally taught how to do a variety of activities. This process of teaching might be viewed as comparable to programming. The second is to challenge the idea that a program is as constraining as the objection assumes. Some programs are closed in that they specify all the responses the computer will make. But other programs are open in that they modify themselves depending upon the results of executing the program. Such programs can be structured so as to generate and then test new variations of themselves (variations that were not explicitly envisioned by the programmer). It seems as least plausible that computers programmed to generate new strategies and evaluate these exhibit creativity in much the same way as humans. The burden, at least, would seem to be on the person who maintained that humans are distinctive to show what this difference consists in.[9]

Objections to Formal Accounts of Mental Processes

Searle and Dreyfus have been two of the more prominent critics of Functionalism, both arguing against the idea that cognition consists of formal pro-

---

[9] Another attempt to demonstrate a difference between humans and computers is based on Gödel's theorem that holds that in any consistent axiomatization of arithmetic there will be undecidable theorems which nonetheless are true. Lucas (1961/1964), for example, argues:

> Gödel's theorem must apply to cybernetical machines, because it is of the essence of being a machine, that it should be a concrete instantiation of a formal system. It follows that given any machine which is consistent and capable of doing simple arithmetic, there is a formula which it is incapable of producing as true—i.e., the formula is unprovable-in-the-system—but which we can see to be true. It follows that no machine can be a complete or adequate model of the mind, that minds are essentially different from machines. (pp. 112-113)

Putnam (1960/1964) countered that this objection rests on a misapplication of Gödel's theorem. The computer system, although it could not directly prove the undecidable sentence, could prove the conditional sentence "if the theory is consistent, the sentence in question is true." And, Putnam maintains, this is exactly the situation which we humans are in and so the computer can do as much as humans can. (For further discussion, see Kirk, 1986.)

cessing of symbols alone. I have already indicated the nature of their objections in the context of evaluating the Computational Theory of Mind as an account of intentionality. Because Dreyfus (1979) explicitly discussed particular attempts in AI to explain cognition in terms of formal models, it is worth considering his position in more detail here. Dreyfus contended that it is likely to be impossible to account for human cognition in terms of formal representations and rules for processing them. He argued for this claim by examining two research programs in artificial intelligence: designing programs to deal with specially designed, limited worlds (micro-worlds) and designing programs using higher level knowledge structures.

Dreyfus examined Winograd's (1972) SHRDLU program as an example of the micro-world project. This program was designed to carry on discourse about a hypothetical world of blocks. Although this program was able to keep track of movements of blocks and to answer various questions about the blocks correctly, Dreyfus objected that this program is only useful in the micro-world and cannot be generalized so as to deal with a broader domain. As Haugeland (1985) noted, there are a host of questions about blocks that SHRDLU cannot answer because it lacks the concepts involved. The program is equipped with a procedure to learn to apply new concepts to the block world, but needs to be taught each of these concepts individually. Generalizing this program to deal with the real world would require introducing definitions for applying each concept in each of a nearly infinite number of domains. Dreyfus took this as evidence that the program is misdirected. Our ability to operate in the world does not rely on combining modularized bits of information each applicable to a specific micro-world. Dreyfus claimed that an actual world consists of "an organized body of objects, purposes, skills, and practices in terms of which human activities have meaning or make sense." "Although there is," he claims, "a children's world in which, among other things, there are blocks, there is no such thing as a block world" (Dreyfus, 1979, p. 163).

Dreyfus sees the endeavors by Marvin Minsky, Roger Schank, and others to develop knowledge structures that integrate individual pieces of information as improvements over the micro-world program. Minsky's (1975/1981) frames consist of nodes where particular information is encoded and relations between the nodes. In a frame for "wedding," for example, some of the nodes contain information that is always true of weddings (e.g., they involve two parties getting married) while others contain information typically true, but which may be altered (e.g., they have attendants). By incorporating modifiable default values for some of the nodes, such structures are capable of directing active investigation and inquiry to determine the appropriateness of various default values to particular contexts.

Despite representing an improvement, Dreyfus ultimately found this approach inadequate because it still requires complete internal control of the system's activity. Dreyfus argued that in human activity many factors remain external, especially those that control the way in which the system confronts an environment and secures knowledge from it. Dreyfus's objection can be seen by considering an attempt to develop a knowledge structure (a script) for going to a restaurant (Schank & Abelson, 1977). The script specifies the typical activities involved in going to a restaurant, but allows for some variations that will occur between different kinds of restaurants (e.g., Continental, and Oriental restaurants.). The script tries to represent all relevant aspects of restaurant experience. Dreyfus contended this is simply hopeless because a human activity like going to a restaurant is largely regulated by factors that are not represented internally. Some of them may be factors in the external environment to which we are sensitive whereas others are learned practices (for example, following the hostess to a seat). Because Schank's program for answering questions about going to restaurants is not sensitive to such influences, the program does not really know about restaurants. To understand cognition, cognitive science, according to Dreyfus, must work with embodied systems, not abstract formal systems.

Dreyfus' contention (which he drew from Heidegger) that some information remains in the environment and is not represented has perplexed many commentators. We can make sense of it by considering Simon's (1969) account of how an ant moves through its environment by following a simple set of routines and not by developing a complex internal map. It may have detectors for determining which path is most level and a procedure that chooses to follow that path. The ant thereby responds to information about the contours of its environment, but does not represent these contours. Pylyshyn (1979/1981) treats Simon's example as showing how control of a system can be partly located in the system's environment without the system representing that information to itself. (See Winograd, 1981, for a related view.) Thus, information does not have to be represented symbolically to be useful to a cognitive system. (See Dreyfus & Dreyfus, 1987, for additional objections to the computational approach based on analyses of human expertise.)

Dreyfus's objections, even if valid, do not totally undermine Computational Functionalism. It is possible to allow that some information is processed in a formal computational system, and other information is found in the environment or learned practices. Computational Functionalism could still account for that processing that does involve formal symbols. To the extent that we forego formal computational accounts, either because we take information to be in the environment or because we employ noncomputational models such as connectionist models, however, we do undercut the claims of Computational Functionalism to give a complete, general characterization of the mind.

Qualitative States and the Qualia Objection

One of the most widely discussed objections to Functionalism is the claim that it cannot account for the affective or qualitative character of mental states. It is claimed that when a computer is programmed to identify visual images, it does not experience the image, and that when it is programmed to play chess, it never feels any anxiety about winning or losing. We might try to remedy this problem by incorporating affective states in our causal analysis of the system. We might posit a homunculus that recognizes when a certain affective state is appropriate and alters the processing in the system appropriately. Critics object, however, that although such a strategy might yield more realistic simulations of human behavior, the resulting simulations will not have the experiences a human does—they won't really feel pain or suffer anxiety.

Nagel (1974/1980) presented this problem vividly by asking the question "What is it like to be a bat?" We can learn in complete detail how the mechanisms in the bat's sonar system operate, yet we cannot imagine what it would be like to sense things through sonar. This is what functionalist accounts miss, he contended[10] (see also Nagel, 1986). Jackson (1982) offered a *Gedankenexperiment* to show us what Functionalism fails to capture. He asked us to contemplate a sophisticated neurophysiologist, Mary, who is deprived of all experiences of seeing colored objects, but yet develops a comprehensive account of the operation of the brain, including how it performs color perception. Although Mary knows everything there is to know about the brain processes employed in color perception, she still does not understand the experience of seeing red. Hence, Jackson concluded, Functionalism fails to account for the qualitative character of mental life.

A number of philosophers have attempted to defend Functionalism against these attacks. Van Gulick (1986) maintained that the affective properties will be higher level functional properties. He also claimed that knowing all there is to know about the lower level properties, we may not yet know about the higher level properties and may have to investigate them separately. But these may still be functional properties which characterize how a system will be able to interact with various types of phenomena. Thus, Van Gulick main-

---

[10] The charge is often made against AI models of cognitive systems that they lack any such subjective perspective. Nagel would charge that there is nothing which it is like to be a machine. Gunderson (1970/1971), however, developed an interesting response to that claim. He held that even though we will not recognize it, subjective experience will arise if we build mechanical systems that use the right causal properties. These systems will, he maintained, insist that they have experiences. Our assumption that we are different is due to what he terms the "asymmetry" between first person and third person points of view. We only enjoy the first person point of view with ourselves, and so cannot imagine how other systems could have such experiences.

tained that the examples advanced by Nagel and Jackson are in accord with Functionalism, not opposed to it.

Another defense focuses on the fact that Nagel's and Jackson's arguments assume that we *know* something when we have a certain kind of experience. It is possible that there is nothing to be known, but only something to be experienced.[11] A related way of presenting this response, due to Lewis (1983a) and P. M. Churchland (1985), is to claim that the word "knows" is used ambiguously in Nagel's and Jackson's objections. It refers on the one hand to conceptual knowledge and on the other to having experience. There is no reason to think that conceptual knowledge necessarily yields experience. P. S. Churchland (1986) offered the example of pregnancy where a similar ambiguity arises. A childless obstetrician may know all the physiological processes involved in pregnancy without having experienced pregnancy. The childless obstetrician is not lacking something that could be known conceptually. She simply has failed to have a certain experience.

These responses all accept the plausibility of Nagel's and Jackson's tales, but question how they should be interpreted. P.S. Churchland also questioned whether it is possible to know everything about a certain kind of experience without knowing what the experience would be like: "How can I assess what Mary [the neuroscientist in Jackson's tale] will know and understand if she knows *everything* there is to know about the brain? Everything is a lot, and it means, in all likelihood, that Mary has a radically different and deeper understanding of the brain than anything barely conceivable in our wildest flights of fancy" (1986, p. 332). This deeper understanding may mean that Mary will already know what the experience of seeing red is like so that Jackson's example could not arise.

Closely related to Nagel's and Jackson's objections to Functionalism are a set of objections that claim that Functionalism cannot account for the particular qualitative characters of experiences commonly reified and referred to as *qualia*. These objections rest on a set of *Gedankenexperiments* that contemplate that our qualitative experience may be altered or totally lacking without any change occurring in the causal processes captured by the functionalist analysis. Block and Fodor (1972/1980) presented one such *Gedankenexperiment* that postulates someone whose functional states are identical to ours but who sees the colors on the visual spectrum in reverse or whose pains feel pleasurable. (This is known as the *inverted qualia* condition.) Block and Fodor maintained

---

[11] Armstrong (1984) compared the situation to a case in which we can describe the figure contained in a puzzle image (e.g., the old woman/young woman drawing) but cannot see the figure ourselves. We might be able to do this because someone had pointed out which lines constituted the nose, hair, and so on, but we had not yet been able to perceive the gestalt. Later we might come to see the figure itself, but we would not thereby learn something new. We simply have a new experience.

that the feeling of pain is critical to the mental state of pain because "nothing would be a token of the type 'pain state' unless it felt like a pain" (Block & Fodor, 1972/1980, p. 244). If these situations could occur,[12] Functionalism would seem to face a serious difficulty, for they would show that something critical to certain mental states would not be captured in the causal relations that figure in functionalist analyses.

Block and Fodor proposed a second *Gedankenexperiment* that contemplates the existence of an organism with the same functional states as us but who has no qualitative character associated with its functional states. (This is known as the *absent qualia* condition.) Block (1978/1980) presented this *Gedankenexperiment* more graphically by proposing the existence of robots in which all the causal interactions found in us are realized but where no qualitative states occurred. One example postulates a human homuncular head in which lots of miniature people carry out each of the tasks postulated in a functional analysis of one of us. Another involves having each citizen of China take responsibility for a particular square of the machine table that characterized one of us and executing that task whenever called upon so that the whole Chinese nation would become a simulation of one of us.[13] Block suggested, using Nagel's phrase, that "there is prima facie doubt whether there is anything which it is like to be the homunculi-headed system" (Block 1978/1980, p. 278). Thus, he claimed that it is possible to satisfy the func-

---

[12] Block and Fodor mention that one response to the inverted spectrum argument is to claim that, for reasons we do not yet know, inverted spectra are impossible. Although Block and Fodor do not pursue this line, Hardin (1985, 1988), in fact, has offered evidence that the phenomenal colors cannot simply be interchanged as the inverted spectrum argument proposes. The reason is that phenomenal colors are not simple properties but have a complex structure which cannot be reversed. Empirical grounds alone, therefore, suggest that the inverted spectrum problem might be of little import.

[13] Block chose the Chinese nation for this simulation because he assumed that only about 1 billion homunculi are needed to staff all the squares of a Machine Table for the Turing Machine simulation, and if not, he proposed that each homunculus could handle a few squares rather than just one. The reason for 1 billion is that that is approximately the number of neurons in the brain. A Turing Machine, however, is perhaps the most inefficient way of carrying out any procedure and so, as the Churchlands argue, 1 billion is likely to be drastically short of the number of homunculi needed:

> It is demonstrable that no T_m realized as described in the population of China could possibly simulate your input-output relations. There are not nearly enough Chinese—not *remotely* enough. In fact, a spherical volume of space centered on the Sun and ending at Pluto's orbit packed solidly with cheek-to-cheek Chinese (roughly 10^{36} homunculi) would still not be remotely enough . . . Even the humblest of creatures are beyond such simulation [using the Chinese nation]. An unprepossessing gastropod like the sea slug *Aplysia California* has well in excess of 332 distinct sensory cells, and thus is clearly beyond the reach of the crude methods at issue. . . . Quite aside from the question of qualia, the Chinese Turing machine couldn't simulate an earthworm. (Churchland & Churchland, 1981, pp. 134-135)

tionalist theory without having any qualitative states. Functionalism, therefore, cannot account for the qualitative states of cognitive systems.

Functionalists who have responded to the inverted qualia and absent qualia arguments have generally pursued one of two strategies. They have either tried to avoid the objections by treating qualia themselves functionally or they have maintained that qualia are partly due to the physical substance which realizes mental functions and hence are not something Functionalism is obligated to explain. I discuss each response briefly.

The first strategy is pursued by Shoemaker (1975/1980) in an attempt to answer the absent qualia argument. He argued that qualia can be characterized at least in part by their ability to cause beliefs about themselves. He argued that without this functional property, we would not know them even through introspection and no qualia problems would arise. The fact that we know of these qualitative states, therefore, shows that they have functional properties and rules out the possibility of totally absent qualia. (See Block, 1980c, and Shoemaker, 1981, for further discussion.) With regard to the inverted qualia argument, Shoemaker took a weaker position. He allowed that in addition to functional properties, qualia may have other properties. If these are exchanged, an inverted spectrum situation results. Shoemaker claimed, however, that admitting inverted spectra in this way does not undermine Functionalism because it is the functional properties of qualia that we in fact use to distinguish objects in the world on qualitative grounds.

The Churchlands, however, take a much stronger position, arguing that the functional criteria of qualia are the ones that define qualia. If there are other features of qualia that could be inverted, they would not be important to what the qualia are. If a feature that was part of seeing blue now became a part of seeing red, we would treat it now as part of the red quale. Thus, the Churchlands maintain that only the functional criteria are important and no real inverted qualia situations ever arise (Churchland & Churchland, 1981).

One thing that has seemed to make qualia difficult for the Functionalist to account for is that they seem to be simple givens of experience, lacking the kind of complexity that would serve to integrate them into a functionalist analysis. Dennett (1978d), however, argued that the monadic character of pain qualia is illusory. The reason the idea of a computer feeling pain has been so puzzling is that we have misconstrued pain as a simple qualitative property. He appealed to the different effects various anesthetics and analgesics have on pain experiences to show us that there really are different aspects of pain. In a similar vein, Lycan (1987) proposed a *Gedankenexperiment* wherein one first administers successively the various drugs to remove different aspects of the pain experience until none remain, and then reverses this process to produce the overall pain experience. Such a decomposition and recomposition of pain would lend credence to the claim that, after all, qualitative states really are complex functional states, not simple monadic states. Further evidence for the functional complexity of qualia is provided by the ability of people to learn to differentiate qualia more finely (e.g., through aesthetic training).[14]

The second strategy for answering the absent qualia and inverted qualia arguments is to appeal to the physical structures in which functional states are realized to account for their qualitative character. This removes qualia from the list of things Functionalism needs to account for. Gunderson (1971) colorfully labeled the qualitative aspects of our mental states "program resistant properties," suggesting that they are due to the basic properties of the mechanism in which programmable properties were realized. He thereby contrasted qualitative properties with the program receptive properties of sapience. One of the more interesting recent arguments for this approach is found in Lewis (1980). He presented two hypothetical cases that seemingly press us to make inconsistent judgments. The first involves a Martian who is made of a different kind of physical mechanism (a hydraulic system) but who has states that are functionally equivalent to pain states in us. The second involves a madman, who is in the same physical state we are in when we suffer pain but who shows none of the behavioral/functional symptoms of pain (in fact, whenever these states occur the madman becomes totally devoted to work and does nothing to try to advert them). Lewis found it intuitive to judge both of these individuals to be in pain, but claims that our grounds for doing so in the two cases are inconsistent. In judging the Martian to have suffered pain we employ a behavioral/functional criteria (the states in the Martian play the same functional role as our pain states) whereas in judging the madman to be in pain we are appealing to the physical state that realizes the pain (the madman is in the same physical states as we are in when we suffer pain). Thus, we seem to be committed to both a functional and a physical criterion for identifying pain states.

To reconcile these apparently competing criteria, Lewis proposed that we use a functional criterion to determine what pain is relative to a species, but that we use a physical criterion within the species. Thus, a kind of state is a pain state for members of a species if it is the kind of state that in normal members of the species functions similarly to the way pain states function in humans. Within a species, pain can be identified with the kind of physical state that in most members of the species instantiates the causal relationships that functionally characterize pain, even if it does not perform that function for a particular member of the species. Lewis also allowed that if there are distinct subgroups within the species in which a different mechanism per-

---

[14] The Churchlands claim that learning about our nervous system will help us learn to differentiate qualia more finely. In appealing to these neurophysiological differences, the Churchlands seem to have departed from a functionalist approach, but this is not the case. They maintained that neurophysiological processes can be analyzed functionally as well so that there is no principled division between functional accounts of mind and of neuroscience.

forms the pain function, we may also use that mechanism in assessing pain in the subgroup. Lewis (1980) applies the same principle to inversions of the color spectrum:

> I would say that there is a good sense in which the alleged victim of inverted spectra sees red when he looks at grass: he is in a state that occupies the role of seeing red for mankind in general. And there is an equally good sense in which he sees green: he is in a state that occupies the role of seeing green for him, and for a small subpopulation of which he is an unexceptional member and which has some claim to be regarded as a natural kind. You are right to say either, though not in the same breath. Need more be said? (p. 220)

Lewis' strategy, however, may not be totally successful. Lycan (1987) introduced two additional cases on which Lewis' analysis seems to give unacceptable results. One involves taking the physical material that normally fulfills the functional role of a pain quale in us and putting it to another use in us. Lewis' account would seem to be committed to saying that we feel pain whenever this material is in the same state as it is when playing its normal causal role. The second involves installing an artificial organ that functioned like the real pain organ. In this case, Lewis would seem to be committed to denying the quale since the person lacks the material state that usually produces pain in our species. The problems Lycan raised are due to the fact that Lewis has tried to reconcile inconsistent criteria for pain. One way to resolve this difficulty is to insist simply on the physical aspects of the state when accounting for the distinctive qualitative character of mental states. Making qualia totally a matter of an entity's physical makeup seems problematic, however. If the person cannot differentiate the states qualitatively, it seems wrong to maintain that the person has experienced different states. The alternative is to return to the first strategy and, like the Churchlands, Dennett, and Lycan, adopt a totally functionalist criterion.

Although both strategies seem to hold promise for resolving the qualia problem, it remains bothersome to many. There seems to be some aspect of experience above and beyond that which can be captured in Functionalism's mechanical models of the operation of the mind. This drives us back to where I began this objection to Functionalism, with Nagel's concern that mechanical analysis can never capture the sense that there is something that it is like to be a certain kind of cognitive system. As a result, the question of qualia continues to be one of the most discussed topics in the functionalist literature.[15]

---

[15] For yet other treatments of qualia, see Malcolm (1984), Armstrong (1984), Maloney (1985b), Heil (1983), Horgan (1982, 1984), and Russow (1982). A closely related issue concerns consciousness. For the most part, cognitive scientists have not tried to explain consciousness because it seems to be such an intractable phenomenon. But some philosophers and other cognitive scientists have begun to analyze consciousness functionally. They have generally advocated a strategy of differentiating aspects of consciousness and explaining each independently. See Dennett (1978c, in press), Bechtel and Richardson (1983), Natsoulas (1981, 1985), Armstrong (1980), and Bricke (1984) for further discusion.

Chauvinism and Liberality Objections

In some respects, Functionalism seems to define a middle ground between Philosophical Behaviorism and the Identity Theory. Like Philosophical Behaviorism, it appeals to behavioral criteria to characterize mental phenomena, but unlike it, Functionalism construes mental states as internal states and grants them a causal role in producing behavior. In countenancing mental states as inner processes, Functionalism agrees with the Identity Theory, but it differs in not insisting that types of mental states be identified with brain states. One of the more interesting criticisms of Functionalism, due to Block (1978/1980), is that this middle ground is untenable and that Functionalism must succumb either to a problem that confronts Philosophical Behaviorism or to a problem that confronts the Identity Theory. Either Functionalism will be like Philosophical Behaviorism in being too liberal by attributing mental states to systems to which they should not be attributed, or it will be like the Identity Theory in being too chauvinistic by denying mental states to systems that do have them. Which problem Functionalism succumbs to depends, for Block, on the form of Functionalism one adopts.

Block contends that Folk Psychological Functionalism will be too liberal. Just as philosophical behaviorism attributes mental states to any system that has appropriate behavioral dispositions, Folk Psychological Functionalism attributes mental states, qualia and all, to any system that we can characterize in folk psychological terms. If, for example, the Chinese nation were to carry out a simulation of the causal interactions that occur in me, we would have to attribute to it the same mental states as are now attributed to me. In particular, Block contended, functionalists must maintain that it experiences the same type of qualia. This, Block claimed, would be too liberal, because it seems absurd to think that this composite entity would have mental states, especially qualitative ones.[16]

The alternative form of Functionalism Block considered is what he called "Psychofunctionalism." It corresponds broadly to the three versions of Functionalism other than Folk Psychological Functionalism introduced at the beginning of this chapter, where the causal *processes* included in the functionalist's analysis are those posited in various psychological or neurophysiological theories. Block contended that Psychofunctionalism avoids the objection of being too liberal, because it rules out attributing mental states to any system that does not use the same processes that produce mental states in us.[17] However, Block went on to argue that Psychofunctionalism, like the

---

[16] For a different attempt to criticize Functionalism by showing its similarity to Philosophical Behaviorism, see Bealer (1978).

[17] Block, however, argued that in fact at least inverted spectra arguments still make sense even given the contents of psychological theory, thus showing that qualia are not proper parts of psychological theories. Block's claim that qualia are not part of psychological theories seems quite peculiar, because the qualia arguments were his primary arguments against folk psychological functionalism and yet he saw these defects as driving us to Psychofunctionalism. If the conclusion is that qualia are not psychological properties, perhaps the Chinese nation simulation of me does manifest psychological properties and folk psychological functionalism is adequate.

Type Identity Theory, is too chauvinistic in that it does not permit us to attribute mental states to organisms to which we should attribute them. For example, we could not attribute them to Martians who might live in much the manner that we do, but use different internal causal processes. But, he contended, we should to be able to attribute psychological states to such organisms if their behavior is appropriate: "surely there are many ways of filling in the description of the Martian-Earthian difference I sketched on which it would be perfectly clear that even if Martians behave differently from us on subtle psychological experiments, they nonetheless think, desire, enjoy, etc. To suppose otherwise would be crude human chauvinism" (Block, 1978/1980, p. 292).

It might seem that we could accommodate the Martians if the causal processes in them were similar to those in us, even if they were exactly the same. Block contended that any such relaxation of the requirement of being like us will lead us to become too liberal. To avoid excess liberalism we need to specify limits on what kind of system is similar enough to us to allow us to attribute mental states, but by imposing any such limits, we risk being too chauvinistic. Block thus maintained that there is no way for Functionalism to avoid either being too liberal or being too chauvinistic.

To emphasize the seriousness of this problem, Block focused on a special case. In any functional analysis, one must specify the causal inputs and outputs of the system. Block claimed the Functionalist cannot do this without being either too liberal or too chauvinistic. We could try to characterize inputs and outputs functionally in terms of whatever happens to provide input and be the output of a system, but this is far too liberal. To show this he imagined a case where financial manipulators might so direct the Bolivian economy that it instantiates the functional relations found in us. If we characterize its inputs and outputs as whatever induces causal processes in it, we are committed to claiming that the Bolivian economy possesses the same mental states we do. But, he commented: "If there are any fixed points when discussing the mind–body problem, one of them is that the economy of Bolivia could not have mental states, no matter how it is distorted by powerful hobbyists" (p. 294). But if we require the system to respond to the very same kind of physical inputs we do and produce the same outputs, we are once again chauvinistic, denying mentality to possible cognitive systems that deal with different inputs and outputs. Without an account of inputs and outputs that avoids both chauvinism and liberality, though, Block claimed that it is impossible to characterize mental system in functional terms, that is, in terms of causal relations between such states and inputs and outputs.

Block may have identified a real limitation of the versions of Functionalism discussed so far. To provide a basis for deciding what kinds of causally interactive systems possess mental states may require us to consider what purpose these processes serve (Richardson, 1979). Invoking purposes in a functional analysis forces us into a teleological perspective. Although many people think that a teleological perspective is incompatible with natural science, a number of recent philosophers of biology have tried to show how one can incorporate a teleological perspective into natural science. In the following section I outline such an analysis.

A TELEOLOGICAL VERSION OF FUNCTIONALISM

The basic tools for a teleological analysis of function statements were introduced in chapter 4, where I sketched how Dennett's analysis of intentionality might be developed within an evolutionary framework. What was critical to that endeavor was treating mental states as adaptive features of organisms and interpreting them in terms of the features of the environment with which the organism must deal in order to survive. This appeal to an evolutionary framework also permits us to develop a general teleological analysis of function. The basic strategy was developed by philosophers of biology such as Wright (1976) and Wimsatt (1972). They both appeal to the fact that if a species has been selected because it possessed a particular trait, then that trait served a need for the members of the species. Moreover, the presence of the trait in current members of the species can be explained by appeal to how it enabled the species to meet these selection pressures. Wright and Wimsatt contend, therefore, that we may attribute to the trait the function of serving that need of the species.

Wright (1976, p. 81) offered the following formal specification of when it is appropriate to attribute a particular function to some entity:

The function of X is Z if and only if:
  (i) Z is a consequence (result) of X's being there, and
  (ii) X is there because it does (results in) Z.

Wright's characterization of function seems to countenance backwards causation because it is what X does that is taken to cause X's occurrence. But this is not the case. When viewed from an evolutionary perspective, the X in clause (ii) refers to an instance of the kind X that is descendent from another instance, and it is that earlier instance which is referred to in clause (i). It is this earlier instance of the type that had the beneficial consequence, and its having that beneficial consequence is what has brought about the current instance. Thus, nothing more than ordinary causation is involved. Wimsatt's analysis of functions is a little more elaborate, but it brings out the relevance of such factors as the nature of the system and environment as well as one's theoretical perspective in attributing functions. Thus, he proposes to analyze function attributions in terms of the schema: "According to theory T, a function of behavior B of item i in System S in environment E relative to purpose P is to do C" (Wimsatt, 1972, p. 32). It is through the purpose and theory values that this analysis becomes teleological. The purpose is given by the selection factors governing a system and the theory specifies both what criteria the system had to satisfy in order to be selected and how the behavior of the item fulfills these criteria.

Wright's and Wimsatt's accounts have the virtue of invoking the function something serves in an explanation of the current occurrence of that entity and yet using only efficient causation. This allows the introduction of a teleological perspective without violating a mechanical view of nature. However, there are two serious objections to this approach. First, Wright's and Wimsatt's positions both entail that something that emerges without an evolutionary history but meets the needs of a system cannot be functional. This is counterintuitive. If we accept the common lore that giraffes acquired their long necks because of the advantage they realized in acquiring food, then, although we could say that the function of the giraffe's neck is to aid it in acquiring food, we could not say the same thing of a giraffe produced artificially by biological engineering because it lacks this evolutionary history. But its long neck is also enabling it to meet the requirements for it to reproduce, and so would seemingly be serving that function for it. (This example is due to Burian, personal communication, December, 1983. See Margolis, 1976, for a similar example and Short, 1983, for arguments against such examples.) Second, Wright's and Wimsatt's analyses also entail that vestigial organs that helped earlier members of a species to meet environmental demands still serve their function even if the environmental demands are no longer operating. Their analyses seem to commit us to counting the gene for sickle cell anemia as functional because of the protection it provided against malaria, although malaria no longer presents a selection force for most contemporary carriers of sickle cell, and being a carrier for sickle cell is a handicap, not an asset.

There is a straightforward way to remedy these problems. Rather than requiring that functions be adaptations (i.e., the product of selection), we need only require that they be adaptive (i.e., they increase the likelihood that the organism *will* reproduce). (This distinction is due to Brandon, 1981.) That is, in ascertaining what the function of something is, we should look at how the trait will benefit the current organism in its quest for survival rather than how it aided its ancestors. There is, however, a significant cost to this remedy. Insofar as we are not appealing to the origin of a trait in ascribing a function to it, we are not explaining its occurrence and should not speak of "functional explanations," but only of "functional analyses" (see Bechtel, 1986).[18]

---

[18] Wimsatt actually introduced several uses of functional statements in addition to the explanatory version we have been considering. One of these is an evaluative use and for this he allows us to look at current selection forces and not historically operating ones. Wimsatt does not sharply differentiate these two versions of function statements and for him the explanatory use is primary. I am not discounting the importance of the kind of evolutionary explanation which Wimsatt and Wright both point to (see also Falk, 1981), but I am arguing that it is the functional analysis that constitutes the primary teleological framework and the one needed for introducing a teleological perspective into psychological analyses of mental states.

Invoking this sort of functional analysis, we can overcome the objections Block raised to non-teleological versions of Functionalism. What the teleological perspective requires us to do is not simply consider causal interactions in identifying functions, but consider how these causal processes are contributing to the *needs* of the organism, as these are specified by environmental demands.[19] If a process is not contributing to the organism's attempt to meet selection forces operating on it, it will not be construed as a function. Consider Block's example of the Chinese nation. When the Chinese simulate my mental states, they are not doing so to meet the same kind of selection forces as operate on me. Hence, we do not need to attribute to the Chinese my mental states. The Chinese do not constitute a system interacting with an environment of the right kind. They are not in the business of processing sensory stimuli about ordinary objects that confront a person in life and planning actions in response. They constitute a social system and if they were to carry out the kind of simulation Block has in mind, the selection force to which they would be answering is the need for income and prestige as a nation. Even here we have a hard time identifying the system in question in an appropriate manner for an evolutionary analysis because very large nations may not have the kind of cohesiveness and continuity that organisms do. The economic system of Bolivia, to consider another of Block's examples, does seem well enough delimited to have enduring cohesiveness. Moreover, it can be construed as evolving in the face of selection pressures. But here the kinds of selection pressures are so radically different than those confronting a person that attribution of mental states to the processes within the Bolivian economy is obviously a mistake.

Block might well respond to these suggestions by contending that they still face the objection of being too liberal or too chauvinistic. This teleological approach requires us to specify the type of selection forces to which a system must be answering for the processes within it to count as mental, and Block might argue that this is impossible. Contrary to Block, however, there is reason to hope for success, even if we cannot produce the appropriate analysis now. To do so we would need to clarify what environmental selection forces are important in determining the future of cognitive systems and develop an account of what adaptive processes are appropriately characterized as mental. Ethologists and evolutionary theorists are well on the way to characterizing the kinds of activities organisms need to do to survive in a variety of environments and general principles of evolutionary processes at this level may be forthcoming. Mayr (1974), for example, distinguished between closed systems, which rely on instincts, and open systems, which can learn. This

---

[19]This evolutionary scheme does not commit us to sociobiology. We can think of cognitive strategies as evolving to meet evolutionary needs without reducing them to genetically encoded adaptations. For a non-sociobiological evolutionary perspective on cultural phenomena, see Boyd and Richerson (1985).

provides a useful dichotomy for differentiating survival strategies. Psychological attributes would only seem to be applicable to those organisms adopting an open strategy and learning what behaviors to perform. Such systems must be sensitive to information about their environment and be capable of processing this information to determine appropriate responses. This suggests that we might be able develop a general account of mental processes in terms of their roles in open systems (e.g., as processes that figure in processing information from an environment which then determines strategies of action).

Block might still raise a chauvinistic worry that evolutionary processes have only been studied in our biosphere and we do not know how to generalize to a totally different type of biosphere. Such a worry, however, would not be peculiar to psychology. We are equally unsure how to transfer biological concepts beyond their home domain in our biosphere. But such uncertainty does not imply that we will be without any principles to settle matters if we encounter processes in another biosphere. If the fundamental principles of our biological and psychological sciences could be adapted to the new context so as to give us useful information, we would be likely to so extend them and expand our conception of life and mind accordingly. If not, we would presumably seek a different framework in which to describe and explain the newly discovered phenomena.

It might seem that a teleological analysis such as this would rule out artifacts such as computers as candidates for mental states. It is not obvious that they evolve in the way living organisms do. I contend, however, that this analysis gives the right answer for judging the mentality of computers. Artifacts are constrained by selection forces. Often these forces operate only in the mind of the designer, who invokes criteria in choosing what system to build. But computers (as composite systems of hardware and software) can be built that are able to adapt themselves over time to the demands of their environments. Self-modifying programs are a step in this direction. The fact that contemporary computers are not closely fitted into an environment to which they are adapting makes attributing mental states to such systems problematic. However, there are no principled obstacles to creating computer systems that interact and adapt much more intimately to the demands of their environment. If we attribute mental states to such systems, we will be less likely to be charged with being too liberal (Bechtel, 1985b).

In the discussion earlier in the chapter I presented Homuncular Functionalism without treating it teleologically. Of the various versions of Functionalism, however, it is the one most naturally interpreted teleologically and has been so characterized by its primary proponents, Dennett and Lycan. As we saw, the Homuncular Functionalist begins with an account of what a whole system accomplishes and then tries to explain that performance by decomposing that system into subsystems (homunculi). A teleological perspective enters with the manner in which we specify what tasks the system is performing. If we do so using intentional idioms and if we adopt an evolutionary perspective on intentionality, we have already introduced a teleological perspective. We are treating mental states as adaptive states of organisms. Such a perspective, moreover, is critical to developing the homuncular account. There are many causal processes going on in organisms and we could well end up explaining features of the organism that are not really of interest. Without specifying what the system was accomplishing through its internal processing, we would lack guidance as to what features of the system we should try to explain (Burge, 1982; Dennett, 1981a). Thus, Teleological Functionalism is a natural complement to Homuncular Functionalism.

Teleological Functionalism also brings the philosophical conception of a functionalist analysis much closer to the tradition of Functionalism in psychology. As noted at the beginning of this chapter, the psychological tradition of Functionalism, unlike the philosophical tradition, adopted an evolutionary perspective and looked at psychological processes in terms of their environmental significance. There are vast differences between the approaches of James and Skinner, for example, but they share this common focus on how activities in organisms render them adapted to the demands of an environment. I also noted at the outset that philosophical Functionalists take themselves to be giving analyses of mental processes as characterized by contemporary cognitivism, a perspective that seems to many to be radically at odds with psychological Functionalism as exemplified by behaviorism. The introduction of a teleological element into philosophical Functionalism, though, suggests that the characterization of mental states in cognitivism may be reconciled with the functionalist aspect of movements like behaviorism. Attempts to characterize mental processes as internal are not inconsistent with attempting to understand these processes in terms of how they permit organisms to behave in their environment (see Bechtel, in press and Schnaiter, 1987). Hence, in addition to showing us how to answer Block's chauvinism objection to Functionalism, Teleological Functionalism opens the prospect of a rapprochement between the internal processing focus of cognitivism and the environmental focus of behaviorism.

SUMMARY

Functionalism now constitutes the dominant analysis of mental events in philosophy of mind. In this chapter I reviewed several prominent versions of Functionalism. I have also discussed some of the major objections raised against Functionalism and the major functionalist responses. Of the objections, Block's objection that Functionalism cannot avoid the dilemma of either being too liberal or too chauvinistic in attributing mental states seemed to show most clearly a limitation to Functionalism. In response to that objection I introduced a teleological version of Functionalism that has been developed within philosophy of biology. I have shown how Teleological Functionalism can overcome Block's objection and, in so doing, bring philosophical Functionalism more in accord with the tradition of Functionalism in psychology.

Postscript

In this volume I have tried to provide a broad introduction to the issues of philosophy of mind and the positions philosophers have taken on these issues. As should be clear, there are long-standing disagreements about these topics. Yet, these issues are of central importance to cognitive science. Implicitly or explicitly, cognitive scientists must take a stand on the issues of whether intentionality can be accounted for naturalistically, of how the mind is related to the brain, and of how mental events are to be identified. This volume has attempted to provide a sufficient introduction to these issues and the views that have been advanced so that other cognitive scientists can enter actively into the discussion. A word of caution is needed, however. Once you engage in discussing these issues, you must assume responsibility for the views you adopt. As you have seen throughout this book, philosophers disagree. Morever, they are fallible, so do not take philosophers as final authorities!

There are other topics relevant to philosophy of mind that have not been discussed or only briefly mentioned in this text. Two of particular note concern innateness and mental images. Regarding innateness, there has been wide ranging philosophical discussion of what it means for a cognitive capacity to be innate and what capacities are in fact innate (see e.g., Stich, 1979, and papers in Piattelli-Palmarini, 1980; and Block, 1980b). With respect to mental images, there are questions about what mental images are and how they might be stored in the head (see e.g., Anderson, 1978; Kosslyn, 1980; Pylyshyn, 1981; Smith & Kosslyn, 1981; and papers in Block, 1980b). Two anthologies that will be particularly useful for anyone seeking a broad perspective on current philosophy of mind are Block (1980a, 1980b) and Haugeland (1981a).

References

Many of the papers listed in this section have been anthologized. Because it is frequently easier to locate papers in the anthologies, I have often indicated an anthologized source as well as the original place of publication. When two dates are indicated for such a paper, the first refers to the original publication date and the second to the date of the anthology. Page references in the text are to the anthologized versions of the papers.

Abrahamsen, A. A. (1987). Bridging boundaries versus breaking boundaries: Psycholinguistics in perspective. *Synthese, 72*, 355–388.

Amundson, R. (1987). *Two autonomous domains*. Unpublished manuscript.

Anderson, A. R. (1964). *Minds and machines*. Englewood Cliffs, NJ: Prentice-Hall.

Anderson, R. E. (1986). Cognitive explanations and cognitive ethology. In W. Bechtel, (Ed.), *Integrating scientific disciplines* (pp. 323–336). Dordrecht: Reidel.

Anderson, J. R. (1978). Arguments concerning representations for mental imagery. *Psychological Review, 85*, 249–277.

Anderson, J. R., Greeno, J. G., Kline, P. J., & Neves, D. M. (1981). Acquisition of problem solving skill. In J. R. Anderson (Ed.), *Cognitive skills and their acquisition* (pp. 191–230). Hillsdale, NJ: Lawrence Erlbaum Associates.

Anscombe, G. E. M. (1965). The intentionality of sensation: A grammatical feature. In R. J. Butler (Ed.), *Analytic philosophy* (2nd series, pp. 158–180). Oxford: Basil Blackwell.

Aquila, R. E. (1977). *Intentionality: A study of mental acts*. University Park, PA: The Pennsylvania State University Press.

Armstrong, D. M. (1968). *A materialist theory of mind*. London: Routledge & Kegan Paul.

Armstrong, D. M. (1980). *The nature of mind and other essays*. Ithaca, NY: Cornell University Press.

Armstrong, D. M. (1984). Consciousness and causality. In D. M. Armstrong & N. Malcolm (Eds.), *Consciousness and causality: A debate on the nature of mind* (pp. 103–191). Oxford: Basil Blackwell.

Austin, J. L. (1956–1957/1970). A plea for excuses. *Proceedings of the Aristotelian Society, 57*, 1–30. (Reprinted in *Philosophical papers of J. L. Austin* (2nd ed.), (pp. 175–204), J. O. Urmson & G. J. Warnock (Eds.). Oxford: Oxford University Press (1970).

Austin, J. L. (1962a). *How to do things with words*. In J. O. Urmson (Ed.), New York: Oxford University Press.

Austin, J. L. (1962b) *Sense and sensibilia* (Reconstructed from the manuscript notes by G. J. Warnock). Oxford: Oxford University Press.

Bacon, F. (1620). *Novum organon.* London: J. Billium.

Bailey, G. (1986). *Cognitive psychology and representational theories of mind.* Unpublished manuscript.

Barnette, R. L. (1977). Kripke's pains. *Southern Journal of Philosophy, 15,* 3–14.

Barsalou, L. (in preparation). *Cognitive psychology: An overview for cognitive science.* Hillsdale, NJ: Lawrence Erlbaum Associates.

Bealer, G. (1978). An inconsistency in functionalism. *Synthese, 38,* 333–372.

Bechtel, W. (1978). Indeterminacy and intentionality: Quine's purported elimination of propositions. *Journal of Philosophy, 75,* 649–662.

Bechtel, W. (1980). Indeterminacy and underdetermination: Are Quine's two theses consistent? *Philosophical Studies, 38,* 309–320.

Bechtel, W. (1985a). Realism, instrumentalism, and the intentional stance. *Cognitive Science, 9,* 473–497.

Bechtel, W. (1985b). Attributing responsibility to computer systems. *Metaphilosophy, 16,* 296–306.

Bechtel, W. (1986). Teleological functional analyses and the hierarchical organization of nature. In N. Rescher (Ed.), *Teleology and natural science* (pp. 26–48). Landham, MD: University Press of America.

Bechtel, W. (in press a). Perspectives on mental models. *Behaviorism, 17.*

Bechtel, W. (in press b). *Philosophy of science: An overview for cognitive science.* Hillsdale, NJ: Lawrence Erlbaum Associates.

Bechtel, W. (in press c). Connectionism and philosophy of mind: An overview. *Southern Journal of Philosophy, 25.*

Bechtel, W., & Richardson, R. C. (1983). Consciousness and complexity: Evolutionary perspectives on the mind-body problem. *Australasian Journal of Philosophy, 61,* 378–393.

Bennett, J. (1976). *Linguistic behavior.* Cambridge: Cambridge University Press.

Berkeley, G. (1710/1965). A treatise concerning the principles of human knowledge. In C. M. Turbaye (Ed.), *Principles, dialogues, and correspondence* (pp. 3–101). Indianapolis: Bobbs-Merrill.

Bernstein, R. J. (1968/1971). The challenge of scientific materialism. *International Philosophical Quarterly, 8,* 252–275. (Reprinted in Rosenthal, 1971, pp. 200–222)

Biro, J. I. (1985a). Hume and cognitive science. *History of Philosophy Quarterly, 2,* 257–274.

Biro, J. I. (1985b November). *Kant and neuro-science.* Paper presented at the 11th Interamerican Congress of Philosophy. Guadalajara.

Block, N. (1978/1980). Troubles with functionalism. In C. W. Savage (Ed.), *Perception and cognition. Issues in the foundations of psychology. Minnesota studies in the philosophy of science* (Vol. 9, pp. 261–325). Minneapolis: University of Minnesota Press. (Reprinted in Block, 1980, pp. 268–305)

Block, N. (1980a). *Readings in philosophy of psychology* (Vol. 1). Cambridge, MA: Harvard University Press.

Block, N. (1980b). *Readings in philosophy of psychology* (Vol. 2). Cambridge, MA: Harvard University Press.

Block, N. (1980c). Are absent qualia impossible? *The Philosophical Review, 89,* 257–274.

Block, N. & Fodor, J. A. (1972/1980). What psychological states are not. *Philosophical Review, 81,* 159–181. (Reprinted in Block, 1980, pp. 237–250.)

Boden, M. (1977). *Artificial intelligence and natural man.* New York: Basic Books.

Boden, M. (1981). *Minds and mechanisms: Philosophical psychology and computational models.* Ithaca, NY: Cornell University Press.

Borst, C. V. (Ed.). (1970). *The mind/brain identity theory.* New York: Macmillan.

Boveri, T. (1903). Über die Konstitution der chromatischen Kernsubstanz. *Verhandlungen der deutschen zoologischen gesellschaft zu Würzberg, 13,* 10–33.

Boyd, R. & Richerson, P. J. (1985). *Culture and the evolutionary process.* Chicago: University of Chicago Press.

Brandon, R. (1981). Biological teleology: Questions and explanations. *Studies in the history and philosophy of science, 12,* 91–105.

Brentano, F. (1973). *Psychology from an empirical standpoint* (A. C. Pancurello, D. B. Terrell, & L. L. McAlister, Trans.). New York: Humanities. (Originally published, 1874)

Brewer, W. F. (1974). There is no convincing evidence for operant or classical conditioning in adult humans. In W. B. Weimer & D. S. Palermo (Eds.), *Cognition and the symbolic process* (pp. 1–42). Hillsdale, NJ: Lawrence Erlbaum Associates.

Bricke, J. (1984). Dennett's eliminative arguments. *Philosophical Studies, 45,* 413–429.

Burge, T. (1979). Individualism and the mental. *Midwest Studies in Philosophy, 4,* 73–121.

Burge, T. (1982). Other bodies. In A. Woodfield (Ed.), *Thought and object* (pp. 97–120). Oxford: Oxford University Press.

Bynum, T. W. (1985). Artificial intelligence, biology, and intentional states. *Metaphilosophy, 16,* 355–377.

Campbell, D. T. (1966). Pattern matching as an essential in distal knowing. In K. R. Hammond (Ed.), *The psychology of Egon Brunswik* (pp. 81–106). New York: Holt, Rinehart & Winston.

Carleton, L. R. (1984). Programs, language understanding, and Searle. *Synthese, 59.* 219–230.

Carnap, R. (1956). *Meaning and necessity.* Chicago: University of Chicago Press.

Chisholm, R. M. (1957). *Perceiving: A philosophical study.* Ithaca, NY: Cornell University Press.

Chisholm, R. M. (1958). Sentences about believing. In H. Feigl, M. Scriven, & G. Maxwell (Eds.), *Minnesota studies in the philosophy of science* (pp. 510–520). Minneapolis, MN: University of Minnesota Press.

Chisholm, R. M. (1967). Intentionality. In E. Edwards (Ed.), *The encyclopedia of philosophy* (Vol. 4, pp. 201–204). New York: McMillan.

Chisholm, R. M. (1984). The primacy of the intentional. *Synthese 61,* 89–109.

Chomsky, N. (1959). Review of Skinner's verbal behavior. *Language, 35,* 26–58.

Chomsky, N. (1966). *Cartesian linguistics: A chapter in the history of rationalist thought.* Cambridge, MA: MIT Press.

Chomsky, N. (1969). Quine's empirical assumptions. In D. Davidson & J. Hintikka (Eds.), *Words and objections. Essays on the work of W. V. Quine* (pp. 53–68). Dordrecht: Reidel.

Chomsky, N. (1986). *Knowledge of language.* New York: Praeger.

Church, A. (1943). A review of Quine. *Journal of Symbolic Logic, 8,* 45–47.

Churchland, P. M. (1979). *Scientific realism and the plasticity of mind.* Cambridge: Cambridge University Press.

Churchland, P. M. (1981a). Eliminative materialism and propositional attitudes. *The Journal of Philosophy, 78,* 67–90.

Churchland, P. M. (1981b). Is *Thinker* a natural kind? *Dialogue, 21,* 223–238.

Churchland, P. M. (1984). *Matter and consciousness: A contemporary introduction to the philosophy of mind.* Cambridge: MIT Press/Bradford Books.

Churchland, P. M. (1985). Reduction, qualia, and the direct introspection of brain states. *The Journal of Philosophy, 82,* 8–28.

Churchland, P. M. (1986). Some reductive strategies in cognitive neurobiology. *Mind, 95,* 279–309.

Churchland, P. M., & Churchland, P. S. (1981). Functionalism, qualia, and intentionality. *Philosophical Topics, 12,* 121–145.

Churchland, P. S. (1978). Fodor on language learning. *Synthese, 38,* 149–159.

Churchland, P. S. (1980a). Language, thought, and information processing. *Nous, 14,* 147–170.

Churchland, P. S. (1980b). A perspective on mind-brain research. *The Journal of Philosophy, 77,* 185–207.

Churchland, P. S. (1983). Consciousness: The transmutation of a concept. *Pacific Philosophical Quarterly, 64,* 80–95.

Churchland, P. S. (1986). *Neurophilosophy: Toward a unified science of the mind-brain.* Cambridge: MIT Press/Bradford Books.

Churchland, P. S. & Churchland, P. M. (1983). Stalking the wild epistemic engine. *Nous, 17,* 5–18.

Cook, T. D., & Campbell, D. T. (1979). *Quasi-experimentation: Design and analysis for field settings.* Chicago: Rand McNally.

Cornman, J. W. (1962). Intentionality and intensionality. *Philosophical Quarterly, 12,* 44–52.

Cornman, J. W. (1962/1971). The identity of mind and body. *The Journal of Philosophy, 59,* 486–492. (Reprinted in Rosenthal, 1971, pp. 73-79)

Cornman, J. W. (1968). On the elimination of 'sensations' and sensations. *The Review of Metaphysics, 22,* 15–35.

Cornman, J. W. (1977). Mind-body identity: Cross-categorial or not? *Philosophical Studies, 32,* 165–174.

Cummins, R. (1975). Functional analysis. *The Journal of Philosophy, 72,* 741–760.

Cummins, R. (1983). *The nature of psychological explanation.* Cambridge, MA: MIT Press/Bradford Books.

Darden, L. & Maull, N. (1977). Interfield theories. *Phiosophy of Science, 43,* 44–64.

Davidson, D. (1967). Truth and meaning. *Synthese, 17,* 304–323. (Reprinted and revised in Davidson, 1984, pp. 17–36)

Davidson, D. (1970/1980). Mental events. In L. Foster & J. W. Swanson (Eds.), *Experience and theory* (pp. 79–101). Amherst: University of Massachusetts Press. (Reprinted in Block, 1980, pp. 107–119)

Davidson, D. (1973). Radical interpretation. *Dialectica, 27,* 313–328. (Reprinted in Davidson, 1984, pp. 125–139).

Davidson, D. (1974a). Belief and the basis of meaning. *Synthese, 27,* 309–323. (Reprinted in Davidson, 1984, pp. 141–154)

Davidson, D. (1974b). On the very idea of a conceptual scheme. *Proceedings and Addresses of the American Philosophical Association, 47,* 5–20. (Reprinted in Davidson, 1984, pp. 183–198)

Davidson, D. (1975). Thought and talk. In S. Guttenplan (Ed.), *Mind and language* (pp. 7–23). Oxford: Clarendon Press. (Reprinted in Davidson, 1984, pp. 155–170)

Davidson, D. (1984). *Inquiries into truth and interpretation.* Oxford: Clarendon Press.

Dennett, D. C. (1971/1978). Intentional Systems. *The Journal of Philosophy, 68,* 87–106. (Reprinted in Dennett, 1978a)

Dennett, D. C. (1975/1978). Why the law of effect will not go away. *Journal of the Theory of Social Behavior, 5,* 169–187. (Reprinted in Dennett, 1978a, pp. 71–89)

Dennett, D. C. (1977). Critical notice of J. Fodor, *The Language of Thought. Mind, 86,* 265–280.

Dennett, D. C. (1978a). *Brainstorms.* Cambridge: MIT Press/Bradford Books.

Dennett, D. C. (1978b). Skinner skinned. In D. C. Dennett (Ed.), *Brainstorms* (pp. 53–70). Cambridge: MIT Press/Bradford Books.

Dennett, D. C. (1978c). Toward a cognitive theory of consciousness. In D. C. Dennett (Ed.), *Brainstorms* (pp. 149–173). Cambridge: MIT Press/Bradford Books.

Dennett, D. C. (1978d). Why you can't make a computer that feels pain. In D. C. Dennett (Ed.), *Brainstorms* (pp. 190–229). Cambridge: MIT Press/Bradford Books.

Dennett, D. C. (1979). Current issues in the philosophy of mind. *American Philosophical Quarterly, 15,* 249–261.

Dennett, D. C. (1981a). Three kinds of intentional psychology. In R. Healey (Ed.), *Reduction, time and reality* (pp. 37–61). Cambridge: Cambridge University Press.

Dennett, D. C. (1981b). Making sense of ourselves. *Philosophical Topics, 12,* 63–81.

Dennett, D. C. (1981c). True believers: The intentional strategy and why it works. In A. F. Heath (Ed.), *Scientific explanation* (pp. 53–75). Oxford: Clarendon Press.

Dennett, D. C. (1982). Beyond belief. In A. Woodfield (Ed.), *Thought and object* (pp. 1–95).

Dennett, D. C. (1983). Intentional systems in cognitive ethology: The "Panglossian paradigm" defended. *The Behavioral and Brain Sciences, 6,* 343–390.

Dennett, D. C. (1984a). Cognitive wheels: The frame problem of AI. In C. Hookway (Ed.), *Minds, machines and evolution* (pp. 129–151). Cambridge: Cambridge University Press.

Dennett, D. C. (1984b). I could not have done otherwise—so what? *The Journal of Philosophy*, *81*, 553–565.

Dennett, D. C. (1984c). *Elbow room: The varieties of free will worth wanting*. Cambridge, MA: MIT Press/Bradford Books.

Dennett, D. C. (1986). The logical geography of computational approaches: A view from the East Pole. In M. Brand & R. M. Harnish (Eds.), *The representation of knowledge and belief* (pp. 59–79). Tucson: University of Arizona Press.

Dennett, D. C. (in press). Consciousness. In R. L. Gregory (Ed.), *Oxford companion to the mind*. Oxford: Oxford University Press.

Descartes, R. (1637/1970). Discourse on method. In E. S. Haldane & G. R. T. Ross (Eds.), *The philosophical works of Descartes* (Vol. 1, pp. 111–151). Cambridge: Cambridge University Press.

Descartes, R. (1641/1970). Meditations on first philosophy. In E. S. Haldane & G. R. T. Ross (Eds.), *The philosophical works of Descartes* (Vol. 1, pp. 181–200). Cambridge: Cambridge University Press.

Descartes, R. (1644/1970). Principles of philosophy. In E. S. Haldane & G. R. T. Ross (Eds.), *The philosophical works of Descartes* (Vol. 1, pp. 178–291). Cambridge: Cambridge University Press.

Donnellan, K. (1972). Proper names and identifying descriptions. In D. Davidson & G. Harmon (Eds.), *Semantics of natural language* (pp. 356–379). Dordrecht: Reidel.

Donnellan, K. (1974). Speaking of nothing. *Philosophical Review*, *83*, 3–31.

Dretske, F. I. (1980). The intentionality of cognitive states. *Midwest Studies in Philosophy*, *5*, 281–294.

Dretske, F. I. (1981). *Knowledge and the flow of information*. Cambridge, MA: MIT Press/Bradford Books.

Dretske, F. I. (1983). Precis of *Knowledge and the flow of information*. *The Behavioral and Brain Sciences*, *6*, 55–90.

Dreyfus, H. L. (1979). *What computers can't do: The limits of artificial intelligence* (2nd ed.). New York: Harper & Row.

Dreyfus, H. L. (1982). Introduction. *Husserl, intentionality, and cognitive science*. Cambridge: MIT Press/Bradford Books.

Dreyfus, H. L. (1985). *Artificial intelligence: The problem of knowledge representation*. Unpublished manuscript.

Dreyfus, H. L., & Dreyfus, S. E. (1987). *Mind over machine. The power of human intuition and expertise in the era of the computer*. New York: The Free Press.

Enc, B. (1983). In defense of the identity theory. *Journal of Philosophy*, *80*, 279–298.

Falk, A. E. (1981). Purpose, feedback, and evolution. *Philosophy of Science*, *48*, 198–217.

Feigl, H. (1958/1967). *The 'mental' and the 'physical': The essay and a postscript*. Minneapolis: University of Minnesota Press.

Feigl, H. (1960/1970). Mind-body, *not* a pseudo problem. In S. Hook (Ed.), *Dimensions of mind*. New York: New York University Press. (Reprinted in Borst, 1970, pp. 33–41)

Feldman, F. (1974). Kripke on the identity theory. *Journal of Philosophy*, *71*, 665–676.

Feldman, F. (1980). Identity, necessity, and events. In N. Block (Ed.), *Readings in philosophy of psychology* (Vol. 1, pp. 148–155). Cambridge, MA: Harvard University Press.

Feyerabend, Paul K. (1963/1970). Materialism and the mind-body problem. *The Review of Metaphysics*, *17*, 49–67. (Reprinted in Borst, 1970)

Field, H. H. (1978/1980). Mental representation. *Erkenntnis*, *13*, 9–61. (Reprinted in Block, 1980)

Fodor, J. A. (1968). *Psychological explanation*. New York: Random House.

Fodor, J. A. (1974). Special sciences (Or: Disunity of science as a working hypothesis). *Synthese*, *28*, 97–115.

Fodor, J. A. (1975). *The language of thought*. New York: Crowell.

Fodor, J. A. (1980). Methodological solipsism considered as a research strategy in cognitive psychology. *The Behavioral and Brain Sciences*, *3*, 63–109. (Reprinted in Haugeland, 1981)

Fodor, J. A. (1981). The present status of the innateness controversy. In J. A. Fodor (Ed.), *Representations* (pp. 257–316). Cambridge: MIT Press/Bradford Books.

Fodor, J. A. (1983). *The modularity of mind*. Cambridge MA: MIT Press/Bradford Books.

Fodor, J. A. (1984). Semantics, Wisconsin style. *Synthese, 59*, 231–350.

Fodor, J. A. (1985). Precis of *The modularity of mind*. *The Behavioral and Brain Sciences, 8*, 1–42.

Fodor, J. A. (1987). *Psychosemantics: The problem of meaning in the philosophy of mind*. Cambridge, MA: MIT Press.

Fodor, J. A., & Pylyshyn, Z. W. (1981). How direct is visual perception? Some reflection on Gibson's "ecological approach." *Cognition, 9*, 136–196.

Fodor, J. A., & Pylyshyn, Z. W. (1987). *Connectionism and cognitive architecture: A critical analysis*. Unpublished manuscript.

Føllesdol, D. (1982). Brentano and Husserl on intentional objects and perception. In H. L. Dreyfus (Ed.). *Husserl, intentionality, and cognitive science* (pp. 31–41). Cambridge, MA: MIT Press/Bradford Books.

Furth, H. (1966). *Thinking without language: Psychological implications of deafness*. New York: The Free Press.

Frege, G. (1892). Über Sinn and Bedeutung [On sense and reference]. *Zeitschrift fur Philosophie und philosophische Kritik, 100*, 25–50.

Gardner, R. A., & Gardner, B. T. (1969). Teaching sign language to a chimpanzee. *Science, 165*, 664–672.

Gassendi, P. (1641/1970). Letter to Descartes. In "Objections and replies." In E. S. Haldane & G. R. T. Ross (Eds.), *The philosophical works of Descartes* (Vol. 2, pp. 179–240). Cambridge: Cambridge University Press.

Gauker, C. (1987). *Thought as inner speech*. Unpublished manuscript.

Geach, P. T. (1957). *Mental acts*. London: Routledge & Kegan Paul.

Gibson, J. J. (1979). *The ecological approach to perception*. Boston: Houghton Mifflin.

Glotzbach, P. & Heft, H. (1982). Ecological and phenomenological contributions to the phenomenology of perception. *Nous, 16*, 108–121.

Goodman, N. (1955). *Fact, fiction, and forecast*. Cambridge, MA: Harvard University Press.

Gould, S. J. & Lewontin, R. C. (1979). The spandrels of San Marco and the panglossian paradigm: A critique of the adaptationist programme. *Proceedings of the Royal Society of London, B205*, 581–598.

Green, G. (in preparation). *Linguistic Pragmatics for Cognitive Science*. Hillsdale, NJ: Lawrence Erlbaum Associates.

Grice, H. P. (1975). Logic and conversation. In P. Cole & J. L. Morgan (Eds.), *Speech acts* (pp. 45–58). New York: Academic Press.

Gunderson, K. (1970/1971). Asymmetries and mind-body perplexities. In M. Radner & S. Winokur (Eds.), *Minnesota studies in the philosophy of science* (Vol. 4, pp. 273–309). Minneapolis: University of Minnesota Press. (Reprinted in Rosenthal, 1971, pp. 112–127)

Gunderson, K. (1971). *Mentality and machines*. Garden City, NY: Anchor Books.

Hamilton, E. & Cairns, H. (1961). *The collected dialogues of Plato*. New York: Bollingen.

Hamlyn, D. W. (1977). The Concept of information in Gibson's Theory of Perception. *Journal for the Theory of Social Behavior, 7*, 5–16.

Hardin, C. L. (1985). *Qualia and materialism: Closing the explanatory gap*. Unpublished manuscript.

Hardin, C. L. (1988). *Color for philosophers*. Indianapolis: Hacket Publishing.

Harman, G. (1973). *Thought*. Princeton: Princeton University Press.

Harman, G. (1977). How to use propositions. *American Philosophical Quarterly, 14*, 171–176.

Harman, G. (1978). Is there mental representation? In C. Wade Savage (Ed.), *Minnesota studies in the philosophy of science. Perception and cognition—Issues in the foundation of psychology* (Vol. 9. pp. 57–63). Minneapolis: University of Minnesota Press.

Harnad, S. (1987). *Minds, machines and Searle*. Unpublished manuscript.

Haroutunian, S. (1983). *The equilibrium model of explanation: Strengths and limitations for an account of cognitive change*. New York: Springer-Verlag.

Hatfield, G. (1986). *Representation and content in some (actual) theories of perception.* Reports of the Cognitive Neuropsychology Laboratory. John Hopkins University. Number 21.

Haugeland, J. (1981a). *Mind design.* Cambridge, MA: MIT Press/Bradford Books.

Haugeland, J. (1981b). Semantic engines: An introduction to mind design. In J. Haugeland (Ed.), *Mind design* (pp. 1–34). Cambridge, MA: MIT Press/Bradford Books.

Haugeland, J. (1985). *Artificial intelligence: The very idea.* Cambridge, MA: MIT Press/Bradford Books.

Heidegger, M. (1962). *Being and time.* New York: Harper & Row. (Originally published 1949.)

Heil, J. (1983). *Perception and cognition.* Berkeley: University of California Press.

Hill, C. S. (1984). In defense of type materialism. *Synthese, 59,* 295–320.

Horgan, T. (1982). Jackson on physical information and qualia. *The Philosophical Quarterly, 32,* 147–156.

Horgan, T. (1984). Functionalism, qualia, and the inverted spectrum. *Philosophy and phenomenological research, 44,* 453–469.

Hume, D. (1748/1962). *Enquiry concerning the human understanding.* Oxford: Clarendon Press.

Hume, D. (1759/1888). *A treatise of human nature.* Oxford: Clarendon.

Husserl, E. (1913/1970). *Logische Untersuchungen.* Halle: Niemeyer. (Translated as *Logical investigations* by J. Findlay, New York: Humanities.)

Husserl, E. (1929/1960). *Cartesian meditations* (Originally delivered in 1929. Tranlated by D. Cairns.) The Hague: Nijhoff.

Husserl, E. (1950/1972). *Ideen zu einer reinen Phanomenologie and phanomenologischen Philosophie, I, Husserliana.* The Hague: Nijhoff. (Translated by W. R. Boyce Gibson as *Ideas: General introduction to pure phenomenology.* New York: Collier Books.)

Jackson, F. (1982). Epiphenomenal qualia. *Philosophical Quarterly, 32,* 127–136.

Jacoby, H. (1985). Eliminativism, meaning, and qualitative states. *Philosophical Studies, 47,* 257–270.

Kahneman, D., Slovic, P., & Tversky, A. (1982). *Judgment under uncertainity: Heuristics and biases.* Cambridge: Cambridge Univerity Press.

Kant, I. (1787/1961). *Critique of pure reason* (N. K. Smith, Trans.). London: MacMillan.

Kaplan, D. (1967). *Transworld identification.* Paper presented at Western Division, American Philosophical Association, April, Chicago, IL.

Kaplan, D. (1969). Quantifying in. In D. Davidson & J. Hintikka (Eds.), *Words and objections: Essays on the work of W. V. Quine* (pp. 206–242). Dordrecht: Reidel.

Kaplan, D. (1978). Dthat. In Peter Cole (Ed.), *Syntax and semantics* (Vol. 9, pp. 221–243). New York: Academic.

Kenny, A. (1970). *Descartes' philosophical letters.* Oxford: Clarendon Press.

Kim, J. (1978). Supervenience and nomological incommensurables. *American Philosophical Quarterly, 15,* 149–156.

Kim, J. (1979). Causality, identity, and supervenience in the mind–body problem. *Midwest Studies in Philosophy, 4,* 31–49.

Kim, J. (1982a). Psychophysical supervenience as a mind–body theory. *Cognition and Brain Theory, 5,* 129–147.

Kim, J. (1982b). Psychophysical supervenience. *Philosophical Studies, 41,* 51–70.

Kim, J. (1985). Psychophysical laws. In E. Lepore & B. McLaughlin (Eds.), *Actions and events: Perspectives in the philosophy of Donald Davidson* (pp. 369–386). Oxford: Basil Blackwell.

Kirk, R. (1973) Underdetermination of theory and indeterminacy of translation. *Analysis, 33,* 195–201.

Kirk, R. (1982). Physicalism, identity, and strict implication. *Ratio, 24,* 131–141.

Kirk, R. (1986). Mental machinery and Goedel. *Synthese, 66,* 437–452.

Kitcher, P. (1984). In defense of intentional psychology. *Journal of Philosophy, 81,* 89–106.

Kosslyn, S. M. (1980). *Image and mind.* Cambridge, MA: Harvard University Press.

Kripke, S. (1963/1971). Semantical considerations on modal logic. *Acta Philosophical Fennica, 16,*

83–94. (Reprinted in Leonard Linsky Ed., *Reference and modality*. Oxford: Oxford University Press, p. 63–72)

Kripke, S. (1971). Identity and necessity. In M. K. Minitz (Ed.), *Identity and individuation* (pp. 135–164). New York: New York University Press.

Kripke, S. (1972). Naming and necessity. In D. Davidson & G. Harmon (Eds.), *Semantics of natural languages* (pp. 253–355) Dordrecht: Reidel.

Lakoff, G. (1987). *Women, fire, and dangerous things. What categories reveal about the mind*. Chicago: University of Chicago Press.

Lewis, D. K. (1966/1971). An argument for the identity theory. *The Journal of Philosophy, 63,* 17–25. (Reprinted in Rosenthal, 1971)

Lewis, D. (1968). Counterpart theory and quantified modal logic. *Journal of Philosophy, 65,* 113–126.

Lewis, D. (1969/1980). Review of art, mind, and religion. *Journal of Philosophy, 66,* 23–25. (Portion on Putnam reprinted in Block, 1980a, pp. 232–233)

Lewis, D. (1972/1980). Psychophysical and theoretical identifications. *Australasian Journal of Philosophy, 50,* 249–258.

Lewis, D. (1980). Mad pain and martian pain. (In Block, 1980a, pp. 216–222)

Lewis, D. (1983a). Postscript to 'Mad pain and Martian pain.' *Philosophical papers of David Lewis* (Vol. 1). New York: Oxford.

Lewis, D. (1983b). Individuation by acquaintance and by stipulation. *The Philosophical Review, 92,* 3–32.

Lewontin, R. C. (1978). Adaptation. *Scientific American, 239,* 212–230.

Linsky, L. (1967). *Referring*. London: Routledge & Kegan Paul.

Linsky, L. (1977). *Names and descritpions*. Chicago: University of Chicago Press.

Locke, J. (1959). *An essay concerning human understanding* New York: Dover. (Originally published, 1690)

Lucas, J. R. (1961/1964). Minds, machines, and Gödel. *Philosophy, 36,* 112–127. (Reprinted in Anderson, 1964, pp. 43–59)

Lycan, W. G. (1969). On 'intentionality' and the psychological. *American Philosophical Quarterly, 6,* 305–311.

Lycan W. G. (1972). Materialism and Leibniz' Law. *Monist, 56,* 276–287.

Lycan, W. G. (1974). Mental states and Putnam's functionalist hypothesis. *Australasian Journal of Philosophy, 52,* 48–62.

Lycan, W. G. (1981a). Form, function, and feel. *Journal of Philosophy, 78,* 24–49.

Lycan, W. G. (1981b). Psychological laws. *Philosophical Topics, 12,* 9–38.

Lycan, W. G. (1981c). Toward a homuncular theory of believing. *Cognition and Brain Theory, 4,* 139–159.

Lycan, W. G. (1984). *Logical form in natural language*. Cambridge, MA: MIT Press/Bradford Books.

Lycan, W. G. (1987). *Consciousness*. Cambridge, MA: MIT Press/Bradford Books.

Malcolm, N. (1984). Consciousness and causality. In D. M. Armstrong & N. Malcolm (Eds.), *Consciousness and causality: A debate on the nature of mind* (pp. 3–101). Oxford: Basil Blackwell.

Maloney, J. C. (1984). The mundane mental language: How to do words with things. *Synthese, 59,* 251–294.

Maloney, J. C. (1985a). Methodological solipsism reconsidered as a research strategy in cognitive psychology. *Philosophy of Science, 52,* 451–469.

Maloney, J. C. (1985b). About being a bat. *Australasian Journal of Philosophy, 63,* 26–49.

Maloney, J. C. (in preparation). *The mundane matter of the mental language*.

Margolis, J. (1976). The concept of disease. *The Journal of Medicine and Philosophy, 1,* 238–255.

Margolis, J. (1977). Arguments with intensional and extersional features. *Southern Journal of Philosophy, 15,* 327–339.

Margolis, J. (1978). *Persons and minds: The prospects of nonreductive materialism*. Dordrecht: Reidel.

Maxwell, G. (1978). Rigid designators and mind–brain identity. In C. W. Savage (Ed.), *Min-*

nesota studies in the philosophy of science (Vol. 9, pp. 365–403). Minneapolis: University of Minnesota Press.

Mayr, E. (1974). Behavioral programs and evolutionary strategies. *American Scientist, 62,* 650–659.

McCarthy, J., & Hayes, P. (1969). Some philosophical problems from the perspective of artificial intelligence. In B. Meltzer & D. Michie (Eds.), *Machine intelligence* (Vol. 4, p. 463–502). New York: Elsevier.

McCauley, R. N. (1986). Intertheoretic relations and the future of psychlogy. *Philosophy of Science, 53,* 179–199.

McCauley, R. N. (1987a). The role of cognitive explanations in psychology. *Behaviorism, 15,* 27–40.

McCauley, R. N. (1987b). The not so happy story of the marriage of linguistics and psychology, or why linguistics has discouraged psychology's recent advances. *Synthese, 72,* 341–354.

McClelland, J. L., & Rumelhart, D. E. & the PDP Research Group. (1986). *Parallel distributed processing. Explorations in the microstructures of cognition. Vol. 2: psychological and biological models.* Cambridge, MA: MIT Press/Bradford Books.

McCloskey, M. (1983). Intuitive physics. *Scientific American, 248(4),* 122–130.

McDowell, J. (1980). Meaning, communication and knowledge. In Z. Van Straaten (Ed.), *Philosophical subjects* (pp. 117–139). Oxford: Oxford University Press.

McKeon, R. (1941). *The basic works of Aristotle.* New York: Random House.

Meinong, A. (1904/1960). Über Gegenstandstheorie [The theory of objects]. In *Untersuchungen zur Gegenstandstheorie and Psychologie.* Leipzig. (Reprinted in R. M. Chisholm Ed., *Realism and the background of phenomenology.* Glencoe, IL: Free Press)

Mendel, G. (1865). Versuche über Pflanzen-hybriden. *Verhandlungen des Naturforschenden Vereines in Brünn, 4,* 3–47.

Mill, J. S. (1846). *A system of logic.* New York: Harper.

Minsky, M. (1975/1981). *A framework for representing knowledge.* (Memo #306) Cambridge, MA: Artificial Intelligence Laboratory at MIT. (Partially reprinted in Haugeland, 1981, pp. 95–128)

Minsky, M. (1986). *The society of minds.* New York: Simon & Schuster.

Mortensen, C. (1978). Review of Popper, K. R. and Eccles, J. C., *The self and its brain. The Australasian Journal of Philosophy, 56,* 264–266.

Nagel, T. (1974/1980). What is it like to be a bat? *The Philosophical Review, 83,* 435–450. (Reprinted in Block, 1980a, pp. 159–168)

Nagel, T. (1986). *The view from nowhere.* Oxford: Oxford University Press.

Natsoulas, T. (1981). Basic problems of consciousness. *Journal of Personality and Social Psychology, 41,* 132–178.

Natsoulas, T. (1985). An introduction to the perceptual kind of conception of direct (reflective) consciousness. *Journal of Mind and Behavior, 6,* 333–356.

Neisser, U. (1975). *Cognition and reality. Principles and implications of cognitive psychology.* San Francisco: Freeman.

Neisser, U. (1982). *Memory observed.* San Francisco: Freeman.

Palmer, S., & Kimchi, R. (1986). The information processing approach to cognition. In T. Knapp & L. Robertson (Eds.), *Approaches to cognition: Contrasts and controversies* (pp. 37–77). Hillsdale, NJ: Lawrence Erlbaum Associates.

Peirce, C. S. (1877/1934). The fixation of belief. *Popular Science Monthly, 12,* 1–15. (Included in C. Hartshorne & P. Weiss, Eds., *Collected papers of Charles Sanders Peirce,* Vol. V. Cambridge, MA: Harvard University Press, pp. 223–247)

Peirce, C. S. (1878/1934). How to make our ideas clear. *Popular Science Monthly, 12,* 286–302. (In C. Hartshorne & P. Weiss, Eds., *Collected papers of Charles Sanders Peirce,* Vol. V. Cambridge, MA: Harvard University Press, pp. 248–271)

Perry, J. (1977). Frege on demonstratives. *Philosophical Review, 86,* 464–497.

Perry, J. (1979). The problem of the essential indexical. *Nous, 13,* 3–21.

Piattelli-Palmarini, M. (Ed.). (1980). *Language and learning: The debate between Jean Piaget and Noam Chomsky.* Cambridge: Harvard University Press.

Place, U. T. (1956/1970). Is consciousness a brain process? *The British Journal of Psychology, 47,* 44–50. (Reprinted in Borst, 1970, pp. 42–51)

Place, U. T. (1988). Thirty years on—is consciousness still a brain process? *Australasian Journal of Philosophy, 66.*

Pollock, J. L. (1982). *Language and thought.* Princeton: Princeton University Press.

Polten, E. P. (1973). *Critique of the psyco-physical identity theory.* The Hague: Mouton.

Popper, K., & Eccles, J. (1977). *The self and its brain.* New York: Springer–Verlag.

Pratt, J. B. (1922/1957). *Matter and spirit.* New York: Macmillan. (Portions reprinted in M. Mandelbaum, F. W. Gramlick, & A. R. Anderson Eds., *Philosophical problems,* New York: Macmillan, pp. 263–283)

Putnam, H. (1960/1964). Minds and machines. In S. Hook (Ed.), *Dimensions of mind.* New York: New York University Press. (Reprinted in Anderson, 1964, pp. 72–97)

Putnam, H. (1962). The analytic and the synthetic. In H. Feigl & G. Maxwell (Eds.), *Minnesota studies in the philosophy of science* (Vol. 3, pp. 350–397). Minneapolis, University of Minnesota Press.

Putnam, H. (1967/1980). Psychological predicates. In W. H. Capitan & D. D. Merrill (Eds.), *Art, mind, and religion* (pp. 37–48). Pittsburgh: University of Pittsburgh Press. (Reprinted as The nature of mental states in Block, 1980a, pp. 222–231)

Putnam, H. (1973). Meaning and reference. *Journal of Philosophy, 70,* 609–711.

Putnam, H. (1975a). Philosophy and our mental life. In H. Putnam (Ed.), *Mind, language, and reality: Philosophical papers of Hilary Putnam* (Vol. 2, pp. 291–303). Cambridge: Cambridge Press.

Putnam, H. (1975b). The meaning of 'meaning.' In H. Putnam (Ed.), *Mind, language, and reality: Philosophical papers of Hilary Putnam* (Vol. 2, pp. 215–271). Cambridge: Cambridge University Press.

Putnam, H. (1978). *Meaning and the moral sciences.* London: Routledge & Kegan Paul.

Putnam, H. (1981). *Reason, truth, and history.* Cambridge: Cambridge University Press.

Putnam, H. (1983). *Realism and reason.* Cambridge: Cambridge University Press.

Putnam, H. (1984). Models and modules. *Cognition, 17,* 253–264.

Putnam, H. (1986). Meaning holism. In L. E. Hahn & R. A. Schlipp *The Philosophy of W. V. Quine* (pp. 405–426). La Salle, IL: Open Court

Pylyshyn, Z. W. (1979/1981). Complexity and the study of artificial and human intelligence. In M. Ringle (Ed.), *Philosophical perspectives in artificial intelligence* (pp. 25–56). Atlantic Highlands, NJ: Humanities Press. (Reprinted in Haugeland, (1981, pp. 67–94)

Pylyshyn, Z. W. (1980). Computation and cognition: Issues in the foundations of cognitive science. *The Behavioral and Brain Sciences, 3,* 111–169.

Pylyshyn, Z. W. (1981). The imagery debate: Analogue media versus tacit knowledge. *Psychological Review, 88,* 16–45.

Pylyshyn, Z. W. (1984). *Computation and cognition: Towards a foundation for cognitive science.* Cambridge, MA: MIT Press/Bradford Books.

Quine, W. V. O. (1953/1961a). Two dogmas of empiricism. In *From a logical point of view* (2nd ed., pp. 20–46). New York: Harper & Row.

Quine, W. V. O. (1953/1961b). Reference and modality. In *From a logical point of view* (2nd ed., pp. 139–157). New York: Harper & Row.

Quine, W. V. O. (1960). *Word and object.* Cambridge, MA: MIT Press.

Quine, W. V. O. (1969a). Existence and quantification. In W. V. O. Quine (Ed.) *Ontological relativity and other essays.* New York: Columbia University Press.

Quine, W. V. O. (1969b). Replies. In D. Davidson & J. Hintikka (Eds.), *Words and objections: Essays on the work of W. V. Quine* (pp. 292–352). Dordrecht: Reidel.

Quine, W. V. O. (1969c). Ontological relativity. In W. V. O. Quine (Ed.), *Ontological relativity and other essays* (pp. 26–68). New York: Columbia University Press.

Quine, W. V. O. (1970). On the reasons for the indeterminacy of translation. *Journal of Philosophy, 67,* 178–183.

Quine, W. V. O. (1973). *The roots of reference.* La Salle, IL: Open Court.

Quine, W. V. O. (1975). On empirically equivalent systems of the world. *Erkenntnis, 9,* 313–328.

Rey, G. (1983). Concepts and stereotypes. *Cognition, 15,* 237–262.

Rey, G. (1986). What's really going on in Searle's "Chinese room." *Philosophical Studies, 50,* 169–185.

Richardson, R. C. (1979). Functionalism and reductionism. *Philosophy of Science, 46,* 533–558.

Richardson, R. C. (1980). Intentional realism or intentional instrumentalism. *Cognition and Brain Theory, 3,* 125–135.

Richardson, R. C. (1981). Internal representation: Prologue to a theory of intentionality. *Philosophical Topics, 12,* 171–211.

Richardson, R. C. (1982). The 'scandal' of Cartesian interactionism. *Mind, 91,* 20–37.

Ristau, C. (1983). Language, cognition, and awareness in animals? In J. A. Secaer (Ed.), *The role of animals in bio-medical research. Annals of the New York Academy of Sciences, 406,* 170–186.

Ristau, C. (1987). *Intentional behavior by birds?: The case of the 'injury-feigning' Plovers.* Unpublished manuscript.

Rorty, R. (1965/1971). Mind–body identity, privacy, and categories. *The Review of Metaphysics, 19,* 24–54. (Reprinted in Rosenthal, 1971, pp. 174–199)

Rorty, R. (1970/1971). In defense of eliminative materialism. *The Review of Metaphysics, 24,* 112–121. (Reprinted in Rosenthal, 1971, pp. 223–231)

Rorty, R. (1979). *Philosophy and the mirror of nature.* Princeton: Princeton University Press.

Rosch, E. (1975). Cognitive representations of semantic categories. *Journal of Experimental Psychology: General, 104,* 192–233.

Rosenberg, A. (1980). *Sociobiology and the preemption of social science.* Baltimore: The Johns Hopkins University Press.

Rosenberg, A. (1986). Intention and action among the macromolecules. In N. Rescher (Ed.), *Current issues in teleology* (pp. 65–76). Lanham, MD: University Press of America.

Rosenthal, D. M. (Ed.). (1971). *Materialism and the mind-body problem.* Englewood Cliffs, NJ: Prentice–Hall.

Rumelhart, D. E. (1984). The emergence of cognitive phenomena from the sub–symbolic processes. *Proceedings of the Sixth Annual Conference of the Cognitive Science Society* (pp. 59–62). Boulder, CO.

Rumelhart, D. E., McClelland, J. L., & the PDP Research Group (1986). *Parallel distributed processing. Explorations in the microstructure of cognition. Vol. 1: Foundations.* Cambridge, MA: MIT/Bradford Books.

Russell, B. (1905). On denoting. *Mind, 14,* 479–493. (Reprinted in Robert C. Marsh Ed., *Bertrand Russell: Logic and knowledge.* New York: Capricorn, pp. 41–56)

Russell, B. (1940). *An inquiry into meaning and truth.* London: George Allen & Unwin.

Russow, L.-M. (1982). It's not like that to be a bat. *Behaviorism, 10,* 55–63.

Russow, L.-M. (1984). Unlocking the Chinese room. *Nature and System, 6,* 221–227.

Ryle, G. (1949). *The concept of mind.* New York: Barnes & Noble.

Savage-Rumbaugh, E. S. (1986). *Ape language: From conditioned response to symbol.* New York: Columbia.

Savage-Rumbaugh, E. S., McDonald, K., Sevcik, R., Hopkins, W., Rubert, E. (1986). Spontaneous symbol acquisition and communicative use by pygmy chimpanzees (Pan paniscus). *Journal of Experimental Psychology—General, 115,* 211–235.

Sayre, K. M. (1986). Intentionality and information processing: An alternative model for cognitive science. *Behavioral and Brain Sciences, 9,* 121–166.

Schank, R. C., & Abelson, P. (1977). *Scripts, plans, goals and understanding.* Hillsdale, NJ: Lawrence Erlbaum Associates.

Schnaitter, R. (1987). Behaviorism is not cognitive and cognitivism is not behavioral. *Behaviorism, 15,* 1–11.

Searle, J. R. (1969). *Speech acts: An essay in the philosophy of language.* Cambridge: Cambridge University Press.

Searle, J. R. (1979). *Expression and meaning: Studies in the theory of speech acts.* Cambridge: Cambridge University Press.

Searle, J. R. (1980). Minds, brains, and programs. *The Behavioral and Brain Sciences, 3,* 417–424. (Reprinted in Haugeland, 1981a, pp. 282–306)

Searle, J. (1981). Intentionality and method. *The Journal of Philosophy, 78,* 720–733.

Searle, J. R. (1984). Intentionality and its place in nature. *Dialectica, 38,* 87–99.

Selfridge, O. G. (1955). Pattern recognition by modern computers. *Proceedings of the Western Joint Computer Conference.* Los Angeles: California.

Sellars, W. F. (1963a). Philosophy and the scientific image of man. In W. F. Sellars (Ed.), *Science, perception, and reality* (pp. 1–40). London: Routledge & Kegan Paul.

Sellars, Wilfrid F. (1963b). Empiricism and the philosophy of mind. In W. F. Sellars (Ed.), *Science, perception, and reality* (pp. 253–359). London: Routledge & Kegan Paul.

Shaffer, J. A. (1965). Recent work on the mind–body problem. *American Philosophical Quarterly, 2,* 81–104.

Shannon, C., & Weaver, W. (1949). *The mathematical theory of communication.* Urbana, IL: University of Illinois Press.

Sher, G. (1975). Sentences in the brain? *Philosophy and Phenomenological Research, 36,* 94–99.

Sher, G. (1977). Kripke, Cartesian intuitions, and materialism. *Canadian Journal of Philosophy, 7,* 227–238.

Shoemaker, S. (1975/1980). Functionalism and qualia. *Philosophical Studies, 27,* 291–315. (Reprinted in Block, 1980, pp. 251–267)

Shoemaker, S. (1981). Absent qualia are impossible—A reply to Block. *The Philosophical Review, 90,* 581–599.

Short, T. (1983). Teleology in nature. *American Philosophical Quarterly, 20,* 311–320

Simon, H. A. (1955/1979). A behavioral model of rational choice. *Quarterly Journal of Economics, 69,* 99–118. (Reprinted in *Models of Thought.* New Haven: Yale University Press, pp. 7–19)

Simon, H. A. (1969). *The sciences of the artificial.* Cambridge: MIT Press.

Skinner, B. F. (1945/1984). The operational analysis of psychological terms. *Psychological Review, 52,* 270–277, 291–294. (Reprinted in *The Behavioral and Brain Sciences, 7,* 547–581)

Skinner, B. F. (1948). *Walden two.* New York: Macmillan.

Skinner, B. F. (1971). *Beyond freedom and dignity.* New York: Knopf.

Smart, J. J. C. (1959/1971). Sensations and brain processes. *Philosophical Review, 68,* 141–156. (Reprinted in Rosenthal, 1971, pp. 53–66)

Smith, E. E., & Medin, D. L. (1981). *Categories and concepts.* Cambridge, MA: Harvard University Press.

Smith, G. E. & Kosslyn, S. M. (1981). An information-processing theory of mental imagery: A case study of the new mentalistic psychology. In P. D. Asquith & R. N. Giere (Ed.), *PSA 1980* (Vol. 2, pp. 247–266). East Lansing, MI: Philosophy of Science Association.

Stalnaker, R. (1976). Propositions. In A. MacKay & D. Merrill (Eds.), *Issues in the philosophy of language* (pp. 79–91). New Haven: Yale University Press.

Stich, S. P. (1978). Autonomous psychology and the belief-desire thesis. *Monist, 61,* 573–591.

Stich, S. P. (1979). Between Chomskian rationalism and Popperian empiricism. *British Journal for the Philosophy of Science, 30,* 329–347.

Stich, S. P. (1981). Dennett on intentional systems. *Philosophical Topics, 12,* 39–62.

Stich, S. (1983). *From folk psychology to cognitive science.* Cambridge, MA: MIT Press.

Sutton, W. (1903). The chromosomes in heredity. *Biological Bulletin, 4,* 231–251.

Tarski, A. (1944/1952). The semantic conception of truth. *Philosophy and Phenomenological Research, 4,* 341–375. (Reprinted in Leonard Linsky, Ed., *Semantics and the philosophy of language.* Urbana: University of Illinois Press, pp. 11–47)

Tarski, A. (1967). Proof and truth. *Scientific American, 220,* 63–77.

Tennant, N. (1984). Intentionality, syntactic structure, and the evolution of language. In C. Hookway (Ed.), *Minds, machines, and evolution* (pp. 73–103). Cambridge: Cambridge University Press.

Thagard, P. (1985). *The emergence of meaning: How to escape Searle's Chinese Room*. Unpublished manuscript.

Turing, A. M. (1937). On computable numbers with an application to the Entscheidungsproblem. *Proceedings of the London Mathematical Society, 42,* 230–265.

Turing, A. M. (1950/1964). Computing machinery and intelligence. *Mind, 59,* 433–460. (Reprinted in Anderson, 1964, pp. 4–30)

Van Gulick, R. (1986). *A functionalist theory of self consciousness: The problem*. Unpublished manuscript.

Von Eckardt, B. (1984). Cognitive psychology and principled skepticism. *The Journal of Philosophy, 81,* 67–88.

Wierzbicka, A. (1987). *'Prototypes save': On the current uses and abuses of the concept 'prototype' in current linguistics, philosophy, and psychology*. Unpublished manuscript.

Wilkes, K. V. (1981). Functionalism, psychology, and philosophy of mind. *Philosophical Topics, 12,* 147–167.

Wimsatt, W. C. (1972). Teleology and the logical structure of function statements. *Studies in the History and Philosophy of Science, 3,* 1–80.

Wimsatt, W. C. (1976). Reductive explanation: A functional account. In R. S. Cohen, C. A. Hooker, A. C. Michalos, & J. Van Evra (Eds.), *PSA-1974. Boston Studies in the Philosophy of Science* (Vol. 32, pp. 671–710). Dordrecht: Reidel.

Wimsatt, W. C. (1981). Robustness, reliability, and overdetermination. In M. B. Brewer & B. E. Collins (Eds.), *Scientific inquiry and the social sciences* (pp. 124–163). San Francisco: Jossey–Bass.

Winograd, T. (1972). Understanding natural language. *Cognitive Psychology, 1,* 1–191.

Winograd, T. (1981). What does it mean to understand language? In D. Norman (Ed.), *Perspectives on cognitive science* (pp. 231–263). Norwood, NJ: Ablex.

Wittgenstein, L. (1953). *Philosophical investigations*. New York: Macmillan.

Wittgenstein, L. (1958). *The blue and brown books: Preliminary studies for the 'Philosophical investigations.'* New York: Harper & Row.

Wittgenstein, L. (1961). *Tractatus logico-philosophicus*. (D. F. Pears & B. F. McGuiness, Trans.). (Originally published, 1921) London: Routledge & Kegan Paul.

Woodhouse, M. (1984). *A preface to philosophy*. Belmont, CA: Wadsworth.

Wright, Larry (1976). *Teleological explanations: An etiological analysis of goals and functions*. Berkeley: University of California Press.

Author Index

Subject Index

160